CHRISTIAN ANTHROPOLOGY

CHRISTIAN ANTHROPOLOGY

AN INTRODUCTION TO THE HUMAN PERSON

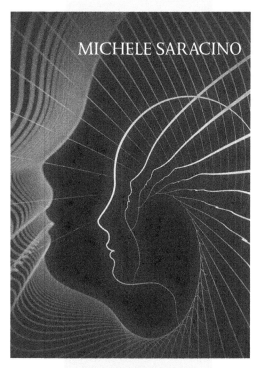

MICHELE SARACINO

Paulist Press
New York / Mahwah, NJ

Cover image by agsandrew/Shutterstock.com
Cover and book design by Lynn Else

Library of Congress Cataloging-in-Publication Data

Saracino, Michele, 1971–
    Christian anthropology : an introduction to the human person / Michele Saracino.
        pages cm
    Includes bibliographical references.
    ISBN 978-0-8091-4925-4 (pbk. : alk. paper) — ISBN 978-1-58768-489-0 (ebook)
    1. Theological anthropology—Christianity. I. Title.
    BT701.3.S268 2015
    233—dc23
                                                              2014037970

ISBN 978-0-8091-4925-4 (paperback)
ISBN 978-1-58768-489-0 (e-book)

Published by Paulist Press
997 Macarthur Boulevard
Mahwah, New Jersey 07430

www.paulistpress.com

Printed and bound in the
United States of America

CONTENTS

ACKNOWLEDGMENTS

Completing this work would not have been possible without the support of my generous colleagues, friends, students, and family. I would like to first thank my colleagues at Manhattan College, especially in the Religious Studies department and the School of Arts, for over a decade of collegiality and friendship. Specific discussions in this book were enhanced by informal and formal engagements with many in the MC community. Beyond Manhattan College, I am deeply grateful for the support and feedback I have received over the years as well as for portions of this book from the local research subgroup of the Constructive Theology Workgroup. Teresa Delgado, Roger Haight, SJ; Jeannine Hill Fletcher; Brad Hinze; Paul Lakeland; Elena Procario-Foley; and John Thiel—we have something special. I look forward to more years of conversation. Chris Bellitto of Paulist Press has been a supportive editor and a wonderful guide on this journey. Chris, thank you for your patience.

This work is unlike any other I have written in that fifty-plus intelligent, wise, and generous Manhattan College students read this entire manuscript as part of their SELF and OTHER course and provided feedback. Alec Argento, Anil Balram, Olivia Blasi, Dan Flynn, Jessica Frost, Samantha Goldstein, Amanda Gomez, Chaveli Hernandez, Lauren Hoffman, Mary Ann Keane, Michael Kelly, James Loures, Brian Martin, Daniel Mascolo, Joshua Matusak, Brittney Mesa, Erica Moore, Quan Nguyen, Nikki Nobile, Caitlin Palumbo, Christian Perez, Natale Recine, Christopher Russo, Kate Shelley, Dominique Turek, Ubadah Abdullah, Eric Ambos, Evan Antonucci, Joel Birnbaum, Carolyn Brazier, Roisin Clarke, Tom Diliberto, Genesis Genao, Alex Guido,

Kelly Huvane, Sara Imbruglia, Joseph Kelly, Eric Lister, Lauren Masucci, Nereida Millan, Brittany Otis, Yesenia Peralta, Marek Saro, Kerry Schuermann, Brittany Tarbell, Cassie Thompson, Giacomo Trevisan, Bonnie Woglom, Kasha Zarzezki, and Zachary Zerio: your suggestions were priceless. Thank you for staying in the conversation. Teaching you was one of the highlights of my time at MC.

All good things for me begin at home. Ken, Roman, and Penelope Einhorn, you are the loves of my life. Thanks for grounding me, making me laugh, and helping me to see the big picture.

INTRODUCTION

Have you ever wondered why you are here or what your purpose is in life? Have you ever thought about why dealing with other people is at times so difficult or why people from different religious and cultural backgrounds tend to conflict with one another? Perhaps you want to know more about the spiritual relationship between human animals and nonhuman animals, or why Christians are taught that only humans can have full communion with God. This book attempts to delve into these questions, exploring the doctrine of Christian anthropology and particularly what it means to be human in light of the changing world and church.

What distinguishes this work from some other texts on the topic of theological anthropology is that it attempts to explain traditional Christian teachings about the human person in a way that is attentive to the needs and realities of all creatures. Most religious teachings on existence are focused exclusively on human beings. And in many ways, this book follows in that trajectory in that it surveys what it means to be human. Nevertheless, in today's day and age it would be remiss not to consider how the lives of all creatures, including nonhuman animals, influence existence. At the present time, we are experiencing a tremendous loss of life in terms of extinction, and so here we ask what it means to be human in the midst of such loss.

The reality that creatures all around us are dying out at an exponential rate undoubtedly impacts human existence. This reality has theological significance not only because Christians are responsible for all life that God created, but also because extinction is changing our environment and eating away at our ability

1

to be free and to create life-giving relationships with God and others. Richard Leakey and Roger Lewin are quite convincing in their work, *The Sixth Extinction: Patterns of Life and the Future of Humankind*, that if we do not change our ways of thinking and behaving, life as we know it will be gone forever.[1] They claim we are in the midst of a sixth extinction spasm, which will diminish much of the world's biodiversity.[2] The last mass extinction decimated the dinosaurs.

What is different about this extinction phase in comparison to the other five on historical record is that humans are the cause of many of the problems, by over hunting and fishing, introducing alien species, and destroying habitats.[3] These mass extinctions are bad news for everyone. In addition to leading to the obliteration of a myriad of species, this trend impacts human beings negatively by depleting food supplies, polluting clean air and water, and displacing human cultures. Due to the far-reaching effects of extinction, these matters not only concern the scientific community, but anyone invested in preserving life. For Christians, life is a priority. Theological treatises on anthropology have a responsibility to attend to these issues and demonstrate a commitment to a more sustainable way of living.

In addition to being attentive to the crises of our times, another feature of this book is that it is devised to be instructor and student friendly. Divided into 13 sections, this primer on theological anthropology roughly correlates with the typical length of a semester. Course instructors can shape their syllabi around this book, organizing the week among lectures, discussions, and exercises. At the end of each chapter, further readings, discussion questions, and exercises are available to aid in integrating the theology presented here with issues related to everyday life. It is important for theology not to be thought of as theory alone; there is a practical side to it, which gives value to living our daily lives with God and others. To aid in integrating theology into the everyday, one of the first exercises suggested for students is to keep a semester-long journal in which they relate personal experience to the weekly readings.

ANTHROPOLOGY, A MISNOMER?

Since many of the aspects of human existence explored in this book are understood in light of the problem of environmental degradation, specifically extinction issues, the descriptive term *anthropology* might be the wrong name for it. Anthropology refers to the study of humans; yet here we are trying to be more inclusive of all creatures. Instead of thinking of this work as a project in theological anthropology, another name to consider is *creation*. The doctrine of creation is a field of study in theology that focuses on God's activity in creating the world as well as the role and responsibility of all of creation. While this book is not necessarily God-centered—and what I mean by that is focused on who God is and how God creates—it is about more than just human creation; it is about all of creation. From humans to orcas to chimpanzees to lemurs to cockroaches to stink trees to grass to dirt, humans are one piece of the cosmic puzzle. Shifting from anthropology to creation broadens our horizon and challenges us to think outside the human-centered box. The language of creation frees us up to imagine a landscape of all things created by God, of which humans are a part, yet do not dominate.

Even with my appreciation for the label of *creation*, I have chosen to keep the word *anthropology* in the book's title. While attempting not to privilege human beings as the best creatures, we will focus on human beings and how humanity needs to change its ways in order to protect life in the broadest sense. Furthermore, at various points in the text, readers will be asked to contemplate whether the sixth mass extinction spasm requires a new type of subjectivity for our context of environmental degradation. Perhaps instead of calling this a theology of creation, it may be more appropriate to conceptualize it as a less anthropocentric anthropology or an antianthropocentric anthropology, in that it refuses to allow the predicament of the human being to be the center of the conversation.

3

Consequently, it attempts to push toward a greener anthropology than we have encountered in the past.

MOVING TOWARD A GREEN ANTHROPOLOGY

Green symbolizes nature and tranquility. In ordinary life, many feel the healing power of green. Green painted walls and green colored furniture have the potential to make individuals feel calm and centered. Going for a walk in the woods has a way of helping us decompress from the pressures of life. This anthropology attempts to tap into the power of green by reimagining what God calls us to be—creatures who embrace the soothing effects of our connection with all of nature. This connection and hence dependence on all creatures needs to be honored rather than degraded. As many of us experience on a daily basis, however, being needy is something that we try to avoid, and dependence is not a trait we are proud of. In fact, at times we regard needing others as a deficit and weakness. However, Christian discipleship in this environmental crisis, plagued with increasingly exponential extinction rates—in the midst of what Seàn McDonagh has named "the death of life"— means at the very least to being able to tolerate being dependent on others.[4] In response to this crisis, Christians today might be open to a new way of framing existence—one that venerates the sacredness of the entire cosmos and human dependence on it. We might call this outlook a green anthropology.

Green is an attractive adjective to describe this existence because of its other connotations. Sometimes we call individuals who are young, innocent, and full of life "green." From a Christian perspective we need to imagine human existence without the trappings of sophistication that force us to pretend we are perfect and beautiful, in control and independent. Like children, all human beings are vulnerable and need others to survive and flourish. Embracing our youthful natures with unfettered love and trust of all others can move us toward a way of being human that is more sustainable for the whole of the cosmos. As Kyle Kramer puts it in *A Time to Plant: Life Lessons in Work, Prayer, and Dirt*, we are all amateurs in this thing called life.[5] This book privileges the perspective of the amateur, the one who continues to be open to new ideas and learn along the way. After all, isn't that what we are all doing anyway? In moving toward a green anthropology, we acknowledge our dependence on all of creation and our limited control over life in general. This may sound innocuous; on the contrary, it is quite radical. It challenges Christians to give up on being the center of the world and in charge of everything around them.

Using the phrase "green anthropology" to describe a nature-oriented posture or our childlike wonder is not without risk. Green has become a marketing tool in consumer culture, often used to get us to buy more products, some of which we don't need. This book acknowledges that context. It is a humble response to that common language we have in culture about the power and need to be green—to be more engaged with the ecological issues of our day—and a modest attempt to have that worldview shape theology. Beyond the academics of it, I have a personal stake in a green anthropology as well. Since he was in preschool, my son has been invested in the plight of sea creatures as our aquatic ecosystems have been stressed by overfishing, pollution, and greed. His love for everything marine and his being a born naturalist has challenged me to see human creaturely existence in a fresh light—in terms of being here to serve rather than master the planet. Perhaps children are the prophets here, in that they take the lead in envisioning a new world of connectedness between human and other animals, and plant life as well. Believers have a responsibility to heed the warnings of the youngest in our midst, as it is their inheritance that we are squandering. Part of the challenge of being human in this time of loss is not only understanding the dismal situation we are facing today, but also, as we will see as this book unfolds, dealing with that loss. In the words of Protestant, feminist, ecological theologian Sallie McFague, in light of today's ecological crisis, we might begin to express our "lament for the planet."[6]

To lament means to regret, grieve, and mourn. This is an important part of being human in relation to the larger cosmos. Until we learn through reflection about what we are doing to our planet and begin to lament the losses we are experiencing, we will not be able to change our ways. Mourning is an important process in moving forward in life, and often includes moments of anger, denial, sadness, guilt, and other feelings and attitudes associated with loss and recovery. The notion may seem out of place in a book like this. However, Christians learning more about their faith are called to do something with the new information. We cannot all change the world. And it is not feasible to bring back extinct species. We can, nevertheless, reflect deeply on which patterns of human sin have led to this situation, grieve those ways of life, and imagine ways of living among all creatures of the planet. These issues are discussed in later chapters. For now it is important to realize that as creatures, we are called to learn what is going on with our planet, think about it from the viewpoint of our Christian commitments to life and justice, and mourn the change and death that is occurring. Any anthropology less than this will keep us on the current negative trajectory without much hope for the future. Only after mourning, can we conceive of a new way of being human.

OVERVIEW

After this introduction, which details what theological anthropology is and why this text moves toward green concerns, the first chapter, entitled "Getting Oriented," helps students navigate the field of theology, mapping key questions and explaining in basic, clear terms what is meant by scripture, tradition, experience, theology, and theologians. Ecclesial councils and philosophical trends are discussed in relation to the modern questions of subjectivity and truth. Moreover, a methodology is outlined for the remainder of the book.

Chapter 2 is entitled "The God Complex." We tend to say someone has a "God complex" when we want to disparage their actions, when we think they have taken their sense of self too far and have no recognition of their limits or the needs of others. However, looking at Sacred Scripture, specifically Genesis 1 with its emphasis on humans being created in the image of God, it becomes clear that all human beings are created with a God complex—the desire to be perfect like God, even in the midst of mortality and human finitude. It is noted that a God complex is not necessarily something negative, particularly if what is meant by "God complex" is being magnanimous, creative, charitable, and so on. Nevertheless, a problem arises when one conflates the theological belief about humans being created in the image of God with the unrealistic expectation to be perfect like God. We see the problems with this perspective in everyday life. For one, in being like God, Christians feel tremendous pressure, especially in a capitalist, consumerist society, to be perfect and to never fail. At the same time, humans must deal with the reality of their creatureliness—of being mortal, finite, and limited. This is the fundamental tension of the human condition, and as such is carried over into the next chapter.

Finitude, which manifests in human frailty and neediness, is part of the human condition. We are creatures and not the creator precisely because we are limited by space, time, and mortality. The third chapter, entitled "You're So Needy," looks at Genesis 2 and argues that a significant dimension of the doctrine of the human person is to embrace this neediness. Jean Vanier's work figures prominently in the discussion, as the Canadian Catholic thinker and humanitarian has devoted his life to demonstrating that vulnerability, far from being aberrant and abject, is a universal and transcultural norm in all creatures. What's more, he explains and illustrates that vulnerability is a catalyst for enacting genuine freedom in our lives. Following Vanier's lead, exposing ourselves to physical, emotional, and spiritual nakedness is what makes us human. This gives way to a mentality about the necessity of vulnerability in everyday life that extends throughout all of creaturely existence, encompassing the panorama of animals and plants of the earth.

As already alluded to, when Christians discuss human existence, a key element in the conversation is that God created human beings with freedom. This is the topic of chapter 4, "Free to Be You and Me." From the start, one point needs to be made plain: for Christians, human freedom is always directed in relation to God and others. When it is not, it does not mean we are bad or necessarily have sinned; rather, it means that we are not free. There are various aspects of life that distort a human being's ability to be free, such as oppression, ignorance, peer pressure, and even social and technological trends—all of which are elaborated on in this chapter. Ultimately, this chapter emphasizes that freedom is not a one-time act or decision. Instead freedom emerges at moments in our life journeys when we are inspired, nurtured, and ultimately converted to be able to say yes to God's grace.

Chapter 5, "Dualism," focuses on a central problem in theological anthropology: the devaluing of the material aspects of existence in an effort to uphold the spiritual aspects. Dualism takes many forms and shapes, ranging from a separation and devaluation of body to soul, of women to men, of Jews to Christians, of blacks to whites, and of nonhuman animals to human animals. Harkening back to the previous chapters on neediness and freedom, this chapter explains how dualism threatens human freedom by setting individuals and groups in competitive relationships with one another, not allowing for relationships based in vulnerability to emerge and flourish.

The discussion of dualism sets the stage for the next two chapters, as dualistic mentalities foster binary oppositions or relationships of contrast that allow for little mixing and moving between the two. We see this when dualistic thinking forces many of us into thinking a person is all bad or all good, our friend or our enemy. Chapter 6, "Friends and Enemies," details how many of our relationships are far from that simple. We often have complicated responses to individuals who are different from us. In this chapter the Bible becomes an important resource for thinking about how to navigate others as friends or enemies; and everyday practices, like eating with those who are different, become ways to convert potential enemies into those whom we regard as our friends. What's more, the field of animal studies explodes the question of who is our friend and who is our enemy beyond the landscape of human animals, to include nonhuman animals as well.

Next, chapter 7, "Blue Is for Boys and Pink Is for Girls," continues exploring how dualism distorts human existence, this time with the focus on gender difference. First, we look at contemporary approaches to gender, specifically whether being a boy or a girl is a product of nature or nurture, meaning of biology or socialization. Then we look at various ways gender is constructed in the Christian tradition, including how the idea of the complementarity between genders often reduces men and women to fixed gender roles and of course leads to an implicit compulsory heterosexuality. Last, Mary, the mother of Jesus, and other saintly figures are analyzed in order to understand how gender can inhibit or foster one's freedom. The emphasis on mothering in the Christian tradition is highlighted as a potential positive metaphor for a Christian's responsibility to nurture and care for the earth.

Chapter 8, "Putting Humpty Dumpty Back Together Again," deals with the Christian belief that humans are born into patterns of brokenness, which in turn constrain our capacity for freedom. Some theologians refer to this as original sin, and a discussion of the fall figures prominently here. From the start of the chapter, it is noted that talking about sin is one of the more difficult topics to grapple with in theology because in today's day and age many of us don't want to appear judgmental and label someone a sinner. However, in order for suffering to cease and for reconciliation to become a possibility, honest talk on the topic of sin needs to take place. Like Humpty Dumpty, we all desire to be put back together again, or at least this is the Christian hope. A first step toward healing is naming the sinfulness we experience. Second, telling our stories and being open to conversion serve as catalysts for reconciliation.

Chapter 9, "The Power of Forgiveness," emphasizes the cross as a transformative moment in the Christian imagination, creating the possibility of forgiveness for all in our lives. Being human from a Christian perspective rests on the ability to be open to forgive and be forgiven as so many of the gospel narratives demonstrate. In order to relate this chapter to everyday life, spiritual and psychological challenges to enacting forgiveness are explored, as well as significant historical events. In the shadow of the Shoah—the Hebrew word for the Jewish Holocaust—and 9/11, it is important to consider how opening the human heart to something other than victimhood is an important piece of becoming human, and how harboring resentment and rage is an impediment to enacting one's freedom for God and others, including the freedom to forgive. Contemporary approaches to trauma treatment come into play in this chapter. Forgiveness is built on the call to relationship and the challenge of loving the other. Hence, starting with the Golden Rule, three important ways of loving for Christians, including *eros*, *philia*, and *agape*, are also defined in this chapter. Each type of love is vital to human flourishing in the face of God and all others—human and nonhuman.

In chapter 10, "Are We There Yet? Reviving a Sense of Vocation in Everyday Life," readers are encouraged to imagine that transforming patterns of brokenness is a lifelong journey. Many of us tend to think of *vocation* as a word that refers to those who dedicate themselves to religious lives, like priests. This chapter extends the idea of vocation to include all believers—each one of us who is called to hope for, imagine, and create a life in which we are free to say yes to God and others. Thinking of what we do with our lives encompasses more than our ideas about getting a job, having a family, or being a student, but also includes thinking about what we are doing with our lives and why we are doing it. Framing our life choices in terms of vocation has the potential to help us be more intentional about the decisions we make and the actions we take. As the chapter unfolds, various frames for understanding vocation in everyday life are explored. Moreover, Christian spirituality, including prayer, the sacraments, and even stories about the saints are emphasized as important signposts and guides for our journey. Ultimately, it is my wish that all readers reflect on how they are living in relation to others with an eye toward whether their journeys are life-giving or not, and if not, that they become empowered to make changes and improvise where necessary.

Every journey comes to an end. A noteworthy characteristic of theological anthropology is that this world is not the end for humans, that we are driven by what some call the beatific vision for a life after death. These questions about the connection between the here and now and the hereafter are the focus of chapter 11, "Happily Ever After." First, biblical ideas about the end are surveyed, and then more modern theological conceptualizations are considered. As so much of the conversation about the end is enmeshed with questions about salvation, I then move to a discussion of what it means to be saved and how certain interpretations of salvation work to exclude other human animals, and perhaps nonhuman animals, from sharing in God's grace. Finally, the reader is challenged to imagine strategies for salvation, which basically refer to ways of living in this world into eternity. I emphasize the contingent and limited nature of human beings as a way of hinting that we know very little about this world and the next. The best we can do is work on being amateurs in this life—with a mind, will, and heart that are oriented toward others. Perhaps that humble posture—that acknowledgment and embrace of being a creature—of being green and an amateur will open us to eternal peace.

NOTES

1. Richard Leakey and Roger Lewin, *The Sixth Extinction: Patterns of Life and the Future of Humankind* (New York: Doubleday, 1995).

2. For more on present extinction rates, see Center for Biological Diversity, "The Extinction Crisis," http://www.biological diversity.org/programs/biodiversity/elements_of_biodiversity/extinction_crisis/.

3. Leakey and Lewin, *The Sixth Extinction*, 234.

4. Seàn McDonagh, SCC, *The Death of Life: The Horror of Extinction* (Dublin: Columba Press, 2005).

5. Kyle T. Kramer, *A Time to Plant: Life Lessons in Work, Prayer, and Dirt* (Notre Dame, IN: Sorin Books, 2010).

6. Sallie McFague, *The Body of God: An Ecological Theology* (Minneapolis, MN: Fortress Press, 1993), 2.

Chapter 1

GETTING ORIENTED

Getting oriented takes work. I am reminded of this every time I use my GPS when driving. If I take a wrong turn or go someplace new, I am surprised by the time it takes the device to recalculate. If I really need to get somewhere quickly, I find myself staring at the screen with a combination of annoyance and terror. *What should I do next? Will I get there on time? Where is help when I need it?* Getting oriented is not just for travelers. Regardless of what we are doing or studying, it is important to become aware of our surroundings. This goes for all aspects of life.

When we swim in the ocean, we need to keep track of our friends back on the shore so we do not drift too far. When we drive, it is a good idea to pay attention to the other cars on the road so we are somewhat prepared if a tire blows or if we hit a pothole. In romantic relationships, it helps to get to know the other person before making a life commitment so we have a context for dealing with conflicts and changes. Pretty much in every aspect of life, taking stock of where we are, how we got there, and where we need to go is indispensable for continuing smoothly on life's journey. Anytime we approach a new topic, it helps to get the lay of the land, so to speak, and to become acquainted with the important issues and terms of the debate.

For some fields of study, getting oriented may seem out of place. It is commonplace to think of the scientist in the lab with her eyes glued to the computer screen or focused on the microscope as not paying attention to anything but her subject. But even scientists ask questions related to their contexts, and make discoveries that benefit specific cultures. Their studies are influenced by their time, place, and the values of the society. Likewise, individuals attempting to learn more about the Christian religion are not exempt from paying attention to their context and the pressing issues of our day. Sometimes with religious matters, talking about how social context influences teachings and beliefs seems to take away from the spirituality of the faith. This book asserts the opposite. The more we pay attention to the world around us, the deeper the level of spirituality we can achieve.

None of us is free from the web of relationships that drive and compose us and our context. Not even Jesus was free from dealing with the signs of his times. He had to negotiate the complexities of living under the Roman Empire. He had to deal with being a Jewish male who had some very controversial ideas. His thoughts and actions were a direct threat to anyone interested in keeping the status quo, particularly the Romans who ultimately killed him because of his countercultural ways. Since Jesus lived two thousand years ago, we are tempted to romanticize his day-to-day existence, and not consider his everyday anxieties. We might think he had all the answers and was unmoved by ordinary pressures and tensions. Nonetheless, holding true to the tradition, Jesus was human and as such had to negotiate his humanity in relation to the needs, wants, and concerns of others.

While we are not living in the Roman Empire today, we are all located somewhere and at sometime, meaning we are enmeshed in cultures that inform who we are and what we want to do in life. It helps to start to pay attention to our surroundings, so we are not punching the screen or the wall when times get tough. How does one get oriented? It starts with candid discussions of various aspects of God and the universe with believers and nonbelievers, not in order to convert others to one perspective or another, quite the opposite, to convert oneself to the needs of others and the issues of the day. We will see as this book unfolds that when thinking about human existence from a Christian perspective, it is important that one explore traditional theological topics, such as the role of freedom and the good of community. Nonetheless, these topics cannot be understood in isolation. Today's social context demands that we complicate this exploration by understanding how these topics are colored by one's social location, including his or her history, race, class, and gender, as well as by the particular trends and happenings of the moment, including environmental degradation and increasing extinction rates. To return to the GPS metaphor, environmental crisis is the orienting point for what it means to be human today. The destination is healing the cosmos and thinking theologically from a green perspective.

Through prioritizing green issues, many of the chapters survey aspects of anthropology with an eye toward implications for the larger cosmos. For example, when speaking about freedom, we will analyze how commonsense assumptions about freedom as something to which humans alone are entitled impact the flourishing and survival of the planet. When pondering how sin and brokenness affect human existence, we will test how our daily practices related to consumption, including the consumption of entertainment and food, exacerbate the devastation of species that is already underway. When surveying our bodies and embodied living, we will consider the way so many contemporary body disorders, such as anorexia, are related to our quest for control and our impatience with the vulnerability that is part of being a creature. When thinking about heaven, the afterlife, and all the things hoped for, we will question what is at stake in claiming that only Christians can be saved. At every turn, we will reflect on these theological topics in relation to our experience. Bradley Hanson, a Protestant theologian, underscores the importance of experience when he describes theology as "a personally involved reflection on a religious faith."[1]

WHAT IS THEOLOGY AND WHO DOES IT?

In an effort to get further oriented, it helps to define important theological terms and ideas in the conversation. We need to be able to read the street signs before we proceed. For instance, what does the word *theology* signify? Most often referred to as the study of God, theology is about bringing reason to faith and faith to reason. It is not merely the act of memorizing creeds, but learning about how core beliefs emerged and what values they hold for the people who find them meaningful. There are various topics in theology, sometimes referred to as loci. They include but are not limited to God, sin, Christology, soteriology, ecclesiology, eschatology, and what we are studying in this book, theological anthropology.

As for the question of who does theology, on the one hand, I want to say that anyone who stands in or around a faith tradition is doing theology—meaning they are personally reflecting on their faith. Not in saying prayers or in fasting, but rather in thinking about those dimensions in critical ways. On the other hand, there are individuals who are trained in theology in the same way that others are trained in medicine or in economics. These theologians by trade today more than ever come from the laity—meaning they are nonclerical. Whereas in the medieval period, only men who were priests or belonged to religious orders were in charge of teaching theology in the universities, today clerics, religious, and lay persons all can be theologians, and ordinarily their training involves obtaining a master's degree as well as a doctorate degree in the academic disciplines of theology or religious studies. Extending this kind of work to lay scholars opens the theological enterprise to different perspectives, including those of women and mothers, many of whom, for a large chunk of Christian history, were silenced and prevented from participating in constructive theological debate.

While professional theologians often take the lead in theological conversations, I am hopeful that individuals from all walks of life, including students, stay-at-home moms and dads, CEOs, lawyers, plumbers, and so on, will begin to see the link between their spiritual lives and the environment in their day-to-day activities. Doing theology is a task for all Christians, not just the pope, bishops, or professional theologians, and by the end of this book, perhaps each one of us will continue to press on with some of the important questions of the twenty-first century: *How do we conceptualize freedom?* *Why are we so negative about being needy?* *Why do we privilege reason?* *Historically, why have we assumed that nonhuman animals and "others" like women and persons of color lack reason?* *What are the theological dangers of this type of thinking?* *How does this thinking interrupt life in the fullest sense of the word?*

NOTHING PERSONAL?

It is important to note the personal aspect of doing theology. Christian theologians are usually Christian and as such, have a unique connection to the subject matter. They want to understand the faith more, and perhaps to make it more accessible to everyday life, or even to critique the shadow side of it. That is different from the anthropologists, who seemingly study culture from afar, not getting involved with their subjects. Unlike anthropologists who keep a safe distance, theologians working on anthropology are already involved, as they are part of the religious tradition they seek to study and reform.

Even though there is a personal stake when doing theology, it is important to keep in mind that the study is still quite rigorous and intellectual. Sometimes in academic circles—meaning among faculty and students in universities—a distinction is made between theology and religious studies; the latter is understood as more objective because there is no personal commitment between religious studies scholars and their subject matter, while there is one between theologians and their field of study. However, there is a problem with this distinction, as major shifts in philosophy, science, mathematics, and the arts due to the Enlightenment have shown that where we stand has an impact on our knowing and being. We can never truly be objective if that means being beyond standpoint. Everyone stands somewhere, regardless of what he or she is studying. In one way or another, it is always personal.

SOURCES FOR THEOLOGY

With the claim that we can all theologize, it is helpful to know what to draw on and where to begin. The sources for doing theology are limitless, but they are often categorized in these three ways: scripture, tradition, and experience. Usually referred to as "the Bible," Sacred Scripture for Christians includes books, letters, prophetical texts, and writings from both the Hebrew Scriptures and the New Testament. These texts serve as stories that reveal meanings and values shared in the Christian community. While the meanings and values may shift from culture to culture and time to time, the inspirational quality of the stories remains.

Reading scripture is an acquired skill. While one can certainly sit with a cup of tea and read the Book of Exodus or the Gospel of John and gain some insights or mediate in prayer, there are scholarly strategies that allow us to know more about the who, what, where, when, and why of the Bible. This knowledge does not take away from the centrality of scripture to Christian living and actually can enhance it. Modern biblical scholars, who are experts in the original languages and are familiar with the cultures of the times, provide commentary to help believers make the text more or less relevant for their lives. While most professional theologians have taken courses in scripture, they still rely on these commentaries to augment their knowledge. Ordinary Christians have access to these sources both in hard copy and online. One such example is the *New Jerome Biblical Commentary*. Another is the *Women's Bible Commentary*. It helps to read along with these scholarly texts to deepen one's understanding of his or her faith.

There are various approaches one may take when reading biblical texts. Generally, we will refer to two main approaches: literal and historical-critical. A literal reading of the text is when one believes the story to be the word of God, meaning exactly what God intended, at face value. There is no concern for who wrote the text and what social pressures may have influenced the writings, or how translation from an ancient language could affect the meaning of the text. A literal approach is also known as a *fundamentalist* one. While there are times when we might refer to literal readings of this or that biblical passage, most of the time, since we are working from an academic perspective, we will be looking at the Bible from a historical-critical approach. This involves reading the biblical passage with an eye toward understanding the social context of the time, and how that context influences both what is written and what is meant. The historical-critical method does not deny that the writings were inspired; rather, it emphasizes that the meaning of what is written is connected to a social world. Readers of the Bible are encouraged to get oriented with the values and issues of the time the story was created before making any universal claims about what is true and right. Our study works best when we compare literal and historical-critical approaches, so we can see how different Christians come to different conclusions on these matters.

Finally, on the topic of scriptural analysis, it is important to note that our coverage of scripture in this book is by no means exhaustive, as only select scriptural passages will be highlighted as talking points to engage issues in theological anthropology. For example, the first three chapters of Genesis are quite important to our discussion and are analyzed across various chapters. Likewise, Gospel passages where Jesus reaches out to those who are different in an effort to build relationships of solidarity are significant to this study, since quite a bit of the conversation is directed toward the relationship between human and nonhuman animals.

In addition to scripture, another source for doing theology is tradition. This refers to the councils, teachings, and practices that have been passed on throughout the centuries. Christian traditions are expansive, and as such, some will figure more prominently than others in this book. For instance, the development of the creed emerging from the Council of Nicea in 325 CE and doctrines about Jesus' human and divine natures crystallized by the Council of Chalcedon in 451 CE are important pieces of the conversation. Understanding the lives of saints as role models for individual Christians is also of great consequence in doing theology. Other significant aspects of the tradition include documents of the Second Vatican Council as well as social justice teachings on the dignity of life and vocation of women, including *Evangelium Vitae* and *Mulieris Dignitatem*, respectively, and some practices, including the sacraments of Eucharist and reconciliation.

As with scripture, there are scholarly strategies for understanding tradition. First, getting a handle on the breadth of tradition is imperative, especially since we are working within and across various Christian denominations, and as a result, particular traditions might depend on a specific confessional stance. While we will work to respect the differences between Christian denominations, we will also strive to build on the commonalities or their familial nature. In his textbook on theology, Hanson uses the notion of Christian families to accentuate the connections among different Christian denominations.[2] In this book, we will read across these families' traditions, not as if they are static and unchanging, but rather with an analytical eye on the signs of the times. In other words, this book takes for granted that traditions are products of history and social contexts, and as a result, change when encountering others with differing perspectives.

Christians have different reactions to the notion that tradition is changing and not static. Some find it disturbing, and others liberating. Change is frightening for many of us, and to think that religious traditions are constantly changing could call into question the very foundations of a person's identity. In my role as a religious studies professor, I assist students in understanding change from an academic perspective, not to destroy their faith, but potentially to deepen it. Embracing tradition is not blindly accepting everything passed down by religious leaders, but hearing those proclamations with openness to them, while at the same time bringing one's own questions to them.

I have learned to *never* blame specific teachers or parents for students feeling confused or disconnected or having a stilted sense of tradition or a limited knowledge of this or that religious tradition. Religion, like sex, politics, and money, is a difficult topic about which to speak freely. It takes energy, time, and willingness to be wrong and challenged or even to offend another. I tell my students as well as my own children that since religion is so difficult to talk about, we must talk about it. Not because every doctrine is true and meaningful for each individual and community, but rather because theological ideas influence consciously and unconsciously the way we relate to one another, for good or ill.

Experience is the last source mentioned for doing theology and the most difficult one to define. In a way, we can intuit what it connotes. The feelings, thoughts, actions, events, and relationships that inform our lives on a day-to-day basis could be thought of as our experience. These dimensions of our reality influence the ways in which we imagine what it means to be human as well as enact our humanity. While the term *experience* is used throughout this book, another way of thinking about this is through the notion of *story*. We all have stories that shape who we are—stories about our family origins, ethnic and racial backgrounds, career trajectories, abilities, and so on. I will return to the notion of *story* as I discuss freedom, vocation, and otherness, but for now, all I want to suggest is that our experience shapes the way we engage God and others. And if we want to change the trajectory we are on in the midst of climate change and mass extinctions, we need to analyze our stories and even rewrite some of them.

THE T-WORD

Since *experience* is such a slippery—hard to define—term, it is difficult to prove as real. Lurking in the shadows of this discussion is the T-word—*truth*. While there is little one can prove about religious belief using the scientific method, the question of who or what has the authority to claim that they are speaking the truth is an important issue. For so many, there is the sense that much of a believer's relationship with God rests on faith, and as such is personal and cannot be proven. Alternatively, others believe that indeed there are truths of religion—beliefs that are nonnegotiable regardless of the social context. Nonetheless, the task ahead of us is neither to say that religious tradition is based on blind faith—so who cares?—nor to say that that it is all true—so we'd better care. On the contrary, our job is to shed light on what Christian tradition teaches about what it means to be a creature and to attempt to understand how those teachings influence individuals and communities.

METHODOLOGY

In working toward a green anthropology, we need to explore the shadow side of the Christian tradition relative to extinction issues. In other words, in order to move beyond this life crisis, we need to pinpoint areas in Christian scripture, tradition, and experience that lead to a neglect of the environment and work against green thinking. Only then, when we face the worst in the religious tradition, are we empowered to imagine a more life-giving way of being human that is inclusive of all creatures. Feminist theologians have long mined the tradition to confront the problematic aspects of it, only they have employed the methodology relative

21

to gender. In what follows, we will use a feminist method for our green anthropology.

In *Transforming Grace: Christian Tradition and Women's Experience*, Anne Carr, an important Roman Catholic theologian of the twentieth century, provides a way for navigating the shadow side of the tradition relative to women's issues that we could easily apply to ecological ones.[3] The first step Carr outlines is that of *critique*, which in many ways we have already described. This is when one studies the tradition and pinpoints the problems, injustices, and incongruencies within Christianity relative to the subject matter. In our case, critique necessitates the following types of questions: Which texts and voices in the tradition occlude the importance of nonhuman animal and plant life to human life? Are there places in scripture, tradition, and experience that validate the human animal having unbridled power over all other animals?

A second step in Carr's feminist method is the *recovery* of the lost voices and history of the oppressed group. In her feminist work, this would involve retrieving lost or muted examples where Christian women held leadership positions and positively influenced the tradition. When applied to ecological issues, we might look at places in scripture and tradition that validate human connections with the larger cosmos. There are obvious places, like Genesis 6—9, where God makes a covenant with all of creation—even nonhuman animals—and the spirituality of St. Francis, the patron saint of ecology. There are less obvious places too, like the theology of the incarnation and church councils.

The third aspect that Carr elaborates on is *revisioning* Christian categories. Scholars working in this aspect of theology look at ways to rethink and reimagine central Christian categories in more life-giving ways for women and men together, and again for us, the larger cosmos. Sometimes this active engagement with Christian traditions is referred to as "constructive theology." Implied in the use of the word *constructive* is the supposition that tradition is always fluid, changing, and influenced by culture and society. It is a structure that believers build upon and further construct in light of their personal theological commitments. Here we might search for new avenues in the tradition to reimagine the environment not as an object to be dominated for our use, but rather as a subject with autonomy.

For decades now, this type of method, which critiques, retrieves, and revisions, has been used in other theological works on environmental degradation. In the inroduction, I referenced Sallie McFague, who focuses extensively on environmental degradation, the role of Christians in helping save the planet, and of course, the need for lamenting the planet. It is important to note both her earlier work, entitled *Models of God*, where she planted the seed for Christians to consider seriously the relation between how we imagine God and our engagement with the planet, in addition to her later projects on the topic, including *The Body of God: An Ecological Theology; Life Abundant; A New Climate for Theology: God, the World, and Global Warming;* and *Blessed Are the Consumers: Climate Change and the Practice of Restraint*, which more fully and deliberately develops theology from the vantage point of the cosmos. Mark Wallace's book *Green Christianity* also tackles key questions in theology related to sustainability of the earth that are of the utmost importance to the future of all creatures. My work is indebted to the school of thought developed in those theologies. Moreover, an attempt is made to weave these insights together and make them relevant for Roman Catholic thought.

In her latest work, one of the most significant Roman Catholic thinkers of the twenty-first century, Elizabeth Johnson, writes about the gravity of Darwin's scientific claims for theology in general and Christians in particular. In her *Ask the Beasts: Darwin and the God of Love*, Johnson passionately asserts that care for the environment, that is, for the natural world, is at the heart of our moral life.[4] We will see in later chapters how Johnson's weaving of scientific thought together with religious claims informs a new way of thinking about conversion and personal vocation. For now, it is important to realize that from a Catholic Christian perspective, care for the environment is essential to Christian discipleship. Until we understand and embrace ecology as a life issue, any anthropology we imagine will be somewhat truncated, incomplete. For all life to truly be respected, and for human beings to come into their full humanity, caring for all others and embracing relationality needs to become a priority.

There are many ways to be in relationship, some of which are exploitative and dominating. However, in the relational humanity I am proposing here, our power is used for others in life-giving ways so that we can flourish together. This worldview is exemplified again in the Catholic Christian tradition, for example, on the United States Conference of Catholic Bishops' (USCCB) website:

> Catholic Social Teaching is a central and essential element of our faith. Its roots are in the Hebrew prophets who announced God's special love for the poor and called God's people to a covenant of love and justice. It is a teaching founded on the life and words of Jesus Christ, who came "to bring glad tidings to the poor... liberty to captives...recovery of sight to the blind" (Lk 4:18–19), and who identified himself with "the least of these," the hungry and the stranger (cf. Mt 25:45). Catholic social teaching is built on a commitment to the poor....Catholic social teaching is based on and inseparable from our understanding of human life and human dignity. Every human being is created in the image of God and redeemed by Jesus Christ, and therefore is invaluable and worthy of respect as a member of the human family. Every person, from the moment of conception to natural death, has inherent dignity and a right to life consistent with that dignity. Human dignity comes from God, not from any human quality or accomplishment.[5]

As we reflect on and lament our ailing planet, in the following chapters I hope to show that for human dignity to truly be respected, we need to acknowledge and embrace the dignity of other species. All creatures are interconnected: human animals and nonhuman animals depend on one another for life to continue to flourish.

Put more directly, in order for all life to be protected, we need to give up the primacy of our own. That does not mean not to care for ourselves; rather, we are called to care for ourselves in relation to others. Here is where the mourning comes in. As we grieve for our dying planet, we are faced with a choice: to keep going on this deadly trajectory of exploiting non human animals and plants to the point of their annihilation and perhaps ours, or to give up our self-centered way of life to make room for life for all creatures. Unfortunately, Christians and others have been socialized to protect themselves at all costs to others. Taking seriously the claims of Christian thinkers across the traditions, we might need to mourn this old way of life for a future to be possible.

LINKING FEMINIST AND ECOLOGICAL CONCERNS

Some may feel put off by the use of a feminist method in a book on the entirety of creation—not just women and not just humans. Here is some background to contextualize the connection between feminist and ecological methods and concerns. Feminist and other liberationist theologians have prioritized the environment for decades now, largely because there is a similarity between the way the earth's body is exploited and commodified and the way the bodies of women and of individuals from other marginalized groups, including persons of color, have been used and abused.

Feminists point out that there is a persistent pernicious tendency to regard women's bodies as more sinful than men's. Women have been perceived as less rational and more trapped by their flesh because of their ability to bear children. They are often regarded as sexual temptresses, and hence their bodies are seen as the gateway to sin. We are confronted with this misogynist thought in literal readings of Genesis 3, where Eve is blamed for the downfall of humanity; in the power inequities exhibited in the "Household Codes" of Ephesians 5; in the misogynist thought of such foundational theologians as Augustine and Aquinas; in the medieval suspicion of witchery as exhibited in the infamous fifteenth-century treatise *Malleus Maleficarum* (*Hammer of the Witches*); and in the contemporary period, where women are excluded from leadership in the magisterium and where women religious (sisters and nuns) are being punished for being too "radical."

This suspicion of women is related to how they are connected to the earthly material world, and how that world has historically been devalued. If we don't value earthliness, materiality, and flesh, then anybody associated with those things will not be valued. So women are devalued. Nonhuman animals are devalued. And even persons of color are devalued. One only needs to reflect on the dehumanization that occurred with the annihilation of Native Americans at the hand of European conquerors and with the enslavement of Africans throughout the Americas. Both groups were thought of as uncivilized and less than human.

We will address these issues in more detail in later chapters, but for now we need to consider more basically that women and other "others" are exploited and used, again much like the earth itself, because materiality is regarded as a bad thing. Getting a handle on this type of oppression within Christianity is extremely complicated, particularly because the tradition, in theory at least, has a positive attitude toward the material world and embodiment. McFague explains this paradox:

> Christianity is the religion of the incarnation *par excellence*. Its earliest and most persistent doctrines focus on embodiment: from the incarnation (the Word made flesh) and Christology (Christ was fully human) to the Eucharist (this is my body, this is my blood), the resurrection of the body, and the church (the body of Christ who is its head), Christianity has been a religion of the body....And yet, the earliest Christian texts and doctrines contain the seeds that, throughout history, have germinated into full-blown distrust of the body as well as depreciation of nature and abhorrence and loathing of female bodies.[6]

So how does one reconcile this reverence of the body in the tradition with the hatred of some bodies, including the earth? Well, even with all its potential to bring us into genuine, rich relationships with others, being embodied comes with baggage. It limits us; it is the ultimate sign of our mortality. And perhaps in our desperation to avoid that reality, our finitude and dependence on others, we sin by turning on our bodies and hating material life. These are some critical insights revealed to theologians by feminist theorists, and they are helpful when trying to understand why

26

in the Christian tradition some human animals are valued far more than their nonhuman counterparts.

SUMMARY

This chapter covers the fundamentals of doing theology, including the processes of engaging in scripture, tradition, and experience. Our world is full of change, and as a result, Christians cannot think of human existence as static. It is a dynamic process that needs to be attentive to real life issues, such as today's situation of global environmental degradation. Fortunately, there are resources in the tradition that can help us move toward a green anthropology. Ultimately, it is up to each believer to navigate his or her own life in this complex world. The ideas presented here are merely some modest tools to get oriented and begin the journey.

EXERCISES:

1. **Keep a journal.**

   Begin a journal to update as you use this book. It could either be a notebook in which you manually write entries or a computer file, whichever you are most comfortable with. From each chapter choose an idea that you find interesting, exciting, or disturbing—in other words, that you would like to explore further. Begin each entry by explaining the idea, referring to the text in question. Then relate that idea to your own experience. Be as personal as you are comfortable with, as the point is to make lived connections with the readings and write on them. Have fun with it! Try to write in the same place/location for every journal entry, perhaps in a natural setting, in a park or forest. Such a locale could enhance your green connections.

2. **Online Research**

   Search the United States Conference of Catholic Bishops (USCCB)'s webpage for writings on environmental justice. After reading, reflect on whether this is the message you have received in your religious education. How could the message be even more prominent?

3. **Think-Pair-Share** (Reflect on these questions silently, find a partner and discuss them together, and then share with the class.)

- List five issues in your life you are most concerned about. Do you think God has a role to play in them? Why or why not?
- Why would anyone want to be a *theologian*? What did that word mean to you before this discussion? Has anything changed for you?
- What makes an individual a human being? Why?

NOTES

1. Bradley C. Hanson, *Introduction to Christian Theology* (Minneapolis, MN: Augsburg Fortress Press, 1997), 4.

2. Ibid., 5.

3. Anne E. Carr, *Transforming Grace: Christian Tradition and Women's Experience* (Harrisburg, PA: Continuum, 1996).

4. Elizabeth A. Johnson, *Ask the Beasts: Darwin and the God of Love* (London: Bloomsbury, 2014).

5. United States Conference of Catholic Bishops, "Catholic Social Teaching," http://www.usccb.org/beliefs-and-teachings/what-we-believe/catholic-social-teaching/.

6. McFague, *The Body of God*, 14.

Chapter 2

THE GOD COMPLEX

Why begin a book on human existence with a chapter on God? While this may seem counterintuitive, in fact the way Christians conceptualize God influences the way they live. Like the other Abrahamic traditions of Judaism and Islam, Christianity upholds the notion that God is a transcendent other who is not limited to time and space. And like adherents of these other important world traditions, Christians believe that God has a personal relationship with and is actively involved with all of creation. Even with these similarities to Judaism and Islam, Christianity has a unique understanding of the Divine in that it proclaims that God became human. This is a game-changer for Christians. At the very most, the doctrine of the incarnation is what defines Christians as Christians. At the very least, it is a significant characteristic of the religion, as Christians not only believe in a god that created the world and loves the world, but also in a god that dwelled in the world through the person of Jesus Christ.

This theological belief about the incarnation, about a god who became enfleshed, is enough to give anyone a god complex, which involves feeling the pressures of being like God and close to God, yet always being human. Indeed one may think that since God became human, somehow humans have special access to God and a privileged relationship with God in comparison to the rest of creation. Moreover, since Christians are taught that human beings are created in the image of God, some may believe they are entitled to more spiritual benefits than their nonhuman companions. This tension between being like God and yet not God has profound effects, and probably all Christians at one point or another have felt the tension of the god complex. Only when

Christians grapple head on with the struggle between the promise of being like God and the reality of ultimately and unequivocally being limited, frail, vulnerable, and mortal—in other words, being a creature—will we be able to begin to imagine an anthropology that is green and sensitive to the plight of all creatures. This chapter attends to these tensions about being like God and not being God, exploring doctrinal ideas about who God is and how those teachings impact Christian discipleship.

FOR BETTER OR FOR WORSE, HUMANS ARE CREATED IN THE IMAGE OF GOD

To begin our conversation on the connection between Christian interpretations of God and what it means to be human, we should look first toward Sacred Scripture. If we turn to the first two chapters of the Book of Genesis, we are faced with two distinct stories of Creation. When we read them from a figurative perspective, as stories that are symbolic of the values of a religious group, we don't need to think of them as contradictory. Instead, they are angles from which we can glean some insight into what it means to be a creature in the presence of God and other creatures. For scholars, these dual narratives about the same event signal that multiple sources were employed in the construction of the Hebrew Bible.

In the first chapter of the first book of the Bible, we find: "So God created humankind in his image, in the image of God he created them; male and female he created them."[1] Scholars understand this text, like most biblical passages, in varied ways. From one perspective, the phrase "image of God" underscores the Christian belief that humans have a spirit or a soul, a nonmaterial aspect that moves them for God and others. Looking at this passage from another angle, when we read that human beings are created in the image of God, we might be inclined to believe that human beings have a built-in desire to be with God and be like God. These two perspectives are variations on a common theme, namely, that human beings are created with a gift from God, with the spiritual adornment chosen by God, one that reflects God's goodness, generosity, and interest in others. Being created in the image of God means having the look of God, or perhaps the imprint of the Divine within us, a force that jettisons us out of our false sense of self—the closed self to which Jean Vanier alludes— embracing instead a sense of self in which we are open, exposed, and vulnerable to being in genuine give-and-take relationships with others.[2]

Sometimes the phrase "the image of God" signals the idea that we are created with grace, the spiritual gift of God by God to enable us to say yes to love and life. Nature and grace are traditional terms in theological anthropology. The term *nature* often refers to the material realm of creation, specifically our embodied being, while the term *grace* emphasizes the spiritual capacity for connections with others. The problem with these terms when they are used generally is that they are often contrasted with each other, making it seem like a creature's material and spiritual realms are two completely separate dimensions of existence, when that is not our reality. Even worse, the spiritual realm of existence is valorized over the material realm of existence. This type of dualistic thinking leads to all sorts of problems, including hating bodies or at least certain bodies, nonhuman animal bodies, which are often understood as lacking grace. In light of these dualistic tendencies, it is important to note that Christians believe that God created the entire world and it is good, a belief that complicates any simplistic division of grace from nature.

Having said that, looking at scripture alone one begins to wonder if only human beings are graced. While it is written that the entire world was created "and it was very good," only human animals are gifted with being created in the image of God.[3] If this idea is taken literally, one could believe that other creatures do not have all the qualities of that image—the spirit, the soul, the ability to love and be free. This signifies a very important distinction between human beings and other creatures, as well as a sense that humans are the closest of all creatures to God; perhaps even the most loved and cherished. This is one negative aspect of the god complex, at least from the perspective of those invested in finding helpful theological responses to the environmental crises

31

facing us today. If we can't say that all creatures are graced and all are in the image of God, then what kind of moral responsibility do we have to them? This is just one of the many questions that arise in this green anthropology.

Being so much like God is not all it's cracked up to be. While it is perfectly normal to want to be special, being created in this image at times may feel more like a curse than a blessing, or at least an awesome obligation. Aside from trying to please our friends, loved ones, teachers, and bosses, this presents a huge responsibility to not only please others, but also to be like God. This becomes challenging when we confuse our orientation to be for God and even like God with believing we are God and forgetting that we are ultimately creatures. This amnesia allows us to think and act like we are God, assuming we can have total control and are capable of perfection. This truly can feel like a curse because all our efforts at perfection are futile. It is not uncommon to hear or utter the phrase "nobody's perfect," which is often said to make people feel better when they have made a mistake. In the moment, it makes sense. We know that everybody has bad days, limits, and faults that prevent them from doing everything perfectly. Yet before long the consolation those words bring fades, and we are off and running, trying to be perfect again.

Advertising campaigns don't help the situation. Everywhere we turn, there is a product marketed to fix this body problem and that social issue—to make us perfect. While many of the products available have the potential to help us, sometimes the underlying message is destructive. It seems as if we are not good enough as is—as finite creatures. The cosmetic industry invites us to buy this or that product to get "flawless" skin. We have our children tutored excessively so they can achieve near perfect test scores. This is not to suggest that pushing ourselves is a bad thing; on the contrary, the problem arises when we hate ourselves for not being perfect and godlike, and feel ashamed about being what we ultimately are; namely, finite creatures.

An important Christian theologian of the twentieth century, Reinhold Niebuhr, claimed that the desire to be perfect and godlike was a basic problem for human beings, of being created in the image of God and yet being finite, of having glorious promise and yet being constrained by mortality.[4] According to Niebuhr, human beings struggle throughout their entire lives with wanting to be different from what they are, with wanting to be God. This is one way of describing the god complex—desiring to be God and experiencing existential suffering because we are not God, but rather are mere creatures. We tend to say someone has a god complex when they are acting conceited and self-centered, when they act like they are more important than we think they are, or when they seem to think they are God. This is the negative side of believing one is created in the image of God. The positive side is when people take the responsibility of being created by God and in God's image so seriously that they work diligently to care for and comfort others.

Part of the journey of being human—or as Vanier puts it, of "becoming human"—is being attentive to the precarious dance between the two manifestations of the god complex. Having an ego isn't bad. In fact, it is healthy and normal. Problems occur when one cannot see beyond his or her own ego, not allowing for others to flourish. The same thing can be said for the god complex. Wanting to be like God can be a good thing in that we challenge ourselves to use our freedom and gifts to the maximum. Challenges arise when we start to believe and act as if we are God and use that to control and manipulate others, and ultimately get frustrated with our creaturely limits.

In the end, the sense of specialness, of being like God, if not attended to, has the possibility of devolving into forms of narcissism where we lose sight of the needs, feelings, and even presence of others. We confuse image and likeness with an ontological reality; in other words, with being. We can begin to think we are God, meaning perfect, infinite, and all-knowing, rather than in the likeness of God. With so many people suffering from esteem issues these days, it might not be too horrible to elevate one's sense of self; however, when feeling good about oneself becomes a license to tromp on others, this is the shadow side of the god complex. Others appear unnecessary, inept, and inconsequential. We may even begin to think we can survive without others altogether— that we do not need anyone or anything, all the various species of the earth. While independence is a good thing in many cases, when it comes at the expense of developing and fostering relationships with others who may be in need themselves, then Christians need to pause.

WHEN FEELING SPECIAL IS NOT ENOUGH

Is it possible for anyone to feel too special? Sure, if an individual's specialness encroaches on the needs of others. Feeling special is an important aspect of being human. We feel special when we feel loved and respected. It builds our sense of identity and motivates us when times get rough. However, when we feel too special or don't recognize the specialness in others, troubles could arise. Again, this is the negative or shadow side of the god complex, when we conflate our specialness with godliness. Interestingly, when reading Sacred Scripture, we find an antidote to this shadow side of the god complex. In Genesis 2, humans are understood to be vulnerable, needy, and best when they are in relationship. When Christians read, "It is not good that the man should be alone," they are affirmed in their dependence on others and even encouraged to find solace in companionship.[5] This is one of those tricky passages in scripture—they all are really—because it could be read in many ways. This passage has often been used to keep women in their so-called place, by confirming that the woman is second in the creation narrative—an afterthought even. Moreover, her "helper" status works to confirm some readings of women's marginal role in society and life. I would certainly not support any such oppressive and misogynist reading, yet I am not overly concerned with woman being portrayed as created second. It shows that Christians believe in a god who improvises and changes course to deal with situations. This is a model for all of us.

Rather than dwell on gender distinctions here, it may be better to emphasize the fact that what we are presented with is a belief in a creator who cares deeply about creation—so much so as to brainstorm, rework, and reimagine; to have a plan B. These are images of God that humans might benefit from exuding. They are signs of hope—of an imagining god; one that surveys the context and adjusts if things are not going as planned; a god that is open to change, flexible, and resourceful. This is a god that not only creates from God's own spiritual being, but creates from the material world, from dirt and flesh. The way God is presented in Genesis 2 opens up the conversation in Christian anthropology to talk about green issues. This is a god who loves the material world enough, or at least values it enough, to create humans from it.

Lastly, it is worth noting that this story also highlights the importance of community in our lives—that others bring authenticity to our everyday comings and goings. What is clear from the Creation narrative in Genesis 2 is that God endorses the human capacity for earthly love and friendship. Creatures are special in their own right as well as in relationship. Moreover, the second chapter of Genesis ends with the words "the man and his wife were both naked, and were not ashamed," giving way to the theological truth that being exposed in all our imperfections and neediness is part of the human condition and God's divine plan, and corroborating Vanier's position of vulnerability being a normative dimension of humanity—one we aspire to in accordance with God's plan.[6] This notion of vulnerability is studied in great detail in the following chapter. For now it is important to note that Sacred Scripture situates human beings in a unique situation of being like God and yet not God, because God ultimately is radically other from all of creation.

GOD AS OTHER: A MODEL FOR ALL RELATIONSHIPS

In navigating the tension between being like God and not being God, it is important to elaborate on the philosophical and theological claims about God's otherness. To be other means to be different from someone or something. We are all different from each other in a plethora of ways. We hold different opinions from one another, have different genetics, families, and cultures, and may even be from different species. The word *other* captures all those distinctions and many more. Sometimes the term *other* seems to have negative connotations, used to describe something as alien, unfriendly, or even dangerous. This alleged negativity is probably a result of the unknown quality of otherness. Something or someone that is different from us is unknowable on some level. That could cause us to fear the other. It is not as though we cannot learn about those different from us; in fact, we do that all the time through informal conversation—getting to know one another—and formal research of different cultures and species. It is just that in some little way or big way they are not like us, a difference that is best respected than denied. When defined in this way, God from a Christian perspective is most definitely other. When Christians are taught about God's otherness, hopefully they are learning that there is a distinction between being the creator and being a creature. They are two different entities. God as Creator is infinite, transcendent, mysterious, and awe-inspiring. As such, the alien nature of God could cause fear and apprehension. However, just like with other "others," it is not as if creatures cannot know about the Creator through reflection and prayer; it is just that being the creator is different than being a creature.

In addition to Sacred Scripture, tradition, including church teachings, public prayer, and the sacraments, provides resources for tapping into what Christians mean by God as other. The Nicene Creed (325 CE) explains that there is one God and this God is the Creator par excellence in that God is the maker of heaven and earth, of all that is visible and invisible. While all creatures have the capacity for reproduction, that is, creation of the same species, God is the one who generates all production. God creates difference and by acting in this way sets the world in motion. Whether God started the process of Creation or actually created creature by creature is not the point here. Rather the focus is on the Christian belief that God created everything, even the matter that made up the world. This concretizes an understanding of a god that is in total control, total creator, and total other. There are no other deities doing godly work. This belief in God as sole creator also relates to the idea of perfection. In being perfect, God lacks nothing, is infinite, and as such, is an "other" to creation. An important point to reflect on is that for most, God's otherness does not lead to God being inaccessible, distant, and utterly foreign. On the contrary, Christians are taught that even in their finitude they reflect God's image. There is an intimacy here that both connects humans to God and keeps God's otherness in mind in order to guard against the negative aspects of the god complex.

THE TRINITY

Another important aspect of the Christian interpretation of God that has a significant effect on creaturely existence is the belief of God in trinitarian terms. The Trinity maintains the otherness of God, while emphasizing the importance of difference and relationality. Christians affirm that while there is one God, this divine other manifests in three persons, as Creator of all, Redeemer or Savior, and Sustainer, or the one who gives life and keeps it all going. Teachings about the Trinity also complicate—in a good way—how Christians live in relation to God and others. After all, if God is a god in relation—a trinitarian god—then connections among oneself and others become a priority for believers. In other words, relationships define creaturely existence. This orthodox Christian idea, as we will see here and in upcoming chapters, runs contrary to much of what humans are taught in their everyday lives about the importance of being independent and self-reliant.

Some easily accept the three-persons-in-one-God formulation as commonsense knowledge. But our facile acceptance of the trinitarian affirmation of the unity and diversity of the Father, the Son, and the Holy Spirit is a result of the theological foundations put down by the early church fathers. There were controversies and struggles that went on in relation to the Trinity, and it was not until 381 CE at the Council of Constantinople that the doctrine of the Trinity was somewhat settled. For our purposes, the primary significance of the Trinity for Christians is that relationship is part of God's being. And in being created in the image of God, believers are called to honor relationships in their own lives.

THE INCARNATION

In addition to the doctrine on the Trinity, Christian teachings about God becoming human—commonly referred to as the incarnation—provide insights into how to live with God and others. Like most theological beliefs, teachings on the incarnation developed over time. In all probability, the first followers of Jesus did not consider Jesus fully divine. After all, these faithful were Jewish and any such thought that a human being was the person-ification of G-D ran contrary to their central claims of monothe-ism. It was more the case that the belief in Jesus' divinity deep-ened as Christianity spread across regions that had interaction with Hellenistic culture. Moreover, it was really during the church meetings or councils of Ephesus (431 CE) and then Chalcedon (451 CE) that Jesus' identity was debated and clarified. At the Council of Ephesus, the role and identity of Mary, Jesus' mother, was discussed. After much debate, she was proclaimed to be *theotokos*—God-bearer—and the mother of God. This is a strong statement because some wanted her to be thought of as *christo-tokos*—the Christ-bearer. Ultimately, it was decided that God-bearer would be more appropriate than all other titles, so as not to understate the divine nature of Jesus.[7]

Notice that what is at stake in this conversation is how much weight is given to the divine nature and the human nature of Christ, and how important it is doctrinally to honor both. Twenty years later, at the Council of Chalcedon, the two natures/one per-son formula was reinvigorated to underscore both Jesus' human and divine natures. By the end of the fifth century, orthodox teaching reflected that "Jesus Christ is 'fully human and fully divine…one [person]…existing in the two natures…without con-fusion, without change, without division, without separation.'"[8] As definitive as this is, this formula did not fully squelch concerns about the right way to interpret the incarnation. To this very day, Christian leaders and scholars continue to debate the nature of the mysterious borders of humanity and divinity. There are many theological questions about the relationship between the two natures.[9] How do the divine and human natures relate to one another and how much emphasis should we allocate to one or the other?[10] How does this relationship between the human and divine natures of Christ affect what it means to be human?

In light of the incarnation, because of the close proximity between the two natures of the one person of Jesus Christ, many Christians look to Jesus for signs as to how to be holy and godlike;

in other words, to imitate Jesus. Here the teachings about the incarnation have a similar effect to the teachings regarding human beings created in the image of God. The idea is that if the divine nature is so close, so connected to the human nature, this reality should offer some sort of road map for Christian living. This type of disposition leads to the *What Would Jesus Do?* phenomenon. The act of imagining what Jesus would do, wear, eat, and so on demonstrates an anecdotal relationship between who Christians say Jesus Christ is and how they attempt to be his disciples in the contemporary world. There is a challenge here. The Christian belief in a god that became human inspires humans to live like Jesus, and accept that they are creatures and hence not God. At the same time, it does not erase our desire to be like God, because God is so close. As with the teachings about the image of God, on the positive side, the incarnation motivates individuals to do their best, and on the not-so-positive side, it leads individuals to feel bad about their limits.

This tension over the proximity between humans and God is enough to give anyone a god complex. Again, what is meant here by the phrase "god complex" is not that humans truly believe they are God, the Creator, or even perfect, but that they find themselves in situations in which they end up going crazy to be perfect and godlike. It is the impossible ideal. And many feel like they have failed if and when they do not achieve these lofty goals. This is not a conscious activity. It is difficult to imagine that when children are asked what they want to be when they grow up, they will respond "God." It is more typically the case that children will answer with doctor, police officer, teacher, scientist, mommy, daddy, or any combination of those and more. Yet somewhere along the way, each one of us in a consumer-driven, global culture starts to conflate being human with being perfect.

THE PROBLEM WITH PERFECTIONISM

Many of us encounter young, beautiful, and bright people practically killing themselves to be perfect. They diet to extremes, work out at the gym for long hours, and then spend all night catching up on their studies so they can ace their exams. Christians need to be really honest about whether believing in a perfect god that becomes human and in a messiah that has no sin exacerbates this situation. Anne Lamott writes about the perils of perfectionism in her insightful work, *Bird by Bird: Some Instructions on Writing and Life*: "Perfectionism is the voice of the oppressor, the enemy of the people. It will keep you cramped and insane your whole life...[and] is based on the obsessive belief that if you run carefully enough, hitting each stepping-stone just right, you won't have to die."[11] In this brief excerpt we can see how even though intellectually we know we cannot be perfect—after all, we are creatures—many of us live as if we can. This is death dealing. There is a paradox to perfectionism in that it promises immortality, but you practically have to kill yourself to obtain it. Just think of how multiple plastic surgeries take their toll on the human body, or how extreme dieting and weight training, including steroid use, negatively impacts one's health. Similarly, testing cosmetics on lab animals has a harmful effect on other creatures.

In his spiritual work on vocation, Kyle Kramer describes perfectionism and perfection as "overrated," meaning that it does not fulfill our deepest desires and bring us full life. As mentioned in the previous chapter, in an effort to move beyond the debilitating effects associated with perfectionism and the need for control, Kramer proposes that we might instead work on becoming "amateur[s]."[12] An amateur is someone who is not the best at their craft, but works hard at it out of love and commitment. This is an interesting way of speaking about Christian discipleship and being human in general, and emerges again in discussion toward the end of the book. Being an amateur is not anything to be ashamed of; in fact, it is worthy of respect. It takes work and never results in perfection, yet we stick with it out of love. Becoming an amateur turns one's life away from a preoccupation with self and toward a connection with others, in that not being hung up on the ideal of perfection opens one to taking risks in relationships. We do not need to be perfect; we need to be present and working. This idea and others like it will become even more important in the next chapters on vulnerability and freedom.

THE POWER OF SYMBOL

Christians do not let the otherness of God prevent them from nurturing a close relationship with God. They use their imaginations to speak about the sacred and mysterious relationship with God and others. Imagination here does not mean something that is not true or intended to be deceitful. That is an important point to make from the outset. It is easy to get confused here because the term *imagination* is used in many different ways. Sometimes children dream about monsters, waking their exhausted parents for solace. Their mothers might reassure them to go back to sleep; after all there are no monsters, it is just their imagination working overtime. In that situation, imagination connotes that whatever the child dreamt or perceived is not real, and hence is inconsequential. When talking about the Christian imaginary or imagination, however, Christians do not believe they are making things up; rather, that they are giving life to the Christian story. The Christian imaginary is at play during prayer, within sacramental life, and in their every day. The way Christians imagine God to be and act is also part of their imaginary.

The belief in a god who became human in the historical person of Jesus Christ heightens the Christian imaginary. It is the closest one can get to seeing God. In other words, Christians get a glimpse into God as they read about Jesus' ministry in the New Testament. However, the divine nature is never fully revealed in the visual sense; after all, God cannot be captured by any one image or portrait. For Christians, God is infinite and a mystery. Yet this fact does not stop believers from using finite words and culturally influenced images to describe God and make God even more accessible.

Imaging God is a distinguishing characteristic of Christianity in relation to the other Abrahamic religions. For example, in Judaism, specifically in the Hebrew Scriptures, there is at the very most an aversion to, and at the very least ambivalence about images of God. On the one hand, in the Book of Exodus, we read that Moses speaks to God face to face: "Thus the Lord used to speak to Moses face to face, as one speaks to a friend," and in Deuteronomy: "Never since has there arisen a prophet in Israel like Moses, whom the Lord knew face to face."[13] Yet at other points in scripture, there is a prohibition to Moses seeing God: "But, he (the Lord) said, 'you cannot see my face; for no one shall see me and live.' And the Lord continued, 'See, there is a place by me where you shall stand on the rock; and while my glory passes by I will put you in a cleft of the rock, and I will cover you with my hand until I have passed by; then I will take away my hand, and you shall see my back; but my face shall not be seen.'"[14] Scholars do not look at these texts as contradictory, just as support for the idea that various sources form parts of the Hebrew Bible. For our purposes, pondering over whether one can really see God and know God in the fullest sense points to the desire to have an intimate connection with God, while at the same time being aware that God is a mystery and unknowable on some level.

Christians navigate this ambiguity by using symbols and images to communicate and celebrate their personal relationships with God—a type of face-to-face relationship of intense intimacy and proximity. These images take many forms, and most importantly here, the particular images used to describe God impact everyday life. To be clear, the ways in which Christians imagine God influence their existence. There are the more obvious correlations between peoples' images of God and their attitudes—for example, if believers employ male language to describe God, they might tend to elevate man's status in life. If they imagine God as a warrior, then that conceptualization could legitimize war in their eyes. If they imagine God as a protector of all of creation, then that conceptualization could foster an ecologically sensitive ethic. These are just examples, and can be interpreted in many different ways.

Some individuals have become so accustomed to using certain language or images to describe God that they think any new images are heretical, meaning that they go against orthodox Christian teaching. However, quite to the contrary, when one becomes overly focused on a particular image of God and confuses that image for God, he or she runs the risk of limiting God to finite language and making God an object. To this point, depending on social context, Christians hold a variety of images of God—some warm and fuzzy, some loyal, some imagining God as a world class negotiator, and still others framing God in terms of a mother or a father.[15] All are orthodox as long as one does not confuse the image for God's total reality.

IMAGINING A GREEN GOD

In light of environmental degradation and the perils of climate change, what if we were encouraged to explore the different sides of God? What might a green God look like? How might one's experience of life be different with a god who is other-species oriented rather than human oriented? How might this change the human condition for Christians and for all creatures of the world? Even more basically, what resources exist to begin imagining God as green? First, in saying that God is green, we are not looking for the color, but rather for a commitment to all of creation. This is not such a reach; as we have already discussed, the trinitarian and incarnational teachings regarding God all reflect a respect for otherness. What is more other than the difference between divinity and all species?

There are other resources for imagining a green God; after all, it is common to speak about religious experience in terms of nature. Some feel God and are moved by their experience of the infinite when by the mountains, at the ocean's shore, under the grand canopy of a rainforest, or even during a bicycle ride through the woods. At these moments when we experience the Sacred in nature it is easy to feel compassion and love for all creatures, believing that we belong to the same sacramental body.

Furthermore, there are various places in scripture that emphasize a green God, so to speak, including Genesis 1 and 2 where God is portrayed as creating all the creatures of the earth and everything is good. However, it is later in the Book of Genesis where a broad sense of the importance of creation is found, specifically in Genesis 6—9, where God makes an inclusive covenant with all of creation to save all of creation—including nonhuman animals. In Genesis 6, we read how God becomes so frustrated with what humans are doing with the gift of life, that God destroys all life and starts anew: "The Lord saw that the wickedness of humankind was great in the earth, and that every inclination of the thoughts of their hearts was only evil continually. And the Lord was sorry that he had made humankind on the earth, and it grieved him to his heart. So the Lord said, 'I will blot out from the earth the human beings I have created—people together with animals and creeping things and birds of the air, for I am sorry that I have made them.'"[16] There is an exception: God recognizes the man Noah as righteous, and tells Noah to build an ark for his family, along with pairs of all the creatures of the earth. According to this story, Noah's family and the animal pairs would start a new life together and God would never again abandon them: "Then God said to Noah and to his sons with him, 'As for me, I am establishing my covenant with you and your descendants after you, and with every living creature that is with you, the birds, the domestic animals, and every animal of the earth with you, as many as came out of the ark. I establish my covenant with you, that never again shall all flesh be cut off by the waters of a flood, and never again shall there be a flood to destroy the earth.'"[17]

Unlike other covenants in scripture, this agreement between God and others is universal and inclusive of all creatures—not just for humans, not just for Abraham's descendants or for Moses and the Israelites, not even the new covenant that Jesus proclaims in the Gospels. The covenant with Noah is a cosmic agreement that starts out with God's wrath, but ends in mercy and promise for all creatures. Perhaps this universal covenant, which groups human animals and nonhuman animals together, is a way to begin to imagine a god who does not distinguish between species in the same way we do. Rather we are presented with a god who cares for and commits to all—a green God.

Like the references to Moses and whether he saw God face to face, this story about Noah and the flood is also ambiguous. On one level, God saves not only human animals from destruction but also nonhuman animals. There is no separation or special feeling toward humans. This underscores the reality that these are all God's creatures, and leads one to be more concerned with all of creation. At the same time, this saving is in light of mass destruction—of God's wrath toward creation. Sure it is great that God treats all creatures the same, but why this massive killing? Another tension related to God and the care for creation is present in Genesis 1, in which God gives humans dominion over all other creatures. Is this biblical text a license for humans to exploit all others, or a warning about the power they have over all non-humans and an implicit instruction to use it wisely? A green image of God and a green anthropology cannot gloss over these difficult moments in the tradition; rather, it needs to grapple head on with the notion that these texts are teaching tools and inspiration for humans to live better. The point is not to live like a god who causes destruction at will, but rather to live like the God who humbly engages all creatures with love and mercy.

SUMMARY

In the first part of this chapter, the complex relationship between God and humanity was explored—one in which humans must balance their desire to be like God with the reality that they are not God. To further underscore this point, we focused on the otherness of God, specifically the notion that the Creator is distinct from creatures on the basis of God being infinite and not being limited by the rules of nature. As the chapter progressed, we looked at how human beings always strive to imagine God, even in the midst of this otherness. It was noted how Christians image God through interpreting scripture, tradition, and the signs of the times. All symbols of the Divine have an influence on creaturely existence by orienting individuals on a specific trajectory. A green image of God may have the power to wake humans from their slumber during this time of environmental degradation and encourage them to be more active in healing the cosmos. While this chapter emphasizes the otherness of God and what that means for humans, the next chapter is an elaboration on the uniqueness of creaturely experience in terms of finitude. It is to the question of human need that we now turn.

EXERCISES:
1. **Complete a journal entry on this topic.**
2. **Online Research**

Go to http://www.google.com/imghp (Google images web-page) and search images for the term god. What types of images come up? Do they match what you would expect? Why or why not? Are they mostly Christian images? How do you know? Then type in the word Jesus. Again, reflect on what types of image come up and how they fit what you have read so far as well as your expectations. You can do the same type of exercise with a visit to your local museum if they display Christian art. If such a museum is not available, visit a local church.

3. **Think-Pair-Share** (Reflect on these questions silently, find a partner and discuss them together, and then share with the class.)
   - How might Christians live life differently if they really believed that Jesus was human in every way?
   - Do you feel pressures to be perfect? If so, in which aspects of your life, and how has the pressure influenced your life?

4. **Creative Time**

With your best pens, pencils, markers, crayons, and paint, create an image of a green God. Share it with others, discussing what you created and why. This should be fun, not pressure. Nobody needs to be perfect—most of us are amateur artists.

NOTES

1. Gen 1:27 (NRSV).
2. Jean Vanier, *Becoming Human* (Mahwah, NJ: Paulist Press, 2008), 120–22.
3. Gen 1:31 (NRSV).
4. For more on this complex, see an elaboration in Michele Saracino, *Clothing: Christian Explorations of Daily Living* (Minneapolis: Fortress Press, 2012), 41–44.
5. Gen 2:18 (NRSV).

6. Gen 2:25 (NRSV).

7. For an excellent discussion of the councils of Ephesus and Chalcedon, as well as others throughout church history, see Christopher M. Bellitto, *The General Councils: A History of the Twenty-One Church Councils from Nicaea to Vatican II* (Mahwah: Paulist Press, 2002), 22–27.

8. As cited in *Constructive Theology: A Contemporary Approach to Classical Themes*, eds. Serene Jones and Paul Lakeland (Minneapolis: Augsburg Fortress Press, 2005), 168.

9. For a survey of theological approaches to the incarnation, see Oliver Crisp, *Divinity and Humanity: The Incarnation Reconsidered* (Cambridge, UK: Cambridge University Press, 2007).

10. For an interesting analysis of the idea of indwelling versus juxtaposition, see Joseph Cardinal Ratzinger (Pope Benedict XVI), *Behold the Pierced One: An Approach to a Spiritual Christology*, trans. Graham Harrison (San Francisco: Ignatius Press, 1986).

11. Anne Lamott, *Bird by Bird: Some Instructions on Writing and Life* (New York: Anchor Books, 1995), 28.

12. Kramer, *A Time to Plant*, 9.

13. Exod 33:11; Deut 34:10 (NRSV).

14. Exod 33:20–23 (NRSV).

15. For an in-depth look into metaphors describing God and how they relate to our ecological crisis, see Sallie McFague, *Models of God: Theology for an Ecological, Nuclear Age* (Minneapolis: Fortress Press, 1987).

16. Gen 6:5–7 (NRSV).

17. Gen 9:8–11 (NRSV).

Chapter 3

YOU'RE SO NEEDY

There are many ways to speak about being a creature, being mortal, and experiencing finitude. We could frame being a creature as being the opposite of God and as being totally other from the infinite. We could talk about how for all creatures life on earth is limited. We are born and die, and hopefully have a number of life-giving years between these two momentous events. Additionally, we could discuss creaturely existence in terms of the laws of physics since most us have experienced the basic axioms of being constrained by space and time. We know that what goes up must come down and that we cannot physically be in two places at once. And while technology certainly allows for face time across wide spans of space, we are still physically in one place and virtually in another. What's more, we cannot stop time or speed it up. It continues on whether we like it or not. All these are important angles from which to explore the finitude of creatures. Ultimately, they all point to a common experience; namely, that all creatures need others. The fact that creatures are limited by space, time, resources, ability, talent, social and political situations, and so on means that we cannot do everything by ourselves. We are dependent on others and, for better or for worse, are needy.

There is no getting around creaturely need. Plants need water and sunlight to grow. Nonhuman animals need plants and other animals to flourish. Human animals rely on others for food, warmth, and companionship. Everywhere we turn we see that every creature is needy; yet, this reality does not go down easy. In fact, it is not unusual for the terms *needy* and *neediness* to trigger a knee-jerk reaction. One of the worst things my husband can say to me is not that I am a bad wife, a mean mother, or a mediocre theologian, but rather that I am needy. That phrase stings the most. I have always been taught implicitly if not explicitly that to be fully human means *not to need*. I should be independent, self-sufficient, in control, and a leader. Perhaps others have similar aversions to being called needy. They may feel like they are being a "nag" or being a downer, that they are holding others back because of their neediness. Some may even feel that if they don't stop being needy, others won't want to be their friends anymore. In many ways, social media and electric technology have exacerbated this situation of not wanting to appear needy, by encouraging us to text instead of call, email instead of write. One student told me that it is too forward to call someone that one is interested in romantically. Texting first is far less needy, and hence more attractive. From a commonsense perspective, being needy is correlative with being undesirable and unlovable.

In all likelihood, many of our responses to neediness are far more nuanced than what has been suggested here. If and when someone calls us needy, they are signaling to us that we are demanding more of them physically or emotionally than they are able to give. We may be asking too much. Perhaps a friend or loved one is hoping that we recognize their needs and give them space. What follows is a discussion of our conflicted feelings about human neediness. This is not meant to exclude other species. Quite the opposite, in exploring the ambivalent feelings human animals experience over being needy, we may gain a better understanding of the place of all animals in the cosmos and create a foundation for our green anthropology.

ORIGINS OF OUR AMBIVALENCE

Why are we conflicted or ambivalent about our neediness? Who is to blame? Enlightenment thinkers like Jean-Jacques Rousseau and Immanuel Kant are often touted as individuals in history whose thought devalued dependence on others, and supported worldviews and societies that valorized independence. It is hard to imagine, however, that this problem of not wanting to need and our antipathy to being needy began just a few centuries ago. While the "turn to the subject" mentality of modernity, with its emphases on self and reason, certainly worsened the situation, it is probably more the case that being torn up about being needy has always been part of the human condition. Recall in the previous chapter how I noted that Reinhold Niebuhr, a prominent American Protestant theologian, argued that a fundamental challenge to being human is the stress caused by our desire to be perfect and godlike, even with the knowledge that creaturely existence is characterized by limits.

Clearly, the fear of being needy runs deep. As such, it is worth exploring where else we learn that it is bad to need. From an early age, those living in a globalized capitalist world are pressured into the mentality that the best way to be human is to surpass limits, overcome barriers, and to be independent to an extreme—to not need. This is why being called needy can be so painful. We learn that our neediness conflicts with the social norm to be in control of everything, on top of everything, and so on. It is not that our parents, teachers, or friends say dependence is bad and failure is deadly. Rather, it is more the case that we get social cues that make our neediness seem shameful and anything less than perfection seem sinful.

I clearly remember running home from high school one day years back, excited to tell my father that I received a 98 percent for my grade on an important exam. I was thrilled to see him bursting with pride. The excitement didn't last long, as he quickly asked, *Why didn't you get 100 percent?* After the exchange, we both had a good laugh. I was used to these expectations, so this is not a bad memory for me or a sad story. Rather this was the norm and the narrative that continues to drive my life today, and I would guess the lives of others. Now I am all grown up, so to speak. A parent myself, I witness my peers struggling with the performance of their kids on the baseball and football fields. They waver between being relieved that their children are holding their own on the field and holding back their parental desires to push their children to do more—to hit harder and to run faster. Parents are supposed to expect more from their children even as they support their efforts. In fact, sometimes in our quest for success we call parents neglectful if they do not support and push their kids to or beyond their limits.

As a college professor, I witness aspects of the downside of this pushing. I meet students who are frazzled from pulling all-nighters to complete their term papers and study for exams, all to keep their high averages and scholarships. I see students who release all their anxiety in binge drinking to the detriment of their health, and perhaps in some instances, to the detriment of others around them. At the college and elsewhere, one can find pockets of conversation about the challenges of maintaining a work/life balance—meaning having a life, whether that is a family or hobbies, and being productive at work and school. Still, substantive discussions over the matter are few and far between. Most of the undergraduates I encounter are burdened by the prospect of having to manage it all—and it sometimes seems like it is just too much to bear.

As we have discussed, and perhaps experienced in our own lives, this is the shadow side of the god complex. We want to be like God or be God, and know we can't. So instead, we "settle" for thinking we can be superhuman. This too of course is impossible, but we are so ashamed of being needy that we run ourselves ragged trying to cover up and hide our limits. When we look at Genesis 2, which in many ways provides an antidote or at least a balance to the god complex engendered in Genesis 1, we see that a significant dimension of the doctrine of the human person is an embrace of this neediness. When God finds Adam lonely—in need—God attends to it. The story does not demonstrate God being angry with Adam for being lonely. God does not judge or blame Adam for not being good enough; rather, God is portrayed as being there for Adam in his loneliness. Neediness is not demonstrated as a sin; rather, as a fact of earthly being. Most important, Adam's need creates the opportunity for a deeper relationship between Creator and creation.

At face value it appears that human neediness is distinct from that of many of the other creatures on the planet. There are plenty of creatures that have been observed in nature that seem to not need as much as humans. For example, after lemon sharks are born, they are forced to survive on their own in the shallow areas of the shore. However, they still need. They need the plants of the seascape to camouflage themselves from predators and they need other creatures for food. Unlike sharks, orca whales are vigilant about the welfare of their young. Orca calves could not survive without their mothers' milk and without learning how to hunt. Both species need, but it is fair to say they have different levels of needing others.

This is a significant point, because one could make the argument that some species have more value than others, depending on their level of interaction with and neediness for another. That is a problematic claim because while there may be different levels of neediness among species, all species need others for flourishing and survival. To make this point clear, let's return to the plight of sharks. Even though they don't need their parents to hunt, sharks of all kinds need their fins to swim. If sharks can't swim, they suffocate and die. What we are finding today is that human animals in particular are denying this need and are mutilating sharks at exponential rates. It is estimated that anywhere between 26 and 73 million sharks are finned each year, a rate that is not being matched by shark births.[1] Fins are used for the delicacy of shark fin soup, and other shark body parts are used in cosmetics and pharmaceuticals. The challenge for Christians today is to accept the neediness of all creatures and to be responsible to that neediness. Why do we choose our wants—here, shark fin soup and wrinkle-free faces—over the other's needs for survival?

NEEDINESS AS A CONNECTOR

If our aversion to neediness was not a problem, there would be no reason for this chapter. However, it is hurting us. In avoiding neediness, we avoid our reality as creatures, and our calling to live in full communion with God and others. We miss out on potentially life-giving relationships. We don't think we need sharks, so we do not necessarily have them at the forefront of our minds when making decisions. The truth is that we may not need this or that individual shark, but we do need the aquatic ecosystems to be in good shape so we can be in good shape—and sharks, like many other forms of marine life, are integral to a healthy ecosystem.

When framed this way, that we need the other and the other needs us, neediness serves as a connector in that it propels us into life-giving relations with others and has the potential to give birth to a host of other relationships. The situation of parents caring for their newborn child comes to mind here. Babies need personal contact, as clinicians have long claimed that touch is a significant factor in development. Moreover, babies need nourishment, and caregivers need to provide that nourishment every few hours. Children who don't get these basic needs met fail to thrive. Providing for these basic needs demands hard work. Caring for young children in particular can be exhausting, especially having to get up for those middle-of-the-night feedings. The parent, particularly the nursing mother, needs sufficient hydration and nutrition too. This catapults the new mother into at least two trajectories of relationship—the intimate one she shares with her dependent child, and the others she shares with the people she relies on for food, including friends, relatives, and most definitively farmers and grocers.

This domino effect of needing is also evident in situations where people are caring for their aging and infirm parents. Adult children cannot sustain care for their elderly parents without proper rest and support. They depend on social workers, friends, family members, their church communities, and so on to keep going. When my mother was in a skilled-nursing rehabilitation facility, I found the network of nurses, therapists, counselors, and other people like me—meaning those children caring for their parents—to be my lifeline. My neediness, precipitated by my mother's need, created an opportunity to build relationships and create community.

Arguably when framed as a connector, human dependence on others—all others, including nonhuman animals and plants—can change the way we think about the entire planet. We might begin to view existence as a network of relationships with the other that requires care and respect, rather than use and abuse. If we are honest about our dependence upon the earth, including our need for clean air and the joy that the beauty of nature brings, then we might pause before overusing it.

EMBRACING THE GRACED NATURE OF FINITUDE

In giving credence to the notion of neediness being a good thing in that it connects us to others, readers are asked to consider how they might embrace the graced nature of finitude in their everyday lives. *Grace* for Christians is an important term in theological anthropology. It refers to God's offer and gift of relationship to creation. It is not something that creatures initiate because they cannot control God. And theologically speaking, orthodox teaching maintains that grace is not something that can be earned. While our actions may enhance our relationship with God, they cannot create it. Grace is that which orients all creatures toward God and sustains creaturely existence. It is the spirit that initiates existence and keeps free existence going. Without God's grace, creation ceases to exist.

Just as we lack total control over grace, we as creatures have limited control over all our relationships. That is not to say that we don't have freedom in them. To be sure, we will see in the next chapter that freedom is a significant aspect of creaturely existence. We are always granted by God the freedom to say yes to the relationships in which we find ourselves. That yes-saying is quite elaborate, painstaking, and context-driven. As such, saying yes to another, whether that other is God or a creature, is only possible when we recognize them as another, meaning when we recognize our limits and our lack of total control over them. We need to embrace our limits—space, time, ability, and so on—before we can reach out in genuine openness and say yes to another. Consequently, finitude—meaning our limits, borders, and needs—creates a context for our freedom to be actualized. When read this way, finitude is a gift in that it puts us in close proximity with the other; so close that our need for and connection to them becomes irrefutable. It draws us into relationship with them.

I am painting a pretty rosy picture here. It would be wrong to glamorize finitude in a culture that seems to despise it. Nonetheless, without exposing ourselves as needy, we can never be in a genuine relationship with God or the other. Genesis 2 becomes relevant here. Again it is in that story where God recognizes Adam's need and tries to satisfy it with the companionship of others. We all need, and human beings in particular need the love of others. We can neither survive nor flourish in this world alone. Embracing neediness and exposing this characteristic to others has the potential to bring us into more life-giving relationships. It has the power to heal our loneliness and create community.

EXPOSURE AS A GOOD THING

It may seem strange to use the word *exposure* when talking about neediness. Everything about the word seems so tawdry—it may bring to mind individuals exhibiting inappropriate social behavior by revealing their private parts, or a shameful moment of being caught cheating or stealing. One is right to wonder if the term *exposure* has too many negative connotations to be considered a good thing, never mind something spiritual. It is precisely because of the discomfort it causes that *exposure* is a helpful term for reimagining human existence as green and other-oriented. In revealing one's humanity to the other—one's neediness, as awkward and unsettling as it is—one creates an opportunity for relationship.

A first step in embracing exposure as a good thing that could move us toward life-giving relationships is ceasing to conceal our human frailties. After all if we cannot accept our own limits, how can we accept and aid others as they struggle with their human frailty? A second step is giving up on the myth that we can somehow control every aspect of our embodied beings. That means we need to let go of the idea that our bodies are machines, and that if we tinker around with them enough they will run just how we want.[2] We need to relinquish the idea that we can control every relationship in our lives and secure some good outcome in them. Sometimes, we can give our all to a relationship and it still dies.

To be sure, exposing the myth of being totally independent, in control of our minds and bodies, and masters of all relationships is dangerous emotional work. Nothing about this orientation toward others, toward an embrace of neediness, is going to be comfortable. The most obvious risk of exposure involves losing the façade of having it all together or the façade of not being lonely. As some have experienced, in order to be attractive to others in a culture of not-neediness, there is a lot of peer pressure to keep the secret that we are in fact very needy.

It is worth trying this as a personal experiment. When with a group of peers, admit to feeling scared about something, perhaps being alone or not being able to achieve a goal. There might be some resistance to your exposing yourself, in the form of people cheering you on, assuring you that you are not alone or that you can achieve your goal. The peer pressure to be okay and in control could make you feel even worse. Alternatively, your admission of neediness could have another, more positive effect. Others might take your admission as an opportunity to share their fears. While very little in consumerist culture predisposes us to this type of exposure, it could prove rewarding and connect us to others in ways we never imagined.

There are times in our ordinary lives in which we are involved in this type of exposure without realizing it. For instance, when we ask for forgiveness from someone or when someone apologizes to us, we are participating in an event of exposure by admitting we need that person and their relationship. There are other opportunities for exposure. After experiencing the breakup of a serious relationship, one's friends and family might encourage one to "get back out there." This usually means to begin going out socially and even dating again. Getting back out there is a precarious situation because it means making oneself vulnerable to loving again and risking the pain and hurt of rejection. It involves exposing oneself to an unpredictable relationship, not necessarily a rocky one, but a difficult one, like most relationships, to fully control. We are at the mercy of the other's actions, likes, and so on.

This is all part of the complexity of dependence. It is not just that we have to admit our need for others. It is also being open to their responses to our admission. Since others have their own minds, wills, experiences, styles, and so on, we cannot always easily anticipate and control how they will respond to our neediness. We are in many ways hostage to the unpredictability of their living and loving. This makes us feel uncomfortable and exposed. To be sure, exposure can take many forms, and here I am emphasizing emotional exposure, which includes a willingness in some contexts to wear one's heart out on one's sleeve, not necessarily being a burden on others, but rather revealing one's humanity in all its need.

Embodying a more humble posture is another form of exposure. Crouching down to speak with children seems to aid in connecting with them. Speaking with students in a relaxed posture with my arms at my sides rather than with my arms crossed seems to make me more approachable. Being attentive to our bodies in space in relation to others—all others, including nonhuman animals—creates a situation of intimacy, which allows a more open engagement to occur. I notice sometimes that if I let a dog approach me before I pet him or her, I have less fear and perhaps the dog has less fear and we have a better encounter. This type of exposure is about deferring to the spatial and sensual needs of the other before trying to get our own needs satisfied. And here it is easy to see that neediness goes both ways. I am needy and so are others, and at times it benefits all to defer to the other's needs before one's own.

Another way people can cultivate exposure in their lives is by making choices for their lives that are live-giving in the long term. To this point, embracing finitude may call us to admit that many of the stories we live by do not always brings us what we need most. For instance, we will see toward the end of the book that in figuring out what we are called to do with our lives—what our vocation is—we first need to be honest about everything we have been told about what it means to be successful and have a good job. Is a successful career one that brings in tons of money, perhaps at the expense of the needs of another, or is it a career that might not pay as much but enables one to lead a modest life and feel good about what he or she is doing and why he or she is doing it? This is a difficult conversation to entertain because often we get our sense of what is job-worthy from our parents and other loved ones whom we trust and respect. In questioning their ideas about success, we risk losing their love as well as their support. However, it could also be the case that such a tough talk could birth a new level of intimacy between the child and parent. This is all very complicated emotional work. There is no one right solution here.

There are other aspects in our lives in which we may find opportunities for exposure, including in our choices of friends and romantic partners. Are we open to friendships that challenge us to think, act, and love in new and hopefully more life-giving ways? Are we able to stay in a friendship during the rocky times, whether that means times of our friend's neediness or, perhaps even more difficult, our neediness? Are we capable of entertaining a difference of worldviews without resorting to leaving the person or hurting them? Throughout this book there is going to be a clear emphasis on the biblical mandate to love the other as one would want to be loved. The other here can be one from another culture, class, religion, or even another species. The risk involved in these relationships is an openness to be uncomfortable, wrong, and converted by the other.

In the chapter on forgiveness and love, we will further explore how exposure can unfold in all types of relationships, including romantic ones. For now it is probably enough to say that in many pockets of consumer culture, we have reduced relationships to a transactional connection, meaning we look at potential partners in terms of what they can do for our image and status. This is not because we are intrinsically mean or hurtful, but because we have a truncated sense of what love is and what it can be. Perhaps exposure in romantic scenarios involves working toward relationships that nourish the whole person, not just our outward appearance. Just admitting that the patterns of relationships we are in are not always life-giving is an act of exposure and an opportunity for transforming our lives.

VULNERABILITY AS A VIRTUE— THE WORK OF JEAN VANIER

So far the idea of exposure has been promoted as a way to embrace finitude and connect with others in an effort to honors God's gift of grace and create a more life-affirming existence. The idea is that if we recognize our dependence on others and our limits as blessings rather than curses, we might find new opportunities to relate with God and all creatures on a deeper level. Another way of talking about this is framing finitude and the vulnerable feelings that accompany finite experience as virtuous. And very simply, here *virtue* and *virtuous* are terms that refer to behaviors that cultivate goodness and life.

Jean Vanier, as previously mentioned, is a Canadian Catholic thinker and humanitarian who has devoted his life to demonstrating that vulnerability, far from being aberrant and abject, is a universal and transcultural norm in all creatures. He is the founder of L'Arche, a worldwide network of residential communities where abled and disabled individuals live in community sharing Christian fellowship.[3] As a young man Vanier was struck by how people with disabilities in some sectors of society were treated, as unlovable, deviant, and unworthy of friendship. These L'Arche communities provide a place for individuals with such disabilities and challenges to live with others in dignity and love, and for others who are more typically abled to learn about humanity and community from their interactions with each other. Most generally, for Vanier, exposing our vulnerability is a catalyst for enacting genuine freedom in our lives. In these L'Arche communities, like in all communities, everyone is vulnerable. The person with challenges needs the other for assistance and companionship, and the more typically abled individuals feel exposed in their fears of the other and are healed by their work together.

Vanier's life work responds in many ways to much of what already has been said here, namely that we are driven by the need for perfection and become paralyzed by a fear of failure. In the end, these tendencies cut us off from connections with others. What is so fascinating about Vanier's written and practical works is that he sees embodied vulnerability—meaning the concrete challenges of eating, praying, and speaking for those who have disabilities—as a moment to embrace our true needy selves and the neediness of others. Living in community with the other and exposing ourselves to the physical, emotional, and spiritual nakedness of the other and ourselves is what makes us human. Nakedness is a metaphor for being exposed. Most of our lives we feel naked, existentially, in that we feel like amateurs, yet we spend tremendous resources, including time and money, on hiding that nakedness. What Vanier's life work shows is that revealing our nakedness is a way to create relationship. When we need assistance with food preparation or even eating, it creates opportunity for community. When we need companionship because we are lonely and perhaps have experienced abandonment, it creates opportunity for community. We will return to Vanier's work in later chapters. For now I am suggesting that we consider this idea that neediness in the form of emotional, physical, and spiritual nakedness has the potential to build community across creation.

NEEDINESS AND THE EARTH

If exposure to the other is a good thing in that it creates community and richer relationships, in the face of mass extinctions, how might we reimagine human animals exposing their needs for all others as a good thing? Could such exposure change the way Christians understand the environment and their place in it? Important to this conversation is the work of Seàn McDonagh, who was previously mentioned in the introduction. His work, *The Death of Life*, calls Christians to be attentive to the ill effects of environmental degradation and poses the exponential extinction rates as a life issue.

Most significant for the discussion here is McDonagh's claim that embracing our neediness can have a positive impact on the world. His point is that in giving up the façade of being in total control, we become oriented to conceptualizing our place on earth with other nonhuman animals and plants in more complex ways. More to the point, becoming cognizant of our dependence on the balance of the ecosystem allows us to live differently or, as he puts it, calls us *to live lightly* in relation to our responsibility to the world, including all the creatures and plants around us. To live lightly means to live in a way that respects the needs of others. To live lightly means to acknowledge that human well-being depends on the well-being of others, so we cannot and do not hoard all resources for our own gain.[4]

This is the difficult task of exposure because it forces human beings to admit not only that we hog resources, but even more, that we have very complicated feelings about giving up that privilege of having and taking in the creaturely hierarchy. With McDonagh's points on the table, Christians are called to give up and change their ways. This giving up is not easy. As stated from the outset, we need to mourn what it feels like to be the center of creaturely existence. We need to mourn our monopoly on the mind and moral superiority. It feels comfortable to live as if human animals are the most valuable creature in the cosmos, as if we are not needy, and as if we have complete domain over territory. Some of us are so comfortable that even talking about the problems of this attitude can be unsettling. But if things are going to change, we need such honest talk and affective openness, so we are ready for a new form of being human.

The language of mourning is helpful here because it would be wrong to admit that humans are not attached to the idea of being privileged in this way. We need to tell our stories about how attached we are to our old ways and how scared we are to live lightly. Such storytelling is ambivalent at best. There is so much to relinquish and, like the Rich Young Man in Mark's Gospel, many of us will walk away grieving. When he asks Jesus what he needs to do to inherit eternal life, Jesus answers, "You know the commandments." After explaining to Jesus that he has kept them his whole life, Jesus replies, "'You lack one thing; go, sell what you own, and give the money to the poor, and you will have treasure in heaven; then come, follow me.' When he heard this, he was shocked and went away grieving, for he had many possessions."[5] In the face of environmental degradation, human animals are called to grieve for their way of living under the pretense of not being needy, in order for a new type of existence to emerge.

VULNERABILITY AND THE CROSS

For Christians, Jesus' ministry and death provide a model for exposing ourselves to neediness, embracing our vulnerability, and mourning our comfortable way of life. Vanier refers to Jesus in the Gospels as a messiah who calls all to the table—not just the popular ones, but the sick, the poor, and the outcasts. In a way, this first century Palestinian Jewish man made exposure his way of life. While Jesus, as he is pictured in the New Testament, could have chosen a very different life, certainly a less dangerous one, he sought out the marginalized and in doing so became marginalized. He made embracing the vulnerability around him what we would call a virtue.

There are so many examples of Jesus being exposed by the needs of the other. Elsewhere, I have referred to Jesus as other-oriented—a disposition that came with a cost: his life.[6] Here let's take a closer look at Jesus' interaction with one particular relentless other. According to the Gospel of Mark, Jesus leaves town for some much needed rest. His celebrity follows him, however, and he is hounded by a Syrophoenician woman. When this foreigner, a Gentile and a woman, "begged him to cast the demon out of her daughter," Jesus responds rather uncharitably, "Let the children be fed first, for it is not fair to take the children's food and throw it to the dogs." Nonetheless, she does not stop there and challenges Jesus to give up the pretense of being better than her; after all, he is equating her "other" status to that of a dog. In a clever and direct way, she responds, "Sir, even the dogs under the table eat the children's crumbs."[7] She does not deny being an other, being needy, and being like a dog; instead she reminds Jesus that we all need. Because of her rejoinder, Jesus is moved—converted even—and her daughter is healed. This encounter is a biblical example of how even Jesus has to recognize need as something worth reward.[8]

Stories of Jesus eating with the tax collectors also demonstrate how Christians should value need as a relationship builder. Here is an example from the Markan Gospel: "As he was walking along, he saw Levi son of Alphaeus sitting at the tax booth, and he said to him, 'Follow me.' And he got up and followed him. And as he sat at dinner in Levi's house, many tax collectors and sinners were also sitting with Jesus and his disciples—for there were many who followed him. When the scribes of the Pharisees saw that he was eating with the sinners and tax collectors, they said to his disciples, 'Why does he eat with tax collectors and sinners?' When Jesus heard this, he said to them, 'Those who are well have no need for a physician, but those who are sick; I have come to call not the righteous but sinners.'"[9] Here human need becomes the priority, not something to be avoided; rather, to be embraced. In both these scriptural stories, Jesus shows that we need others, and that for deep relationships to develop one is obligated to be open to being wrong, insecure, and stripped of social status in order to attend to another's feelings of vulnerability and need.

Nowhere is vulnerability more sacralized than in the crucifixion, where Jesus dies at the hands of the Roman Empire in a most humiliating and tortuous way for those in need. His death was political punishment for his inclusion of the needy into his mission. He was upsetting the apple cart, so to speak, or disturbing the status quo by insisting that the marginalized deserved compassion and care. And for this hospitality to others, he was persecuted. Christians are taught to believe that he felt the pain of the crucifixion, dying by mutilation and suffocation. He did not avoid his human frailty on the cross; he chose it freely. That was part of his yes-saying. As a result, the cross becomes a symbol for Christians of the power of embracing human vulnerability. The Christian belief in a messiah who publically suffers and dies, is mocked and scorned by Roman authorities, and is taunted for not getting himself off the cross, is reverence for the power of human frailty.[10] Jesus is shown to reject all worldly desire for a boundless existence; and in solidarity with all of creation, dies like we all will someday. It is important to note that while Christians believe that Jesus made the decision to embrace this death, not all suffering in life is voluntary. Thus Christians need to be careful when conflating suffering and death with exposure. For example, one would not want to glorify the suffering associated with poverty or exploitation. These are not choices to which one says yes; rather, due to complex situations some end up in dire straits.

SUMMARY

So far we have studied two influences on creation, the Creator's infinity and creaturely finitude. We looked at the human animal's ambivalence toward finitude when it presents as neediness, and suggested that human beings need to relearn what it means to be a creature, to have limits, and to be dependent on others—not with a begrudging tolerance but with a graceful posture toward neediness. It is not as if trying to do better on a test is a bad thing. It is not that we should not push ourselves to be all that we can be. Rather, the problem is when we hate ourselves for "failing" to go it alone, to be even better, or to be in total control of ourselves, and we end up feeling sad or angry and cut ourselves off from life-giving relationships. In other words, we end up hurting ourselves. In the next chapter on freedom we will explore the dynamic relationship between creator and creation, and reclaim finitude and neediness as a motivator for genuine freedom.

EXERCISES:
1. **Complete a journal entry on this topic.**
2. **Think-Pair-Share** (Reflect on these questions silently, find a partner and discuss them together, and then share with the class.)
   - Think about your living space. List several things you own that you consider needs, versus things you want. How does it feel to imagine your life without your wants? Is it a loss?
   - Do you think individuals with physical and emotional challenges today are otherized and marginalized? If so, why and how?
3. **Creative Time**

   Get into small groups. As a group create a script about dealing with conflicts with others and/or admitting one has failed and been wrong. Perform the skit in front of the large group. After the applause, discuss as a large group how exposing one's vulnerability unfolded throughout the entire creative process.

NOTES

1. Oceana: Protecting the World's Oceans, "Shark Finning," http://oceana.org/en/our-work/protect-marine-wildlife/sharks/learn-act/shark-finning.

2. For more on the problem of controlling one's body, see Susan Wendell, *The Rejected Body: Feminist Philosophical Reflections on Disability* (New York: Routledge, 1996), 93–106.

3. For more on L'Arche, see http://www.larcheusa.org/.

4. McDonagh, *Death of Life*, 119–52.

5. Mark 10:17–22 (NRSV).

6. Michele Saracino, *Being about Borders: A Christian Anthropology of Difference* (Collegeville, MN: Liturgical Press, 2011).

7. Mark 7:26–30 (NRSV).

8. For more on the intricacies of this relationship, see Claudia Setzer, "Three Odd Couples: Women and Men in Mark and John," in *Mariam, the Magdalen, and the Mother*, ed. Deirdre Good (Bloomington: Indiana University Press, 2005), 75–92.

9. Mark 2:14–17 (NRSV).

10. See Mark 15:21–32 (NRSV).

Chapter 4

FREE TO BE YOU AND ME

Most value freedom as one of the most important aspects of being human. The ability to choose our destinies and create our lives with integrity is indispensable to finding peace and happiness. In particular, Christians are taught to believe that all human beings are created by God with the capacity for freedom. In many ways, accepting this belief is the easy part. Defining what Christians mean exactly by freedom is far more complicated. It is not a one-time act; rather, it is a gift of the capacity to say yes to God and others throughout one's lifetime. Karl Rahner, a prominent Roman Catholic theologian of the modern period, is known for this idea of freedom as the potential to say yes or no to God. In *Foundations of Christian Faith*, he explains freedom as that "which is actualized in a free 'yes' or 'no' to that term and source of transcendence which we call 'God.'"[1] This is not a willy-nilly nod to God; quite the opposite, it reflects a deeply introspective and spiritual commitment that involves conversion and fortitude. Needless to say, defining freedom in this way—as saying yes to God—is countercultural. It goes against what many of us have been taught, namely, that freedom is our right to do whatever we please, whenever we please, wherever we please, and with whomever we please.

Part of the confusion over what freedom is and what it is not arises due to the conflation of an individual's capacity for freedom with rights. We tend to simply collapse freedom language into rights language. We tend to read freedom as our basic right of being alive. However, for Christians, this approach obscures the belief that it is God alone who grants creatures freedom. Hence, freedom is neither something one deserves, nor something that is automatically given, that is to say, an entitlement of being part of the world. On the contrary, freedom is a *gift* in the purest sense of the word—a gift to be cherished and used with care. Today we exchange gifts for many occasions. Gifts are used to celebrate birthdays and weddings, to show our gratitude, and even to say we are sorry. A gift is something one offers another not out of duty, expectation, or fear, but out of love. And it is with this same spirit of love that Christians believe God bestows freedom unto creation.

It is noteworthy that our discussion of freedom connects with previous chapters, in that it sheds light on the qualities associated with the Creator and creation. Related to God's being, Christian teachings on freedom support the Christian belief that God is good, loving, and generous, so much so that God gives creatures not only the gift of life, but also a respect for their own desires. We get a sense of a god who lets creatures be different, and doesn't try to control them. Related to the identity of creation, teachings on freedom support the claim that human beings are not puppets controlled by God's strings, a sentiment that harkens back to the previous discussion of exposure. Just like God lets creation be creation without exerting total control over it, human beings are called to relinquish the need to dominate all others in their life. We practice freedom God's way when we let others act freely, too.

FREEDOM AS RESPONSIBILITY TO THE OTHER

God's gift of freedom, while not able to be repaid or reciprocated by humans to God, certainly comes with great responsibility in that one cannot truly experience freedom without enacting that freedom in relation to others. As discussed in earlier chapters, it is the difference of the other that calls us into relationship and demands us to act. The need of the other ignites our freedom. Without the other, we would just be talking to and acting for ourselves. When freedom is situated in relation to the other, Christians cannot keep up the façade that freedom is the right to do whatever, whenever, and with whomever. Instead, Christians are prompted to ask: *What kind of freedom is genuine freedom?*

This is not an easy question to answer. In an effort to comprehend the magnitude of the responsibility that comes with being free, Christians might look first and foremost at how Jesus enacts his own freedom in the Gospels. Also, Mary the mother of Jesus provides a model for human freedom, as she is portrayed throughout the tradition as making some difficult choices when faced with freedom as responsibility. In a more contemporary Catholic Christian look at freedom, one might again turn to the work of Jean Vanier, who claims that true freedom only emerges in serving others. Lastly, doctrinal claims about the incarnation are significant to the conversation.

SNAPSHOTS FROM THE TRADITION

Previously Jesus was described as other-oriented in that he is often portrayed in the Gospels as tending to the sick and other outcasts in society, including tax collectors, unmarried women, foreigners, and so on. One might say he used his freedom to make connections across difference. He engaged in the world by serving the despised—not the elite—of the community. The message in the Gospels about freedom seems to go against so much of what many of us hear from childhood on—to look out for number one, that charity begins at home, and that it's a dog-eat-dog world (so we'd better be the top dog). Counter to much of this commonsense logic, in the Gospels Christians encounter a messiah who employs his power and resources to benefit those in need. In this way, charity catapults us far away from our comfort zones, situating us in complex relationships with others.

Take for example Jesus' message in the Gospel of Luke regarding whom we should share our food and space with: "When you give a luncheon or a dinner, do not invite your friends or your brothers or your relatives or rich neighbors, in case they may invite you in return, and you would be repaid. But when you give a banquet, invite the poor, the crippled, the lame, and the blind. And you will be blessed, because they cannot repay you, for you will be repaid at the resurrection of the righteous."[2] This famous passage shows that the path to Christian discipleship is being an agent for others, even if that is contrary to societal norms. As a result of his countercultural message, Jesus' enactment of freedom landed him in lots of trouble. Likewise, Christians are called to this sort of risk-filled freedom in their everyday lives. Such risk-filled freedom in the contemporary world might involve making special concessions for immigrants, refugees, and the poor in our midst. It might mean rethinking personal attitudes toward those less successful around us; instead of blaming them for their failures, supporting them in their successes. It might involve taking personal and public stands against hate crimes or other contentious and controversial issues. This is the level of countercultural work Jesus was involved in two thousand years ago.

In addition to Jesus, Mary also is portrayed in scripture and the tradition as engaging her freedom for others at a great cost to her reputation and even life. Mary figures quite prominently in the Christian imagination. Especially for Catholic and Orthodox Christians, the mother of God weighs heavy on the minds and hearts of believers. She is a model for how to be in relationship with God and humanity—by completely embracing freedom as vulnerability. According to Christian teachings, it is not as if Mary rejects a sense of purpose and freedom that is associated with responsibility; in fact, she is portrayed as reveling in it. When the angel Gabriel announces that she is with child, the Son of God, Mary voices a clear yes: "Here am I, the servant of the Lord; let it be with me according to the word."[3] Like Jesus' yes-saying, Mary's yes-saying is not an easy road. A young Jewish woman being unwed and pregnant brings scorn and potential violence against her. Yet even with all the peer pressure to conform to standards about marriage and sexuality, the Gospels portray Mary as willing to be exposed and vulnerable for God and for others. She is a model of service for all Christians.

Vanier is a contemporary Catholic thinker who uses Sacred Scripture to endorse a sense of freedom that is at the service of others, and as a result, is quite critical of the individualistic interpretations of freedom with which many of us are familiar. For Vanier, freedom is born in our exposing our frailties to the other. We may be born human, according to Vanier, but we have to become human by opening up to vulnerability in ourselves and others so genuine freedom can emerge. It is the fear of our own imperfections, weaknesses, and needs, as well as those of the other, that prevent us from being truly free. This is difficult because at times it feels as if we live in a culture of unchecked and unquestioned competition. Contemporary consumer society fears any weakness and certainly fears failure, giving way to a distorted sense of freedom—one in which we use our power and resources to dominate the other. Constantly bombarded by the media about who we should be and how we should act, many of us feel like complete failures if we cannot attain the images on the screen. We feel inadequate if we cannot *Just Do It* like the Nike advertisements suggest or if we cannot get that big house and designer clothes that we see on reality television shows. We become paralyzed by these feelings of failure; they become obstacles to our making changes and building positive relationships in our ordinary lives. For Vanier, rather than fostering relationships, this perverse sense of freedom causes us to become held up within ourselves with no connection to others. It forces us to constantly compete with instead of love the other. It can drive us crazy because we will always be wondering if we have enough or are good enough. It leads to a lonely existence. Moreover, we are left with the opposite of freedom; we are imprisoned by our own fears.

THE INCARNATION AND FREEDOM

We have already looked at scripture with an eye on how freedom is explained. Now it is important to look at specific church teachings on freedom not just in relation to Jesus' ministry, but in relation to his being, too. Here teachings on the incarnation, specifically on the belief that God became human in the historical person of Jesus Christ, come to the fore. Simply put, the central question is *how does Jesus exercise free will?* To answer this question, we have to explore how the hypostatic union, which refers to the teaching that Jesus is of two natures—divine and human—complicates the discussion of freedom.

As one would imagine this is a delicate conversation because if Jesus is human, which he is believed to be, then he is created like any other creature with freedom. However, Jesus is not really like any other creature, in that for Christians he is believed to be

divine also. Consequently, one must provide for the reality that
the divine nature has a will too. The conversation gets thorny
when one starts to question if the divine will trumps the human
will or perhaps vice versa. Back in the seventh century, this
became somewhat of a controversy in that some believers made
the claim that Jesus had one will, a belief that came to be referred
to as monothelitism. This idea of the one-willed Jesus became
quite prevalent, so much so that a meeting of church leaders
referred to as *Constantinople III* was held from 680–81 CE to settle
the dispute. At the meeting it was proclaimed that Jesus was of
one person with two natures and two wills, ultimately marking
anyone who believed in the one-will theory, namely monothelit-
ists, as heretical.[4]

The question of wills, of who has them and how many they
have, is tremendously important for those interested in
Christology and anthropology, especially as related to questions
of ecological degradation. For Christians, what is at stake in the
discussion over Jesus having one or two wills is his humanity. For
if he did not have a human will and a separate divine will, it
might be the case that he really was no more than a puppet of
God. The orthodox belief in two wills keeps the otherness of the
human/divine relation intact and protects the intimacy between
the two. Again, the underlying assumption is that Jesus is only
fully human if his will is his own, and it follows, if he is truly free.
If Christ only has one will, and it is a divine one, then Jesus is not
an enfleshment of God and a creature of God, just a robot of God.

Scripturally, this point is best illustrated in the Gospels when
Jesus travels with his disciples to Gethsemane to pray. Jesus is
shown to contemplate his mission, leaving his disciples for a
while in order to make sense of what he has to do. Alone in his
struggle, knowing what he is being called to do, and in fear of
arrest and torture, Jesus is portrayed as asking that his father's will,
that is, the other's will, be followed. See for example the Gospel
of Matthew: "My Father, if this cannot pass unless I drink it, your
will be done."[5] Immediately following, Jesus is betrayed by Judas
and arrested by the Roman authorities. In the midst of an intense
narrative, we sense the importance of these two wills as well as the
significance of Jesus' personal freedom.

It is not too strong to suggest that teachings on the incarnation and the theological belief in the two wills give rise to a model for understanding difference today. This will become more apparent in later chapters, but still carries weight here. Through the hypostatic union, the divine and human natures lived side by side—as creator and creature—with no separation and no confusion. This relationship of difference bears witness even if analogously to the challenges and opportunities in living in relation with all species. When we live so close to another, it is easy to overtake the other, that is, to make your wants their wants, to make your needs their needs. However, as we see in the incarnation, others live side by side without aggression and narcissism. Jesus' divinity does not overpower his humanity. His humanity does not lessen his divinity. Here we have a model for living with the other—a model from God. To be in such intimate proximity with the other and not overwhelm the other is God's gift to creation, and creation's gift to God and others.

OBSTACLES TO GENUINE FREEDOM

Even with all these snapshots from the tradition to assist in enacting other-oriented freedom in one's life, it still is a difficult process. And it would be wrong to assume that individuals who refuse to embrace this sense of freedom are somehow mean, detached, lazy, or ignorant. It is more the case that there are many obstacles and pressures that prevent people from even imagining freedom as other-oriented, never mind enacting it in their everyday lives. We are hindered in our efforts at genuine freedom by bias, peer pressure, and limited resources.

BIAS

The term *bias* conjures a commonsense idea of being against one person or another, or put simply, having a favorite. Here bias takes on an alternative connotation as it is understood through the lens of Bernard Lonergan, a prominent Canadian Catholic theologian of the twentieth century. When Lonergan uses the term *bias*, he does not refer to a simple preference, like having a bias against certain cars or a bias for one type of cuisine over another. Rather, bias, according to Lonergan, is an intellectual blind spot, something that obscures one's field of vision and, most importantly, one's understanding. Lonergan actually uses the term *scotoma* to speak about bias, a classical notion that refers to something that compromises our vision. For Lonergan, these blind spots make it problematic for an individual to fully understand the situation and act accordingly. These blind spots can manifest in the life of the believer in a number of ways.[6]

For example, Lonergan speaks about *dramatic bias*. This type of blind spot is caused by psychological factors, leading to the repression of vital information, prohibiting us from having insights about ourselves that would reveal negative feelings of fear, prejudice, and anger. This probably sounds similar to Vanier's thought on how fear of the other and fear of failure has the potential to imprison someone, meaning keep them closed off from life-giving relationships with God and others. What's more, fear can manifest for Lonergan in an apprehension about being wrong in this or that situation, preventing one from finding out new and more information on the issue. Many of us have experienced this situation of being too embarrassed to ask for more information. However, when read from the perspective of Lonergan, this fear leads to a context of unknowing that, in turn, negatively impacts our capacity for freedom. On one level, fear impacts our ability to act freely, and on another level, the lack of good information prevents us from being confident in our decisions.

In addition to dramatic bias, Lonergan speaks about other forms of bias including (but not limited to) *individual bias* and *group bias*. Individual bias blocks us from seeing beyond our own needs and desires to such an extent that we refuse to be accountable to the larger community. This leads to extreme self-centeredness and egoism. Individual bias can escalate into *group bias*, in which one group cannot see past its own agenda, leading to disparity and injustice within the larger community. All of these biases are important to our discussion of the power differential between human animals and nonhuman animals, including what human animals know about other animals, feel about other animals, and how human existence is framed in relation to nonhuman animals. Ultimately, bias prevents us from using our freedom in the service of others.

PEER PRESSURE

At times, with all the pressures on us, it is difficult to tell if we are truly free. It comes down to this simple question: How do we know if we really are exercising our free will or if we are being pressured by social norms and institutions to make the decisions we make? Take for example the decision of what to eat. In choosing what to eat, are we really free in consuming this or that food product, or are we constrained by resources in our lives, like time, money, and creativity, and hence coerced into consuming certain products and in certain ways? Or in terms of romance, are we really free to love who we want in this world, or do social norms put us on a path in life that seems to control our course? We may think we are choosing a particular path in life because we think it is good for society and ourselves, but sometimes it is hard to know.

When it comes to attempting to be free as God calls us to be, we are exposed to the naked truth that ultimately, in Roger Haight's words, we are "semiautonomous." We are not capable of existing by ourselves or meant to live that way at all; rather, we are in complex webs of relationships with God and others that influence our freedom. An important Catholic thinker of our time, Haight explains clearly and simply that "there is no pure freedom," as "each person is both free and unfree, free and determined."[7] What he means by this is that freedom is always dreamed and enacted in the midst of relationships, desires, pressures, emotions, and values. This is not necessarily bad news for us; rather, it is an eye-opener. We need to be aware of the complexities in our journeys of freedom and try to navigate those waters with grace, saying yes to being in the image of God.

LIMITED RESOURCES

Another reason being free to be you and me is so difficult is that in today's fast-paced world, we are taxed with so many burdens on our time and energy that this task—engaging *freedom* in the fullest sense of the word—is a low priority or just plain exhausting. Learning about situations in all their complexity before we act is time consuming. We live in a world of texts, images, and sound bites. To get beyond this interrupted and abbreviated information pattern involves creating time and stamina for research and fact-checking. Through no fault of our own, time and energy are often the very things we lack.

Sometimes our fatigue looks like apathy. Many times, however, we are not apathetic in that we don't care or have feelings related to the question of what to do and how to be. On the contrary, we probably have very strong feelings or very confused feelings that overwhelm us. Yet our freedom is restricted by fatigue and overload from life. In these cases, instead of judging others or ourselves in our seemingly futile attempts at engaging freedom, perhaps we could help ease the load for all by creating a context where we feel less tired and less overwhelmed.

In addition to the time and energy crunch, engaging freedom is sometimes difficult because there is no stock pattern on how to be free. This is probably self-evident, but worth highlighting. Freedom unfolds uniquely for each individual. We are not all alike. We do not have the same abilities to say yes, the same talents to say yes, the same resources to say yes, and the same social support to say yes. As such not all yes-sayings look alike; and in some cases saying yes may not be possible. There are a variety of reasons that prohibit one from saying yes to the responsibility of being human and of being a creature with obligations to God and others. One instance worth contemplating is the situation in which individuals cannot say yes because of past hurt and trauma. It may be the case that people who have experienced trauma in the clinical sense cannot open to life even if they want to—they may be riddled with pain, anxiety, and extreme stress. Some Christian theologians are beginning to take the concept of trauma quite seriously in their discussions of freedom, most probably because of the rich scholarly dialogue between the fields of psychology and theology.[8] Referring to trauma as an inability to say yes is not intended to leave one hopeless, but rather to show how much work is involved in enacting freedom in our broken world.

TECHNOLOGY'S IMPACT
ON FREEDOM

In the previous section technology, specifically social media, was noted as something that complicates our sense and enactment of freedom. This question is worthy of deeper reflection. The issue here is whether we are free to be you and me through technology. Do all these technological advancements in communication enhance or erode our freedom? As one might expect, the answer to this question is mixed.

On the one hand, if people feel pressured to perform and pretend to be someone they are not, then this technology probably is not enhancing their freedom. For instance, if people feel like they have to have a ton of "friends" on Facebook, they may consciously spend a lot of energy developing their profiles, being witty, and so on. While this may seem pessimistic, it is imaginable that some people might feel invisible and not really part of things if they aren't posting, sharing, and tweeting. In a *New York Times* article, psychologist Sherry Turkle refers to this phenomenon as an "I share, therefore I am" mentality.[9] This is where one's identity and agency is a direct result of his or her virtual presence. Conversely, if people do not post or tweet or so on, they feel like they are not present and not being active in the community.

Another point on diminished freedom and e-technology is related to resources. One needs to have time and energy to enact freedom and say yes to God and others. The "always on" demands of electronic technology eat away at quiet time and meditative time.[10] Sometimes I find myself vigilant about listening for my phone, waiting for the other to call on me. Emmanuel Levinas, an important Jewish thinker of the twentieth century, talks about waiting for the other as a good thing. However, I am pretty sure he did not conceptualize this waiting for the other in terms of a smartphone. Indeed, working and waiting for the phone can be exhausting. What if we put our energies into something else? Do we feel comfortable leaving our phones at home and going for a walk in the woods or a swim in the ocean?

Related to the question of freedom and resources is the pressure some feel to buy the latest technology, even if it is too costly and they cannot afford it. In many ways in our global consumerist society, to be human means to consume food, time, and products. If we keep with the "I share, therefore I am" mentality, then to be human depends on having the technological capability, data plan, and so on to share. Freedom here is potentially curtailed by the pressure to purchase the latest technology—all in the race to be heard.

NOW FOR THE GOOD NEWS

The effects of technology are not all bad. Students frequently comment on the flip ways we speak to each other via texting or emailing, claiming that we use a tone on electronic technology that we would never dream of in a face-to-face encounter. While this may seem like a bad thing, perhaps this technology allows us to be present with the other in conflictual ways that many of us would never do in real life: it is our electronic courage, so to speak. It could be the case that the face-to-face affective encounters that are imagined in this book really do not happen very much, and that electronic technology is a vehicle for expressing our disagreements, hopefully in an honest and civil way.

There are other aspects of electronic technology that assist in our being human. While some may be concerned with preserving the "embodied" experience of being present, not all would agree. For those who have physical and emotional challenges that prevent them from getting out and about to meet others and for those who struggle with social relationships, digital communication is a blessing. It allows them to be present and contribute to the community in meaningful ways. What's more, electronic technology enables one to reach large numbers of individuals and groups, giving way to a new wave of cyber-activism and support. It feeds our desire for agency and enables us to say yes to God and others.

Probably the most moving testimony to the power of electronic technology I have encountered is in Deanna A. Thompson's book *Hoping for More: Having Cancer, Talking Faith, and Accepting Grace.*[11] As she chronicles her journey living with cancer, she speaks about the power of websites that allow loved ones to update others on the status of critical medical events. In a chapter entitled "Embraced by the Virtual Body of Christ," Thompson relays the importance of prayers from people all around the country and explains how that web of support gave her courage and helped her to keep going. This is the power of electronic technology. It can connect and motivate individuals and groups at exponential rates and across distances far and wide. In this way, presence and being connected take on a unique, even graced, meaning.

CONVERSION AS THE WORK OF FREEDOM

We probably already intuit from the discussion above that overcoming obstacles to enacting freedom in today's unique day and age takes a great deal of intellectual, psychological, and spiritual effort. It may seem strange to say that freedom, which is a gift, takes work. When I receive a new gift, the last thing I want to do is work at it. I just want to use it. In fact, I get annoyed when I have to assemble my new gift or read the directions because that all takes time and energy—two things that I tend to run low on with the demands of everyday life. Nonetheless, learning about my new gift and knowing the potentials and hazards of it certainly are important to my ultimate happiness. Likewise, honing one's capacity for enacting freedom takes a lot of painstaking intellectual, emotional, and spiritual work, but as it develops, it is potentially rewarding. From a realist's perspective, there is no way around it. We need to work at understanding the situation before we can act in an appropriate manner. Even with work, we may mess things up. We could choose a path that offends or bothers a loved one. And then we have to do the emotional work to make things better with them. We cannot truly be free until we understand and deal with what is at stake in our choices and decisions.

Already mentioned in reference to his work on bias, Lonergan's thought on the topic of conversion provides strategies for tackling the work involved in being free.[12] He claims that for human beings to be authentically subjects and authentically free, they need to be opened or converted intellectually, morally, and religiously. This is not an uncomplicated process, especially since many people associate the term *conversion* with the situation in which an individual changes from one religion to another. For example, a person might convert from Christianity to Judaism if he or she is marrying someone who is Jewish and if he or she was not particularly religious as a Christian. However, Lonergan is pointing to something different, not a quick change but a lifetime of attempting to understand the world around us.

Employing Lonergan's work as our starting point, Christians are challenged to accept that authentic human living in relation to God and others demands not just thinking, but also thinking about one's thinking, learning about one's surroundings, and making the most informed decisions possible.[13] When read this way, one could make the claim that true freedom is only possible not just when it is at the service of others, but also when it is enacted by an individual who understands the situation in all its complexity. Such understanding is not achieved in an instant; rather, it occurs through hard work and a process of intellectual conversion. It is far from obvious what or whom to say yes to when read from this perspective. Instead of taking the situation at face value, a person working toward intellectual conversion attempts to learn about and understand the person and situation in question without rushing toward a judgment about them or taking action. And for Lonergan, one can only judge who or what something is once all the possible questions related to the issue have been answered.

This view of human understanding provides a critique of the way many of us navigate our lives. As already alluded to, many of us live by images, sound bites, texts, posts, and other quick looks, whether we like it or not. After all, this is the technological moment we find ourselves in; if we refuse to participate we risk getting left behind. While Lonergan's work predates this electronic age, it still challenges Christians to ask whether that type of information is enough to say yes. Think about a news program on television or on the web. The presentation is usually divided into segments or links that rarely foster knowledge of the big picture; rather, they offer diversions and gossip angles that are potentially distracting. While the proliferation of technology certainly has its place, it may be the case that the lack of depth associated with modern forms of communication prevents us from knowing the complexity of people and situations. Lonergan's emphasis on the importance of intellectual conversion subverts this type of knowing by mere looking, privileging an alternative way of knowing in which we gather information, reflect on that information, verify the information, and correct our perspective if we have the wrong information. This openness to being wrong may seem to go against cultural pressures to be right, certain, and unwavering in our views.

Being open to more complex ways of knowing, that is, experiencing intellectual conversion, encourages one to live and act differently, to open to the needs of others and the greater values of the human good. This is where Lonergan's claims about moral conversion come to the fore. Moral conversion moves one from a closed, egoistic sense of what is good to a more communal sense. For example, related to a green anthropology, if we learn something about the sixth mass extinction spasm that scientists claim we humans are contributing to, then we might want to begin to change our ways. Hence, intellectual change stirs moral change.

The third aspect of conversion according to Lonergan is religious conversion, which relates to falling in love with God, and is characterized by a complete reorientation of mind and heart toward God and others. It is not unusual for Christian thinkers to use the love metaphor to describe faith relationships. With love comes a willingness to be there with the other and to be firm in one's commitment to the other. It demands an openness to difference as well as an acceptance of the emotional dissonance that difference brings. It involves conflict—dealing with feeling uneasy and uncomfortable in some stages of the journey with the other. Religious conversion embraces the plurality of feelings associated with love and intimacy—of living with others. Without an openness of heart in this way, we are unfree—tethered to negative feelings, destructive patterns of behavior, and blind spots.

I like to think of this religious conversion as an embrace of the ambivalence of life—or as my son once put it—the "happimess." He was not mistaking his words. He did not mean happiness. He meant happimess as a way to describe that some of the best times in life are the messiest and the most emotionally complicated.

They are at once negative and positive—a mixed bag. Sometimes we might feel like heading the other way from a relationship because the messiness of all our unmanageable feelings tied up with it is so unsettling. But freedom depends on navigating complex feelings. We know this implicitly from ordinary life. For example, if an individual fails to exhibit feelings, we begin to worry. We ask if that person is cold or even if he or she has a clinical disorder. This concern is anecdotal evidence of the importance of feeling in one's potential for freedom. Life is textured by all different types of emotion, including joy, anger, fear, and so on. This does not mean they are all good or comfortable; yet they are all part of everyday existence. Saying yes to God and others depends on welcoming all of the happimess of life.

TAKING STOCK OF PERSONAL CONVERSIONS

Whether people are religious or not, there is a good chance they have experienced some aspect of conversion and experienced a moment of freedom. Related to our green focus, perhaps you have had an experience with a nonhuman animal that caused your views to change on the human animal/nonhuman animal relationship. Or perhaps on a service trip you witnessed how deforestation in some areas of the world is destroying human cultures as well as biodiversity. It is important to make time to reflect on these experiences, as they shape the way we enact our freedom.

I have experienced one such conversion regarding the place of trees in the contemporary ecological crisis. For years I have heard various bits and pieces about the importance of forests for alleviating some of the devastating effects of global warming. But it was not until I spent time reading about trees and being with trees that I had any transformation in action. After reading Jim Robbins' book, *The Man Who Planted Trees: Lost Groves, Champion Trees, and an Urgent Plan to Save the Planet*, things changed.[14] His work encouraged me to entertain the premise that reforestation, the process of replanting trees, is one important way out of this environmental mess we have created. His work forced me to question my own biases related to trees and their place in life. I began to ponder how dichotomous thinking, which separates humans from the rest of creation, blinded me to imagine trees as existing for anything other than human use—for our pleasure.

My conversion began as Robbins, a science journalist for the *New York Times* and other prominent venues, educated me (and all his readers, for that matter) by explaining how forests support all of creation by filtering water and air, mitigating flooding, and possessing medicinal properties. Unfortunately, we have decimated many of the world's forests due to industrialization. What tugs at me most are the assertions that there is a lot we do not know about trees. Some scientists claim that their aerosols reduce stress and disease in humans, and moreover that trees may communicate with one another. These new ideas opened me to a renewed way of living among trees, giving me a deeper appreciation for Robbins' sentiment, "It's unforgivable how little we know about [trees]."[15]

Applying the idea of conversion to ecological concerns brings to mind Elizabeth Johnson's work *Ask the Beasts*, particularly the section in which she declares that in light of environmental degradation, "We need a deep spiritual conversion to the Earth."[16] This may not happen overnight; yet for Johnson it is necessary in order for humans to change the trajectory they are on regarding the death of the planet. Echoing Lonergan's typology, Johnson calls for conversion on three levels. She first describes intellectual conversion as that which allows for one to transcend anthropocentricism. And then there is ethical conversion, which necessitates seeing morality beyond the landscape of human need. Lastly, for Johnson, there is emotional conversion, which refers to the process of affectively connecting with all of creation.[17] My conversion after reading Robbins was an emotional one, which slowly gave way to intellectual and moral conversion. Many of us have these types of changes of mind, will, and heart. We need to talk about them if we want human existence to take a new shape. To be sure, saying yes to God and others is inextricably connected to being open to these conversion moments. They are the stuff of human freedom.

FREEDOM AND
NONHUMAN ANIMALS

So far we have only dealt with human beings and the question of freedom. In working toward an inclusive notion of grace, one in which God creates all of creation with goodness and for life, it might seem apropos to ask if nonhuman animals have the capacity for freedom. And if the answer is yes, one might ask what yes-saying for nonhuman animals looks like; in other words, how does it unfold? In attempting to answer this, a first response might be that freedom is God's gift to give and is it not anyone's role to say God gives freedom to this species and not another. After all, how would we recognize freedom in nonhuman animals? In relation to dolphins and elephants and other socially oriented nonhuman animals, we might be moved to argue that they enact freedom in the way they organize hunts, play, and grieve; but I am not sure what purpose that type of reasoning serves. Certainly there are theorists who are trying to make these sorts of claims, namely that nonhuman animals think and feel analogously to human animals, which paves the way for a discussion about nonhuman animals as subjects with freedom and agency.[18] And one would think these are important connections to make, especially if one wants to dismantle an anthropocentric anthropology.

However, imagining nonhuman animals as subjects—with freedom and all that personhood encompasses—is a wrong move to make in the effort toward a green anthropology. From the beginning, I have argued that the problem is with human activity harming the environment, not with other animals. So the freedom of the ant, lobster, or great white shark really is not the main concern here. It is not how they should say yes or if they say yes that is our concern, but rather, whether our human yeses are leading to their demise. When put this way, focusing on whether nonhuman animals are free or not has the potential to distract us from the main topic: human beings are called to change—to live lightly—in the midst of the sixth extinction spasm.

Moreover, focusing on the question of nonhuman animal freedom may be a mistake because it imports all sorts of human assumptions into a nonhuman world. Many of us become entranced when watching documentaries about the wild, seeing nonhuman animals acting so much like us. We recognize human emotions in the baboon and something analogous to human communication in the dolphin. There is a danger in over-identifying with the other in that we can miss signs of the other's difference, uniqueness, and need. When we look for ourselves in the other, we risk impinging on the other's unique being. These issues about animal subjectivity and otherness are at the foreground of the conversation in the next chapter. For now, I am proposing that the notion of human freedom is what needs to be problematized, particularly in a world that seems to be dying at our hands.

SUMMARY

So far, being dependent on others and enacting freedom have been highlighted as important aspects in human existence. Furthermore, embracing one's responsibility to the other was emphasized as a way to engage one's freedom, as illustrated in scripture and tradition. In many ways much of our talk has been just talk, as we have seen that there are stumbling blocks to enacting freedom, including bias, social pressures, and limited resources. Conversion is one way of beginning to work toward freedom. However, conversion is a grueling process. And at the root of these obstacles to freedom is an insidious theoretical and practical problem that mutes our potential for risking exposure in relationships and asserting ourselves in the world, namely, that of dualism. It is to that problem that we now turn.

EXERCISES:
1. **Complete a journal entry on this topic.**
2. **Think-Pair-Share** (Reflect on these questions silently, find a partner and discuss them together, and then share with the class.)
   - Is Vanier's sense of freedom—at the service of others— the one with which you are most familiar? If not, what is your working definition of freedom?

- Explain how freedom is portrayed in the media, in politics, and in school settings.
- Do you believe nonhuman animals have the potential for freedom? How do you know? Is this the right question to ask when it comes to rethinking what it means to be human in light of mass extinctions? If so, why? Are there better questions? If so, what are they?
- Analyze your feelings about Facebook and/or Instagram. Does your self-worth correlate to your number of Facebook friends? How do your photos work? Is there any sense of pressure when it comes to what you post and how you post it? If so, is that positive or negative? Does it impact your freedom?

3. Creative Time

Write your own personal stories of conversion. Recall a period in your life when you felt imprisoned by negative feelings, destructive patterns of behavior, or intellectual blind spots. Discuss the catalysts for your conversion. Or perhaps describe an obstacle that prevents you from overcoming those aspects in your life that inhibit your freedom. These stories can be as personal as you like; and as such there should be no expectation to share them.

NOTES

1. Karl Rahner, *Foundations of Christian Faith: An Introduction to the Idea of Christianity*, trans. William V. Dych (New York: Crossroad, 1994), 97.

2. Luke 14:12–14 (NRSV).

3. Luke 1:38 (NRSV).

4. For a deeper look into this controversy, see Christopher Bellitto, *General Councils*, 28–30.

5. Matt 26:42 (NRSV).

6. For a discussion of the four avenues by which bias occurs, see *Collected Works of Bernard Lonergan*, eds. Frederick E. Crowe and Robert Doran, vol. 3, *Insight: A Study of Human Understanding* (Toronto: University of Toronto Press, 1992), 214–20.

7. Roger Haight, "Sin and Grace," in *Systematic Theology: Roman Catholic Perspectives*, eds. Francis Schüssler Fiorenza and John P. Galvin, 2nd ed. (Minneapolis, MN: Fortress Press, 2011), 384, 394.

8. See Serene Jones, *Trauma and Grace: Theology in a Ruptured World* (Louisville: Westminster John Knox Press, 2009); and also Jennifer Erin Beste, *God and the Victim: Traumatic Intrusions on Grace and Freedom*, American Academy of Religion Series (Oxford: Oxford University Press, 2007).

9. Sherry Turkle, "The Flight from Conversation," http://www.nytimes.com/2012/04/22/opinion/sunday/the-flight-from-conversation.html?_r=0.

10. Ibid.

11. Deanna A. Thompson, *Hoping for More: Having Cancer, Talking Faith, and Accepting Grace* (Eugene, OR: Cascade Books, 2012).

12. See Lonergan, *Method in Theology* (Toronto: University of Toronto Press, 1971).

13. For more on the link between understanding and subjectivity, see a seminal work of Lonergan, *The Subject* (Milwaukee, WI: University Press, 1968). There he discusses the modern "neglect" of the human subject in philosophy and theology. By using the term *neglect*, Lonergan signals the way philosophers have insufficiently explored the dimensions of being human by ignoring the complex process of cognition.

14. Jim Robbins, *The Man Who Planted Trees: Lost Groves, Champion Trees, and an Urgent Plan to Save the Planet* (New York: Spiegel & Grau, 2012).

15. Ibid., 200.

16. Johnson, *Ask the Beasts*, 258.

17. Ibid., 258–59.

18. For example, see Virginia Morell, *Animal Wise: The Thoughts and Emotions of Our Fellow Creatures* (New York: Crown, 2013).

Chapter 5

DUALISM

Few would argue with the fact that the categories of the *mind* and the *body* are useful. They provide frames for exploring aspects of human existence. For example, we may use the term *mind* to signify mental processes and states, such as reason, consciousness, and thinking, and the term *body* to signify animal flesh, emotion and feeling, and our daily embodied practices, such as eating, sleeping, and so on. However, upon further reflection, we realize that these two aspects of human existence are not separate at all. They are interconnected. We think with our mind and body and we eat with our mind and body. Without enough sleep or proper nutrition, we are unable to think clearly and make good decisions. All sense and feeling is connected to the life of the mind. Yet even though we experience and understand the mind-body connection, we sometimes fall into the trap of dualistic thinking. Simply put, dualism is the separation of the mind from the body, and the valorization of everything associated with the mind over everything associated with the body. It is one of the biggest problems for being human in the midst of God and others because it could lead us to hate our bodies or the bodies of others—both human and nonhuman others. When this happens, dualism has the potential to disrupt our ability to say yes to God and others; in other words, to be free.

The most common form of dualism in philosophical and theological discourse is mind-body dualism, which is sometimes referred to as the binary between mind and matter, between the soul and the body, and between reason and emotion. In each of these cases, the physical aspects of existence are devalued and deemed less important than the spiritual ones. There are other manifestations of dualism in human existence, including the dichotomies between being masculine or feminine, white or black, straight or gay, friend or foe, good or evil, and victim or per-petrator, just to name a few. These types of extreme contrasts force one to adhere to one role or another, not allowing for a diversity of stories within human experience. For instance, while one might identify as a woman, this does not mean she should not be free to engage in activities that are typically characterized as mascu-line. It is peer pressure that enforces rigid gender roles. Moreover, at one moment in life our actions may result in something posi-tive, while at other times they may result in pain and brokenness. Christians are taught that no one individual is all good or all evil. Rather, the struggle of being human is opening oneself to say yes in the face of bias, peer pressure, and limited resources. This chap-ter focuses on how rigid binary oppositions—also known as dualisms—thwart human freedom by distorting reality, limiting it to either/or typologies that end up creating situations of pain and brokenness.

How is freedom thwarted exactly? If we fail to realize that these categories, such as mind, body, masculine, feminine, and so on, are just that—human-made categories—and start to believe and live as if they are descriptive of nature, then we run into trouble. If we do not regard these categories as provisional and always based in a changing social context, then we could feel pressure to consign certain individuals into particular categories, such as rational, male, straight, victim, and so on. These either/or cate-gories—especially those related to one being either rational or emotional—restrict our freedom to embrace who we are and con-nect with others in diverse ways. They force us into preformed scripts and roles that can feel like shackles. In other words, dual-ism prevents us from enjoying true freedom.

Most of us have grown up with this binary thinking, so it may seem strange to question it. Even if these simplistic contrasts make us uncomfortable, we may not have the resources—emotionally or intellectually—to get beyond them. We may even end up passing them on to others. Dualistic thinking is a trap we find ourselves falling into when we don't have the time or energy to think about what we are saying and why we are saying it, and what we are doing and why we are doing it. We use binary oppositions to describe reality when we don't have the emotional, intellectual, spiritual, or psychological energy or skills to grapple effectively with the complexity of individuals and relationships. We end up understanding creaturely existence in either/or terms. Again, for example, we may find it easier to force a person into the male or female category than to imagine an individual having both masculine and feminine qualities. Either/or thinking makes navigating life simpler in the short run. After all, it is easier to put people in a box, so to speak, than to find out who they are, including their likes and dislikes—some of which may seem confusing and contradictory. We are not bad people for doing this—in fact, thinking we are bad signals more of the dualistic legacy. It is more the case that we are constrained by the pressures of life, and use dualisms to make it through the day. In the sections that follow, three threads of dualism are explored, including how dualistic thought unfolds in Christianity, how it leads to hatred of bodies, and ultimately how it impacts human and nonhuman relationships. Perhaps we can move beyond a sense of reality in either/or terms and embrace a more holistic and complicated view of life.

CHRISTIANITY'S ROCKY RELATIONSHIP WITH DUALISM

The classic mind-body split appears in some of the great philosophies of our time, including those of Plato, Descartes, Kant, Rousseau, and others. All these thinkers in one way or another have privileged mental activity over bodily activity, that is to say, reason over emotion, and in doing so have created a philosophical context in which it becomes difficult to argue that the body is important and integral to being free subjects. While most of us don't go through our days thinking, *My mind is split from my body!* we in all probability have at some point or another experienced the negative effects of this mentality. Consider how some of us stress over how to control the unruly aspects of embodied existence. We don't want to be perceived as being too fat, too old, too hairy, too dirty, or too emotional. Scholars specializing in the field of disability studies argue that perceptions about what is human and what is not are connected to pressures in consumerist culture to have full control of our bodies, including ability, size, endurance, and so on. This is referred to as the myth of control. Dualistic thinking fuels this myth by justifying the idea that if an individual could just get control over his or her body—control *being* a catchall term for monitoring flesh, feelings, and frailty— then he or she would be better, more lovable, and more desirable.

While much of Christian theology has been influenced by philosophical thinking that privileges mind over matter and reason over emotion, it is important to keep in mind that according to orthodox Christian teachings, dualism is a heresy. Christianity's struggle with the heresy of dualism and dualistic strands of thought has a long history. The religion of Manichaeism, which began in the third century CE, touted a dualism so rigid that all matter was considered evil, and the only hope for redemption was death in this world and release of one's soul. Manichees practiced rigorous ascetical practices, including strict prohibitions related to food and sex. Interestingly, St. Augustine was a Manichee for years until he converted to Christianity. This biographical fact certainly sheds light on Augustine's continued struggle with body and materiality in his understanding of sin, even as he became a devout Christian and theological giant. Later in Christian history, specifically in the medieval period, the Cathars developed as a Christian dualist sect that was ultimately dismissed and suppressed by the institutional Catholic Church due to its extreme teachings.

To be sure, Christianity is a religion that historically and even in the contemporary period must grapple with how to interpret embodiment and materiality. There is no avoidance of the issue. Bodies are everywhere in the Christian tradition. There is the human body of the believer, the ecclesial body (the church), and the incarnate body of Christ. Moreover, orthodox teachings reflect that matter is good and connected to the spiritual realm. After all, Christians believe that God created creatures from the earth and that that is a good thing. Christians are taught to love and emulate a god that became enfleshed. All Christians celebrate sacraments in which God's grace breaks into the world, setting the stage for a sacramental imagination that feels God in the world, not against the world. And some Christians honor the clothing and body parts of dead holy ones called saints, a practice referred to as the veneration of relics.

Even with all this positive talk about materiality, Christians are not immune from the trap of dualistic thinking. Dualism has plagued Christianity from its beginnings, and even in orthodox theology we find traces of it. The mind-body problem surfaces in conversations about the soul and spirit of the believer, in that the separation between the mind and body is correlated with the distinction between the soul and the body. The soul is the term Christians use to represent the spiritual essence of an individual —the trace of the sacred in human beings. One might imagine how it is easy to think of the soul as totally disconnected from the body, with the soul being more important to the individual than the body. This is particularly true when the soul is conflated with the mind and reason.

Things become even more complicated when we talk about death and the soul. When we die, we know our bodies decompose; yet Christians believe that the soul lives on. In that respect it is difficult *not* to be dualistic, because it appears at face value that because the soul lives on it is by default more important. That is not true according to orthodox teachings; still common Christian practices encourage these sorts of faulty assumptions. One such practice is when believers pray for the souls of the departed. This tradition is quite prevalent and poignant; yet there is no consistent, public prayer for their bodies. This one-sided concern might give the impression that for Christians, a person's soul is what really matters.

Common beliefs about the resurrection of the body also lead to ambivalence about the importance of embodied being in creaturely existence. For example, Christians are taught to believe that all will be resurrected with their bodies for a final judgment. At face value, this teaching on bodily resurrection seems to raise the status of the body. Nonetheless, scriptural passages on the resurrected body are less convincing about the value of real, fleshy bodies. For instance, Paul, a missionary of the early Jesus movement, explains in his First Letter to the Corinthians that human beings are resurrected in a spiritual body.[1] This is not the body that we are used to, with scars and age spots. It is not the body we are accustomed to living with twenty-four hours a day, seven days a week. In another example, this one from the Gospel of Luke, the disciples encounter the risen Jesus, yet they are unable to tell from his appearance that it is him. It is only when he eats with them that they recognize him: "When he was at the table with them, he took bread, blessed and broke it, and gave it to them. Then their eyes were opened, and they recognized him."[2] His body does not signal his identity. It is almost as if his spirit and actions matter more. These are two examples in scripture of the ambiguity of the role and essence of the body in the afterlife. While not necessarily dualistic, there certainly is the sense that real fleshy bodies are not as important as souls. As we can see, Christianity does not exist in a vacuum, and as such is not free from the dangers of dualistic thinking.

BODY AS THE ENEMY

This may seem like a strange heading. Many of us don't consciously hate our bodies or think of it as the enemy. In fact it could be argued that we love our bodies so much that we spend exorbitant amounts of time and money on perfecting them, or at least trying to. We work out at health clubs and eat healthy foods in an effort to respect our embodied selves. We take care of babies' bodies with diligence and care. No soap is too gentle for newborn skin. In addition to honoring our bodies through exercise, maintaining a healthy diet, and grooming practices, we tell the importance of embodied being through ritual practices of piercing, tattooing, and even circumcision. In these ways the human body becomes transformed into a canvas on which we share our most intimate hopes and dreams. Here our bodies are sites of creativity and love, worthy of our care.

But at the same time as we are attentive to taking care of our bodies, we get messages from an early age that bodies and material life are dirty and dangerous. We become afraid to talk about sex with our parents and teachers, and with little good information about what we are feeling sexually and otherwise, we start to resent our bodies. These are moments in which dualism rears its ugly head. Our bodies become the site of all our uncertainty over what it means to be a desiring or desirable person. This confusion manifests in many ways. We may repress our desires. We may obsess over our appearances. If we want to get really specific, we may even bathe ourselves often and with the most potent products to make sure that no part of us is offensive. And as commercials seem to show, it appears that soap is not enough, so it is necessary to apply perfumes and body mists to further conceal our bodily odors. We are coaxed by consumerist strategies to believe that the aging process is something we can control, making plastic surgery and Botox treatments standard. We hate our bodies for getting tired, for having limits. And much of the neediness we avoid as discussed in the third chapter is tied to emotional and physical vulnerability.

It is not uncommon to think that girls and women face more peer pressure than boys and men when it comes to controlling their bodies. Nonetheless, in a book entitled *The Adonis Complex*, clinicians analyze the harmful effects of the gym culture on men and boys.[3] They claim that analogous to the anxiety women and girls feel over the burden to be thin and beautiful, their male counterparts feel pressure to be big and muscular to an extreme, giving rise to a type of disorder they call bigorexia. A common feature of all who suffer from body image disorders is a compulsion to control and master their bodies in unhealthy ways, and a fear that if they cannot, they are failures. Bigorexia is a sickness in which males work their bodies to be buff and big at all costs, using steroids and weight training to an extreme.

The pressures of bigorexia, like those of other eating and body-image disorders, have the capacity to ruin relationships, not to mention an individual's health. Harkening back to the chapter on neediness, there is not an acceptance of bodily vulnerability; hence many of us are in a constant battle to look a certain way and act a certain way. Bigorexia, like other body disorders, feeds on the fear of vulnerability, and at the root of it is a fear of ordinary embodied existence. This is where the dualism comes in, when we begin to see our body as an enemy. It is our enemy because we are in a constant battle with it to be better, good enough, loveable, and for some, to be worthy of God's grace.

HAVING A BODY VERSUS BEING A BODY

Stephanie Paulsell writes about the challenges of dualistic thinking in her work *Honoring the Body: Meditations on a Christian Practice*. She names a tension that many of us live with throughout our lives, the struggle between "having a body" and "being a body."[4] A dualistic mentality encourages us to live like we *have* a body. When we have something we feel ownership and power over it, and tend to treat it like an object separate from ourselves that is for our use and enjoyment. I have a car. I have a pen. The car and pen are other than me; they are for my use. Paulsell challenges her readers to engage the world not as if their bodies are objects, but as if they are part of their identities—a basis for their existence and essential part of their well-being. When we live life in terms of *being* a body, we are more apt to care for our bodies in life-giving ways, not just in a fight for control. We love them, forgive them, and care for them. They are who we are.

Most of us probably have a view that falls somewhere in between feeling like we have a body and we are a body. While we know intellectually that we could not live without the warmth generated from our fat, we hate being thought of as fat or even as having an average body size. And while we are well aware that the aging process is natural and part of the cycle of life, we don't like getting older. Perhaps our eyesight seems diminished and we have trouble reading texts and restaurant menus. We may have some age-related arthritis in our knees from wear and tear, which means we have trouble keeping up with some others in our lives. In these scenarios not everyone is content to say, *Oh well, there's nothing I can do about it.* If we do have that sentiment, we may experience push back from others. They may tell us outright, *Of course you can do something about it. You just need to push yourself more. After all fifty is the new forty!* While all these reactions are quite normal for our culture, they are made more extreme and dangerous by dualistic thinking in which we see our bodies as objects to be tamed.

If we thought of existence as being a body rather than having one, then our perceptions of embodied self and other might change. We might not feel the unending pressure to stop the aging process. If we thought of our beings as inextricably connected to our embodied natures, we might be less obsessed with sculpting our bodies into unhealthy perfection, either through too much dieting or ingesting steroids. If we really got on board with a sense that material existence is existence, it might be the case that our relationships with ourselves, other individuals, and even nonhuman animals would change—for the better. Perhaps we might be one body among many, no better and no worse, inclusive of all creatures. We would be more tolerant and even seek out individuals who are less than the idealized perfect body type and build relationships across borders.

A SLIPPERY SLOPE

Dualism does not end with us despising our own flesh. In fact, we could start to hate others' flesh too. This happens when particular individuals and groups are lumped together as closer to flesh, material, and body than others—as practically soulless. Here the Christian missionary movements across the Americas come to mind. For instance, when the French missionaries accompanied leaders to North America and the Great Lakes Region in the seventeenth and eighteenth centuries, they saw their mission as saving the souls of the indigenous peoples. The native's way of life was seen as base and animalistic. Interestingly, one reason the missionaries typed the Indians as heathens was because of their deep connection to the earth and nonhuman animals.

There are other examples of this slippery slope between dualistic apprehension about the body and specific individuals and groups. Women throughout the ages have often been understood to be less rational than men and to be ruled by their emotions. Most probably because of their capacity to have children, they are also often tied more to body issues and seen as less capable of engaging in intellectual life. They cannot seem to escape their biology. This made the accusations of witchery against women throughout the ages all the more plausible. Their bodies were seen as the devil's playground. The slippery slope does not end with women. If we reflect on the catastrophic history of chattel slavery in the United States, where persons of color were traded as objects and their bodies poked and prodded as those of nonhuman animals are, we can detect more evidence of one group being devalued and exploited in relation to the other on the basis of a supposed intimate relation to materiality. These are just a few instances where certain human animals are seen as fleshier, and hence as less human, than others. It is as if reason is the marker of subjectivity and value. And only some individuals are understood to be capable of reason, while others are not.

Keeping in mind Vanier's spiritual writings, one may anticipate how this dualistic mentality could devolve into a situation in which some individuals, for example, persons with intellectual and emotional challenges, could be typed as less than human. While few would want to make these claims in this way, this is one way in which a dualistic mentality could unfold. Clearly this idea that only some humans have value—and that value is based on a constructed notion of reason and intelligence—could have disastrous effects. To continue with the metaphor of the slippery slope, as one moves toward a green anthropology one begins to see how, if the soul, and hence spirituality, is valued over the body, and thus materiality, then it is possible to dismiss the significance of nonhuman animals in creation. What is the answer then? Does one insist that nonhuman animals have souls, the capacity for reason, and are free subjects? Or does that line of reasoning just strengthen the destructive effects of mind/body dualism?

BEYOND BODILY LIMITS

As we reflect on the question of dualism as it relates to body, materiality, and emotion, we might consider how digital life influences one's experience of materiality and embodiment. These issues are hinted at in chapter 3 on neediness and become prominent in chapter 4 on freedom, coming to fruition here when speaking about dualism. Simply put, in this section we evaluate the role of the body in digital life. Is it the case that with increased communication with others through Skyping, texting, gaming, and so on we are more present in our relationships because we have more opportunities to connect? Or is it more that we avoid embodied being—

the happimess of corporeal experience through digital life—through carefully constructed words and profiles?

TELL ME HOW YOU REALLY FEEL

In strands of dualism in Western philosophy and theology there is an aversion to feeling, and beyond that, a sense that any emotion is a sign of weakness. In an age of emoticons, we are urged to ask whether we are experiencing a certain sense of avoidance of genuine affect as we participate in digital life. Emoticons are pictorial representations of the mood of the individual writing or posting the message. A smiley face means we are happy. A frown means we are sad. There are a myriad of emoticons, and while posting, a writer inserts the emoticon to show his or her expression. Hence in digital life one does not read the other person's actual body language, but rather interprets his or her virtual body language. In our study here, we need to reflect on whether these emoticons make emotion more acceptable or less. Do we really know how the other feels through emoticons? If so, fine. If not, then how can we be for the other if we cannot feel for them? Is this more dualism in that we are avoiding and devaluing concrete emotion and human interaction?

One aspect of digital life that clearly impacts our attitudes toward corporeal existence is the construction of profiles, virtual personas, and avatars. When creating a profile, people put their best foot forward, so to speak, by uploading the most attractive pictures of themselves and listing the most interesting and exciting activities they are involved in, all in a tone that is intended to wow the other encountering the profile. Some wonder if it is easier to cover up "real" emotions and human frailties through careful construction of a profile. When this is the case, this cover-up reveals itself as a lingering effect of dualism, namely, the discomfort with embodied being and the messiness of life. Critics of this aspect of digital life argue that both emoticons and profiles, while pragmatic, have the potential to work against our ability to connect with others in deep, meaningful ways, as outlined in the chapter on vulnerability and neediness. Put more strongly, social networking sites have the negative potential to foster light, breezy relationships instead of intimate, embodied ones. We can hide our body language through our virtual bodies and posts, texts, and the like, and this veiling of our true selves leads to a superficial existence. The casual way in which some of us engage many of our friends, enemies, and others through electronics facilitates our flight from neediness—our flight from getting down, dirty, and real with one another.

Roger Scruton, in "Hiding Behind the Screen," writes that "by placing a screen between yourself and the friend, while retaining ultimate control over what appears on that screen, you can also hide from the real encounter—denying the other the power and the freedom to challenge you in your deeper nature and to call on you here and now to take responsibility for yourself and for him (sic)."[5] What Scruton means by the "real encounter" presumably is the flesh and blood encounter, in which one can talk back with body language and a material urgency that at this point our electronic communication technology seemingly cannot hold.

Scruton's remarks bring to mind our analysis of the biblical story of the Syrophoenician woman. Recall how she challenges Jesus to deal with her material and cultural otherness in a face-to-face encounter. He could not escape her by shutting down his screen or application like we can today. Would her command have had the same import if written by text or email? Would Jesus have felt as judged and compelled to act differently if he were not face-to-face with this triple other? Scruton argues that email, Facebook, texting, and gaming allow for "risk avoidance," which is the "avoidance of *accountability*, the refusal to stand *judged* in another's eyes, the refusal to come *face to face* with another person, to give oneself in whatever measure to him or her, and so to run the risk of rejection."[6] Scruton's claims harken back to our previous discussion about the need to move beyond the myth of control in our world, in order to be open to saying yes to the other in the midst of ambiguity and uncertainty.

An overall theme of this book is the importance of becoming open to emotions, and even prioritizing them, in everyday interactions with one another. It has been argued that being open to others is not just about being nice or intellectualizing the situation, but also about recognizing the feelings we have about others—the positive and negative ones; the happimess—so we can move through them to an even deeper relationship. Only then can we have "real" relationships based on vulnerability and mutual exchange. Reflecting on Scruton's claims, electronic technology and virtual reality call into question all presuppositions about real relationships in an affective, embodied way.

ELECTRONIC INTIMACY

In addition to the question of how feelings are relayed in digital life, there is the issue of being present. Few could argue with the fact that electronic technology provides us with more opportunities to connect with others from whom we have been distant, perhaps due to geography or busy schedules—in other words, to be present. However, the question here is not about whether or not electronic technology allows us to connect. It is about the quality and substance of the connections and what is meant by bringing us "closer" to others.

Increased contact times (multiple texts and emails) and zones (social networking sites, phone, email, text) seem to imply an enhanced sense of closeness with the ones with whom we communicate. To this point, my friends, family, students, and coworkers can reach me at any time and through any number of devices, which is different than the reality of a decade ago. I often find myself responding to my students while getting gas for my car, or waiting at the bus stop for my children. I have more contact with my students now than at any other point in my teaching career. We communicate via technology on weekends, at late hours, and even over holidays. Moreover, with the increasing number of threads and responses, my communication style seems to be more casual. By the third email response, I may just answer the question, forgoing the "Dear Student" opening. The sheer volume and informal style of our communiqués might lead one to believe that the professor-student relationship is closer than ever.

However, I am no closer with these students than with students from of any other point in history. In fact, I find that since I have more electronic communication with them and less one-on-one embodied conversations, I am not as connected to them as in the past. And by that I mean that I am less emotionally close. When students come into office hours and we sit down together talking face-to-face, a richer sense of togetherness occurs. We meet each other in our embodied humanity. Neither of us can hide from the other. If they appear tense, I can tell from their body language, eyes, hand gestures, and so on. If I am annoyed by their disregard for the class materials, they can tell from my tone. When they are stressed, I attempt to reassure them with my body responses, with unfolding my arms and with a smile. All the while, I try to tell from their embodied responses whether they are comfortable. Perhaps it is just me, but I cannot quite tell that online. So much potential emotional intimacy is lost through electronic technology.

Already mentioned, Sherry Turkle notes the potential to evade the genuine, embodied give-and-take of relationship through technology. She writes, "We expect more from technology and less from one another and seem increasingly drawn to technologies that provide the illusion of companionship without the demands of relationship. Always-on/always-on-you devices provide three powerful fantasies: that we will always be heard; that we can put our attention wherever we want it to be; and that we never have to be alone."[7] There is an unbounded sense of the self that emerges through this technology, which, if unchecked, could lead to narcissism. Technology is not necessarily a bad thing; rather, it is when we fail to reflect on how it works and when we get too self-congratulatory about being connected that things could devolve. To be sure, what is being discussed here is not a new conversation, as most of us have engaged in tongue-in-cheek conversation about how many Facebook friends we have and how many likes we've received on a post. Still, even in the midst of casual critique, we march on using technology more and more with what appears to be little sustained reflection on how this electronic intimacy changes the way Christians might imagine vulnerability and exposure.

Ultimately being present in the physical, embodied sense is something that has great significance for Christians. We have explored how sacramentality refers to God's presence in the world, in creation, and in our everyday lives. The incarnation promises the Divine's commitment to creation through the presence of Jesus Christ. Every Sunday, Christians worldwide ritualize God being present in the here and now in communion. Christians long for that sense of feeling God through prayer and sacraments, and in nature, in love relationships, and in church. Facing others—being present—has the potential to call them into question, to obligate them, to orient them for self and others. Like all others, Christians value people being present in the intellectual, spiritual, and embodied sense. I want my children to be engaged and present in family life. I want them to pay attention. What needs to pursued at greater length is how being present manifests in virtual ways.

MORE TRACES OF DUALISM IN EVERYDAY LIFE

In addition to creating all sorts of unjust social inequities and creating ambivalence about the importance of embodiment and emotion, dualistic thinking feeds an unhealthy desire for certainty. We tend to sound stronger, smarter, and more powerful if we don't waver or change our minds or even see the other's perspective. Certainty is synonymous with being right. It follows then that if we can safely organize our world into categories that are bounded and secure, then we will be regarded as firm and all-knowing. But as already discussed in relation to freedom, knowing what to do and how to act is not an easy process. Furthermore, certainty is in many ways an unattainable goal. We might want things and people to fit into categories neatly; to have the situation be either black or white, so to speak, because we believe we can move faster in our everyday relations with others and feel good about ourselves. The problem here is that our need for clarity might be hurtful to another who does not fit the box. We are in danger of making all sorts of assumptions about the other, ruining the possibility of a long-term, genuine, truthful relationship with them, and instead opting for a superficial, easy exchange or at least a story that makes us feel good about ourselves. Unwittingly, we may be participating in our own pain and suffering by keeping up the pretense of the box. Perhaps true freedom and genuine life-giving relationships are a result of embracing the gray, the uncertainty of who self and other are.

This is not a treatise blaming this or that group or this or that person. We are all in danger of dualism. I say "in danger of" and not "guilty of" because danger highlights how a dualistic world-view hurts all parties. Guilt tends to blame one person only and leads to the false conclusion that aside from the one feeling guilty, no one else in the situation really suffers. But dualistic thinking is a problem for everyone. Everyone suffers. It thwarts positive relationships and limits our freedom by forcing us into limited options when relating to God and others.

I have experienced this in my life in many different ways. Every so often a teacher encounters a student who does not fit in a box. He or she may sit in the very back of the class, come in late, seem dazed, refuse to participate in class discussion, and yet still may perform very well on examinations. This presents as a difficult situation, especially in courses in which a student receives credit for class participation. A student who does not participate in a class with an instructor who wants to create a sort of faith community can lead to tension, and even negatively affect the tenor of the classroom. Not really knowing the student, it is much easier for the teacher to assume that the student hates the course. Giving them a frame and putting them in a box makes the situation a bit more manageable. However, this is not a positive response. It limits the possibilities; it shuts down any chance for change and conversion for any of the parties involved. When and if the teacher gets to know the student, the instructor may acquire new information that changes the picture. Perhaps the student's girlfriend just broke up with him and he is devastated, or her father was diagnosed with a serious illness. These situations do occur, and it is up to the instructor to work at meeting students where they are and talking with them.

In sum, the reason dualistic thinking is so dangerous is that it forces one to understand the world in fixed categories, with little room for nuance. It legitimizes calling one student "good" in relation to another; calling people who are different heathens because they do not adhere to cultural norms; or even labeling someone not human because of uncontrollable physical attributes such as race, class, gender, ability, and so on. While many of us are comfortable with categorizing creatures because that is what we are used to, we probably don't like it when it happens to us. We experience our lives in a more nuanced way. What is being proposed is not a comprehensive rejection of any and all categories or labels. In fact, many can be helpful and our understanding of them is a sign of human development. If young children cannot categorize shapes and colors, caregivers may worry that they are not reaching the proper developmental milestones. However, with maturity comes the ability to see the gray, or the connections between categories. Not everything is good and not everything is bad. And while such a realization could catapult us from our comfort zones, it is an important realization, especially if we want to break out from the shackles of dualistic thinking and enact freedom in the fullest sense possible.

A LANE CHANGE

One of the effects of mind/body dualism is a complete disconnect between human animals and nonhuman animals, and the assumption that unlike human beings, nonhuman animals do not have the capacity for reason, freedom, and living in full communion with God. This assumption creates less of a moral obligation to them, in comparison to their human counterparts. Acknowledging that this human animal/nonhuman animal dualism has resulted in problems for our world, one might think that a green anthropology would reframe nonhuman animals as free subjects with the capacity to think, feel, and act, analogously to humans. Proponents of to this argument might feel empathetic to their nonhuman companions, prodding humans to consider the plight of nonhuman animals when making decisions.

Much of the literature in the expansive field of animal studies leads toward these sorts of conclusions, that nonhuman animals have an analogous subjectivity to humans. In some ways, they think like us, act like us, and feel like us. Through this line of reasoning, animal studies scholars attempt to overcome the negative effects of the human animal/nonhuman animal dualism, the idea being that since the various species are similar and connected, we must find a new way of living together. While I see the merit of such claims, in this last section of the chapter, I am proposing a lane change. Instead of imagining nonhuman animals as just like us, we might do well to embrace their otherness. This does not mean we should focus on them being closer to nature or without the capacity for reason; rather, we are called to admit that they are different or other and be open to our feelings about their otherness.

Dwelling on nonhuman animal otherness may seem like a strange move. Why would one even consider claiming the nonhuman animal as other, especially since everything labeled "other" seems to be automatically stigmatized? This is the essence of dualism, right? A dichotomy between human animals and nonhuman animals has been set, we feel forced to choose which one has more value, and many of us have chosen human animals. Giving human animals more value because of the way they think, act, and feel, that is, the way they engage their freedom, has secured the turf and ego of the human animal. It is arguable that the human animal/nonhuman animal border is another one of those constructed borders that work to keep one side empowered and dominant over the other. It is analogous to the border patrol that occurs when we talk about the relationships between men and women, whites and blacks, straight and gay people, and even the two natures of the person of Christ. The border that creates a chasm between human animals and nonhuman animals seems to fuel our ignorance of and apathy toward mass extinctions today.

So with all this in mind, why would someone invested in a green anthropology not want to claim all animals as subjects, on the human animal side of the border? For one, so much about human subjectivity is wedded to damaging assumptions about what is normative—like the capacity for reason—that moving other species into that category does nothing to acknowledge the problem. We don't change the fact that the mind is privileged over matter, or that reason is regarded as more valuable than feelings, just by imagining nonhuman animals as thinking creatures. Quite to the contrary, we make the capacity for reason an even more important characteristic when we imagine nonhuman animals as reasonable. Claiming that nonhuman animals can think like us, and hence are worth as much as us in the grand scheme of things, privileges reason above all else. It continues to support a hierarchal relationship between the mind and the body. Put another way, situating nonhuman animals as subjects does little to dismantle the dualism that drives exploitative anthropologies. What we are attempting to do in this chapter by problematizing dualism is to break free of the habit of privileging the mind over everything else and create a space for talking about the connections among thinking, feeling, and acting. It is for all these reasons that instead of focusing on nonhuman animals as the same as us, we might want to consider their otherness.

What is their otherness exactly? We don't know—that is what makes them different. They may look like they are thinking, feeling, and acting in similar ways to us, but we do not know. All we know is that they evoke emotion in us, and those feelings can spark a new way of relating to them. In allowing ourselves to feel for them and talk about the queerness of our feelings for them, we, that is, human animals, are potentially converted to a new subjectivity.[8] At the very least we are drawn out of the habit of binary thinking and freed to imagine new ways of living with nonhuman animals.

It may also be the case that paying attention to how we are changed by our feelings for the nonhuman animal other could lead us to recognize and mourn the privilege of thinking we are the ones in charge of or of importance at the supposed human animal/nonhuman animal border. The difference of nonhuman animals causes a unique concern and empathy for them, which could push us to transcend our position of privilege at the border. In the discourse of Emmanuel Levinas, they (nonhuman animals) might become our concern without them collapsing into us.[9] Levinas was a Jewish thinker concerned for ethics in a post-Shoah world, where Jews and Judaism in certain circles continued to be deemed other. Here his ethics could apply to a green anthropology, in that the human subject becomes moved to act on behalf of the other precisely because he or she is other. While an enhanced or new type of intellectual knowing, like the one we are introduced to in Lonergan's work on conversion, certainly has a role in the fight against environmental degradation, it might benefit all of creation to grapple head on with how the difference of nonhuman animals makes us feel and act.

If we buy into the idea that the otherness of the nonhuman animal has the potential to change us and make us more responsible when it comes to green concerns, it is important to ask what the first step is in this new way of being. For one, we might admit our true feelings for nonhuman animals and how they influence human life, perhaps even how a particular non human animal or Proponents of story has changed us. This is another way of speaking about conversion—this is the conversion based not only in intellectual knowing, but also in receptivity to feeling. A second, more difficult step toward a new way of being with nonhuman animals, and really all others, is admitting that *feelings are important*. We all have feelings about this or that matter, this or that animal, and so on. Often our feelings are confusing and uncomfortable. Dualism devalues the role of feeling in human freedom. However, here I am suggesting otherwise, particularly that reflecting on our feelings creates a space for more life-giving relationships with God and all others.

For example, feelings of love transcend the categories that we tend to force all animals into—human and nonhuman. When we love, this dualistic mentality fades away. I cannot help thinking of the story of Louis Herman, an expert in dolphin cognition, who was asked if he would ever work with dolphins again after two of his subjects died from infection. He responded, "I loved our dolphins...as I'm sure you love your pets. But it was more than that, more than the love you have for a pet. The dolphins were our colleagues. That is the only word that fits....When they died, it was like losing our children."[10] These sorts of emotionally charged stories about human and nonhuman animal relations may be more powerful catalysts for changing how we think about nonhuman animals and their place in the world than merely imagining nonhuman animals as just as smart as us.

Our true love stories about nonhuman animals also have the potential to help us embrace the complicated feelings we may experience about giving up privilege and place in the creaturely hierarchy. As argued in an earlier chapter, Christians working toward a green anthropology are called to mourn what it feels like to be the center of creaturely existence. If we lump nonhuman animals together with human animals, we do not need to change our minds about our minds. We can keep thinking that reason is the highest value of existence. And when we do this, we not only devalue nonhuman creatures with different affinities for cognition, but also implicitly devalue human creatures with different and perhaps less developed affinities for cognition. For real change to occur, in other words, to overcome the insidious effects of mind/body dualism, we need to let go of the idea that human beings are superior because of their minds, and hence are guaranteed the top billing in the drama of life. We need to be open to the possibility of love for nonhuman animal others as well as open to the responsibility born of love relationships. We cannot and should not keep our love stories secret. We need to tell them in a way that bears witness both to the importance of feelings and the place of the nonhuman animal other in our midst.

Like we discussed in chapter 3, such storytelling is not always easy. It brings up complicated emotions about who we are and who we want to be. We may find that we need to change and that need scares us. We might even need to grieve. Recall how in the Gospel of Mark, Jesus directs a young man to give up all his possessions—an order that left the young man full of grief. In the face of mass extinctions, we too are called to grieve, surrendering ourselves to the mystery of brokenness and the grace of healing. As we hope for new life, Christians are called to carry the cross within them—after all, the cross is a symbol of brokenness and healing. Perhaps the crosses of some individuals will look a bit different than traditional renditions of the crucifix. They may have the fins from all the mutilated sharks on them in place of Jesus; they may have Herman's dolphins. The possibilities are endless. Whatever one's image, overcoming dualism allows us to talk about nonhuman animals as other with respect and awe, and ultimately with an openness to how they call us to be human in the fullest sense of the word.

SUMMARY

Above we have explored one of the biggest problems in being human; namely, dualistic conceptions of the person and the world. To feel more in control and to make things easier to navigate, we tend to divide the world into spiritual and material realms, issues related to mind and related to body, reason and emotion, and human and animal. These dichotomies are overly simplistic in that there are always connections between the two seeming disparate entities. Embracing the gray areas is one way to develop oneself as a subject for the other. In the next chapter, a specific dichotomy, that between friends and enemies, is investigated with an eye toward imagining Christian community in a pluralist and diverse context.

EXERCISES:
1. **Complete a journal entry on this topic.**
2. **Think-Pair-Share** (Reflect on these questions silently, find a partner and discuss them together, and then share with the class.)
   - Discuss what you have been taught about having feelings and showing them. Is part of the message you learned related to the idea that an emotional person cannot be reasonable or intelligent? In your experience, are there gender assumptions at play?
   - Do you see your body as a friend or enemy? What lessons have you learned about messy bodies, dirty bodies, and out-of-control bodies?
   - Watch a documentary about nonhuman animals in the wild. Analyze how it is narrated. Does the narrator use language to persuade the viewer that the creature is like human beings? What kind of emotional effect does that have on you?
   - Watch a news program involving a hot political or religious event. Reflect on how the terms *liberal* and *conservative* are employed. This is another either/or relationship that gets used often. What do those positions mean according to the program? Is there any room for the liberal individual to have conservative views or vice versa? If so, how? If not, why?
3. **Creative Time**
   Devise an artistic work, such as a drawing, painting, or poem, that reflects a world without dualism.

NOTES

1. 1 Cor 15:35–49 (NRSV).

2. Luke 24:30–31 (NRSV).

3. Harrison G. Pope, Katharine Phillips, and Roberto Olivardia, *The Adonis Complex: How to Identify, Treat, and Prevent Body Obsession in Men and Boys* (New York: Simon & Schuster, 2000).

4. Stephanie Paulsell, *Honoring the Body: Meditations on a Christian Practice* (San Francisco, CA: Jossey-Bass, 2002), 16–20.

5. Roger Scruton, "Hiding Behind the Screen," http://www.thenewatlantis.com/publications/hiding-behind-the-screen (accessed December 31, 2013).

6. Ibid.

7. Sherry Turkle, "The Flight from Conversation," http://www.nytimes.com/2012/04/22/opinion/sunday/the-flight-from-conversation.html?_r=0.

8. Donna Haraway, a feminist scholar who has written extensively on the ways in which gender dualism functions in culture, also explores how dogs have changed humanity. See *The Companion Species Manifesto: Dogs, People and Significant Otherness* (Chicago: Prickly Paradigm Press, 2003); and see Haraway, *Simians, Cyborgs, and Women: The Reinvention of Nature* (New York: Routledge, 1991).

9. Emmanuel Levinas, *Otherwise than Being or Beyond Essence*, trans. Alphonso Lingis (Pittsburgh: Duquesne University Press, 1998), 11–12.

10. Morell, *Animal Wise*, 177.

Chapter 6

FRIENDS AND ENEMIES

Keep your friends close, but your enemies closer. Few can forget these famous words uttered by Don Corleone, the head of the legendary crime family in *The Godfather* film saga. What the Don means is that we can never trust those we consider to be our enemies, so we need to keep watch over them to make sure they do not hurt us or the ones we love. The Don's words only work because of the dualistic mentality previously discussed, in which we feel forced to group individuals into an either/or binary in order to make life easier. Building on our insights from the last chapter, here we will confront the challenges posed by the friend/enemy dualism. To be sure, from a young age many of us feel pressured to categorize people in our lives as either our friends or our enemies, creating relationships of contrast that do not allow for relationships to evolve. Far from making life easier, the friend/enemy dualism, like all dualism, ultimately makes life more difficult by thwarting one's freedom and ability to develop life-giving relationships.

The truth of the matter is that like the Don suggests, we tend to spend most of our leisure time with people with whom we share common interests and who bring us peace and joy; in other words, with our friends. Indeed, the notion of "friend" is an idea that we learn quite early in life. From the moment children become engaged with the world, they begin to notice that their parents have certain people with whom they tend to spend their free time. And once children start attending school, they learn quickly that making friends is an important aspect of their educational experience. As a child we may have had one best friend or many friends or no friends at all. These relationships, like familial ones, can be quite powerful and can influence our life experience in deep ways.

For children, the concept of "enemy" tends to develop later, particularly when people start to speak about "bad guys," for example in the context of superheroes that fight and triumph over villains. It is fair to argue that the notion of enemy makes more sense because of the idea of friend. We understand friends in opposition to enemies, and as a result, a friend/enemy dualism develops. In other words, friend versus enemy becomes one of those binaries that help to organize our lives. As implied in the discussion of mind/body dualism, it is not that the word *enemy* is intrinsically bad, but once we declare someone an enemy, the dualism is so strong that it is tough to imagine that person any other way—to ever think of them in neutral terms or even as our friend. Moreover, sometimes enemy language is used to impute blame onto someone, making them the ultimate perpetrator and the other the ultimate victim. This does not allow for all individuals to take responsibility in their relationships, or at the very least attempt to figure out what happened, how they got to this point in the negative relationship, and if there is anything they can do to make the situation better.

There are other scenarios in which the friend/enemy dualism surfaces; for example, when individuals are so afraid of others that instead of dealing with them, they label them as their enemies. This could happen when we encounter someone who is different from us by race, religion, country of origin, or even by sexual orientation. We may feel unsettled or afraid, or perhaps in encountering that other, our own identities are called into question. The encounter may encourage us to think about the complexity of our stories in relation to the other's. It is much easier to quickly categorize others as friends because they are so much like us, or label them as enemies because they are so different from us, than to get to know them and in all probability realize that they are both similar to and different from us.

The problem with the friend/enemy dualism from a Christian perspective is that it does not allow for an individual to change from enemy to friend, or to be both at the same time. What this dualism results in is a belief that the enemy is bad to his or her core or ontologically evil, a sentiment that goes against so many of the Christian teachings on love and forgiveness. Christians are called to question the Don's advice. For the mob boss, the reality is that once someone is an enemy, they are always an enemy. The only option is to watch the enemy, so that they do not hurt anyone again. This surveillance is the main way to feel powerful and in control. Christians are called to a different sense of power: not one of control, but one of mercy, in imitation of Jesus' earthly actions.

As we delve deeper into these issues related to who is your friend and who is your enemy, we will explore several questions. First, we will look at how friendship emerges in everyday life. Then, we will examine Sacred Scripture on the question of friends and enemies, with an eye toward the biblical mandate to welcome the stranger into our lives and to love our enemies. Several strategies for answering the call to "love one's enemies" are presented here. These strategies include developing practices of self-care, working toward embracing emotional conflict in negative relationships, and creating opportunities for renewed relationships with our enemies by breaking bread together. Finally, we will reflect on the impact of this dualism on connections between humans and nonhuman animal others.

FRIENDSHIP IN EVERYDAY LIFE

Friendship in our ordinary lives is probably more fluid than the Don's comments suggest. For example, when my children talk about who they are friends with and who they are enemies with, I attempt to explain to them that their enemy today may be their friend tomorrow. It is important to keep in mind that all relationships have high notes and low notes. The high notes are the times when everything between friends is going smoothly, whether the friends happen to be in similar places in life or just plain in sync with one another. The low notes are when friends are at different places in life—for example, when one friend has a good job and the other is unemployed, potentially causing jealousy and tension between the friends. These high and low phases are part of any relationship. And it seems unreasonable to say that someone is your enemy just because things are out of sync.

Such fluctuations are found in romantic relationships and even faith relationships, so much so that it is not uncommon for individuals who are committed to their religions to go through periods of struggle and doubt. This does not necessarily mean the end of the faith relationship; rather, it presents an opportunity for deeper introspection and greater awareness. Not all introspection is comfortable though, in that one may be confronted with another's needs or one's own biases.

For example, perhaps one discovers that his or her friend is gay. At first he or she may feel quite confused, and may ask questions like, "How could I not have known?" and "Why did my friend not tell me?" The person may begin to question the foundations of the friendship and wonder if the relationship was built on a lie. In such a situation, it may seem easier to walk away than to confront the friend. It may be less painful to accuse the friend of being deceitful—or even to label the friend as an enemy—than to deal with the larger reasons for the secret. Maybe the friend who is gay did not feel safe telling the other about his sexual orientation because he had heard that friend make negative comments about gays and lesbians. This would all come out in an honest exchange. Many confusing emotions would certainly arise. Walking away from the relationship rather than dealing with the messiness of it might seem like the best option, especially if associating with one's gay friend publicly leads to questions from others. In order to insulate oneself from criticism about being friends with someone gay, one may drop his or her friend and even ostracize him. It is difficult to overcome the peer pressure to *not* associate with a specific individual or group because they have been deemed other, a problem, a source of pain, or just not popular enough. This is the challenge of human existence. We all need others, so much so that at times we may forgo the good of the community to satisfy our needs through superficial relationships. In doing this we become hostage to the friend/enemy binary.

Since we hear so much about the problem of bullying today, it might be beneficial to elaborate more on the effects of peer pressure on friendships. One of the worst parts of growing up, which can last even into adulthood, is the formation of cliques. It seems that for a short while, when they are toddlers, children are allowed to be friends with whomever and whatever they choose. As they "develop," however, they are forced in subtle and not-so-subtle ways to choose strategically the types of people they want to hang around with, and to build alliances. I put "develop" in quotes because from a Christian perspective, and the perspective of many other religious worldviews, for that matter, it does not seem to be a sign of progress or maturity to start limiting the creatures we call our friends.

Perhaps strategies and alliances are not always enacted with malicious intent; rather, they represent a step in basic survival. We need alliances to survive—a concept that we often see illustrated in popular reality shows and literature. In the popular fiction series *The Hunger Games*, the protagonist, Katniss, is forced by the government to participate in a torturous reality program in which contestants, referred to as tributes, fight in a giant arena in order to be the last one alive.[1] The tributes' survival depends on their ability to be manipulative and make temporary alliances with the most useful contestants. Even as she feels pressured to ally with certain individuals in order to survive, Katniss manages to connect with others with care and compassion. While this novel is clearly fiction and set in a hyperbolic context of apocalyptic devastation and political dictatorship, many of us experience these pressures in our ordinary lives. At one time or another, we feel coerced to choose our friends wisely and create our enemies strategically for our own survival and gain. Still at other times, we take the risk to do otherwise and choose with our heart.

Even if we want to resist peer pressure, it is very difficult to be the lone person who stands up for a person or cause when it *seems* that everyone else is against them. We can never really be sure how someone feels or thinks. A person may feel constrained by forces about which we know very little. These pressures exist in every aspect of life. When going along with the crowd, also referred to as "group think," occurs in the workplace, it could result in coworkers feeling pressured to corroborate the story that one person is bad and the other is good in order to gain positive favor with colleagues or even the boss. When this happens at school, students may feel coerced into defending the perpetrator of—or even being an accessory to—a bullying event, instead of advocating for the victim, because they do not want to become bullied too. When this happens within the national context, citizens could feel constrained to go along with the least controversial view in an effort to prove their loyalty, instead of questioning the broader political agenda.

In order for the friend/enemy dualism not to have the last word on relating to others, we need everyday human beings to become prophets and stand up so others can be free. We find these prophets at certain points in history. One only needs to reflect on the life of Martin Luther King Jr. to grasp the importance of taking a stand so others can be free. King was born in Georgia in 1929, growing up under the insidious Jim Crow restrictions, or laws of segregation. As an adult he became a minister and eventually went on to become one of the most powerful and prophetic civil rights leaders in U.S. history. King's activism came with a personal cost; he was arrested, jailed, and eventually in 1968 assassinated. But his life and death were not in vain; he mobilized a country and the world to advocate for freedom for all and against injustices everywhere.

When reflecting on Jean Vanier's work, specifically his sense of authentic freedom as emerging only when we are in community and at the service of others, then we see even more clearly that a short-term gain of acceptance eats away at our fundamental capacity to be free. Instead of capitulating to this friend/enemy binary, Christian scripture and teaching shows that in order to build healthy relationships all around us, we need to expose and overcome any convenient, fabricated, and self-serving stories about the enemies in our lives. Truth be told, at some points in our lives, we have all probably displayed kind acts of friendship, while at other junctures we may have played the part of the bad guy or gal. Raising these objections to the friend/enemy dualism highlights an important point. While living in a world where there are clear boundaries between who is good and who is evil can be a strategy for *surviving*, it may not be the best practice for *flourishing* in relationships with others—that is to say, for respecting God's grace and human freedom by living a life for others.

FRIENDS, ENEMIES, AND OTHERS IN SACRED SCRIPTURE

Scripture provides resources for how to navigate complicated relationships with friends, enemies, and all the connections in between. In this section, we revisit some of the gospel passages that portray Jesus as an other-oriented person, and more specifically as an individual who in many ways rejects a friend/enemy dualism. Furthermore, we will look toward the Hebrew Scriptures for insights as to how to enact hospitality toward those who present as a threat or as our enemy. Both the Hebrew Scriptures and the New Testament offer strategies for dealing with the conflict that often ensues with an encounter with a perceived enemy. In every scenario, whether between God and God's people, among differing groups, or even at the interpersonal level, Sacred Scripture fosters a broad ethic of hospitality, which extends to diverse individuals and communities, even those that threaten our comfort and safety.

JESUS ON FRIENDS, ENEMIES, AND OTHERS

Already we have seen how Jesus is portrayed in the Gospels as being other-oriented, meaning demonstrating compassion for the poor and marginalized in his lifetime. The story of the Syrophoenician woman is a text that shows Jesus being challenged to practice what he preached—loving others. Is it feasible to claim that the sick, needy, tax collectors, and the precarious women whom Jesus treated with respect and love are more rightly conceptualized as his enemies? While *enemy* probably is too strong a word, it is certainly accurate to think of those others as threats to his safety and status. After all, hanging out with those types got him into lots of trouble with the people in power. It is like the saying goes: "With friends like that, who needs enemies?" However, Jesus is shown to be present and in solidarity with these enemy/others, consequently disrupting any fixed understanding of friend or enemy.

In contrast with Don Corleone's dictum to keep one's enemies close, Jesus is portrayed as changing the question. For Jesus, being

116

faithful is not about having friends or enemies necessarily, but is about a radical sense of hospitality that is displayed in the Golden Rule: "Do to others as you would have them do to you."[2] Both the Lukan and Matthean Gospel editors situate the Golden Rule in a deeper discussion of how to deal with one's enemies. And here enemy should be understood in the more typical sense of one who has hurt another and now is that person's enemy. In Luke's Gospel, Jesus is noted as saying, "Love your enemies....If you love those who love you, what credit is that to you? For even sinners love those who love them....But love your enemies, do good, and lend, expecting nothing in return. Your reward will be great."[3] Christians interpret this as part of the cost of discipleship, framing this as a call to work through and relinquish the anger and resentment that separates one from the other.

Equally challenging is the biblical mandate to not only love one's enemies, but also to not judge them. Implicit in the command *not to judge* is the notion that we all have burdens we carry and things we are ashamed of—no one is free from that. So why do we judge others and in doing so, create a barrier between us and them? Let's turn our attention here to Matthew's Gospel, in which Jesus asks, "Why do you see the speck in your neighbor's eye, but do not notice the log in your own eye? Or how can you say to your neighbor, 'Let me take the speck out of your eye,' while the log is in your own eye? You hypocrite, first take the log out of your own eye, and then you will see clearly to take the speck out of your neighbor's eye."[4] These are some harsh words expressed by Jesus—a clear mandate not to judge others. Isn't that what we often do when we deem someone our enemy? Aren't we judging them without any sense of how other parties and factors may figure into the equation—into their perceived wrongdoing and our hurt?

From this brief exploration of scripture, we can pinpoint a couple of lessons from the Gospels regarding dealing with friends, enemies, and others. First, we see that many of these other-oriented Jesus narratives emphasize the importance of being hospitable in Christian discipleship. Hospitality is not only giving to others but also being open to receiving someone's love, compassion, and friendship. Second, there is a direct call to love those we consider our enemies. This is different than the call to invite the marginalized—the poor, the crippled, the lame, and the blind, as referred to in the Gospels—into one's home. It involves even more; namely, dealing with those in our everyday life about whom we have very strong and often negative feelings because they have hurt us in one way or another. This is probably the most radical aspect of the gospel messages on friends and enemies. It should be noted that this is no easy task and may take some real-life strategies to make it work. By the end of the chapter, we will explore some of these strategies.

LESSONS FROM THE HEBREW SCRIPTURES

It is not as if Jesus grew up in a vacuum. He grew up Jewish and was educated in the Torah, which is Jewish law. Part of the law is to be faithful to the covenants, to the pacts of mutuality and respect, such as the one exemplified in the Noahic covenant between God and all of creation, and in the Abrahamic covenant between God and God's people. Moreover, Jewish law on hospitality goes beyond these covenantal obligations to include an obligation to be open to others who are not part of a specific covenant, even those individuals that are viewed as a threat.

In the Hebrew Bible, there are various places where God is portrayed as calling people to be gracious toward strangers. In the Book of Exodus, one reads, "You shall not oppress a resident alien; you know the heart of an alien, for you were all aliens in the land of Egypt."[5] In the Book of Deuteronomy: "You shall also love the stranger, for you were strangers in the land of Egypt."[6] In the Book of Leviticus, both these commands are integrated into one: "When an alien resides with you in your land, you shall not oppress the alien. The alien who resides with you shall be to you as the citizen among you; you shall love the alien as yourself, for you were aliens in the land of Egypt: I am the Lord your God."[7] In each of the passages, God commands believers to not just tolerate the others in their midst, but rather embrace them, even if these others are foreigners, meaning unknown and hence potentially dangerous. The sticking point of the argument is that God's chosen people, the Israelites, were once alienated from others. Put another way, in each of these stories a memory is invoked, one about the Israelites being lonely, oppressed, and exploited. The reason this call to hospitality works is that if people remember the pain they felt when they were mistreated, one presumes they would not want others to feel that way. It is a story about the need to show compassion, rather than to judge. It is a call to feel for the other before labeling them in any particular way. It is a mandate against the friend/enemy dualism.

Even with these positive threads in the tradition on relating to others, the world has witnessed traumatic events caused by one group making another into the enemy. For example, throughout history members of the Jewish community have been exploited, marginalized, tortured, forced to convert, and even murdered all because they were framed as evil others—more as objects than as people. Writing in light of the Shoah, Martin Buber explores the danger of conceptualizing a person as an enemy and an object. According to this famous Jewish philosopher, when we think of someone as an "it," we lose all sense of responsibility to that person—all moral obligation fades away. No one is expected to treat a pen or a towel with respect. Those items are for human use. When they are no longer useful, we can discard of them. This is the potential outcome of dualistic thinking, namely that an individual or group can be so demonized that they are no longer understood as human. This allowed the Nazis to treat Jewish prisoners as objects, as inhuman, and as "its."[8] This is the horror of the Shoah in particular and of genocide in general.

After 9/11, persons of Arab descent faced and perhaps continue to experience the threat of being labeled enemies, even as "its." This label has had terrible consequences. For one, it has restricted freedom. It probably comes as no surprise that after the traumatic events of that September morning, many Arab and Arab-American parents feared for the safety of their children and were hesitant to let them go out in public places because there seemed to be an assumption that anyone of Arab descent was the enemy—that they were terrorists, and thus expendable. Many were even afraid to go to work or attend classes. This is just one example of the danger of dualistic thinking, of seeing people as one's friend or one's enemy, as either being all good or all bad. It is worth considering that neither the one being accused of the wrong-doing nor the one making the accusations is free in this situation. Both are scared by the supposed actions of the other and constrained in their everyday lives.

TOWARD LOVING OUR ENEMIES

Loving our enemies is challenging. The friend/enemy binary creates a situation in which we do not even need to question why we call the other our enemy. The perceived enemy has hurt us or someone we need or love. We are the victims, and the other, meaning the perpetrator, is our enemy. When the lines are drawn so starkly, how does one begin to follow Jesus' commandment and love his or her enemies? One way is to find out more about the situation by asking some tough questions. *Why did this person hurt me? Are they suffering? Is there some deep-seated issue to which I have been inattentive?* This sort of questioning chips away at the bias that prevents us from knowing the totality of the situation. This sort of questioning makes us vulnerable in a way that invites the other into a potentially more open and responsive relationship. While in many cases such interrogation of the motives of the self and other will not bring friendship, it may work to destabilize the idea that the other is all evil.

Another reason why loving the other, that is to say, doing to others as you would have them do to you, is challenging, is that sometimes we do not take such good care of ourselves. We treat ourselves as the enemy. Perhaps we are hard on ourselves because we feel like failures in our personal or professional lives. Perhaps we feel so burdened by the stressors of life that we cannot care for ourselves, never mind attend to the needs of others. In these cases, loving our enemies is impossible because we cannot even care properly for ourselves. That is why caring for oneself is so important. If one does not care for oneself, then he or she cannot live out the Christian mandate to be for others, including others who are his or her enemies. Self-love is a first step toward loving the enemy. If we ever feel like failures or feel overburdened by life, loving anyone is practically impossible.[9] With all these challenges to loving others, it is helpful to note strategies for negotiating these thorny relationships.

ALLOWING FOR "ME-TIME"

If valuing and loving oneself are prerequisites for loving others, especially those difficult persons in our lives, we need to find strategies for developing self-care and self-love. In general, we need to allow for "me-time," that is, a place, space, and time for engaging in activities that bring peace and make us feel good about things in general. Perhaps this would involve making time to pray and mediate. Keeping a journal is another way of creating a context for taking care of oneself. In these quiet moments, it becomes possible to take stock of all the good things one brings to relationships as well as of the places that need care. Even more basically, making sure one is getting enough sleep and enough exercise and eating healthfully are all ways to set the stage for dealing with contentious relationships in the most positive ways possible.

OPENNESS TO CONFLICT

In our effort to love our enemies through questioning the other's motives for hurting us and creating time and space for self-love, there will come times where we need to confront our perceived enemies. This is a moment of conflict. What I mean by conflict is not outright violence, but an openness to the tension of the situation, specifically to the feelings that cause disturbance and enmity. Sometimes facing a negative situation head on mitigates crises from erupting into violence. Confrontation comes with its own challenges, especially if the individual one confronts is in a position of power or control. Here, one might recall the lessons learned from the Syrophoenician woman in the Gospels. This triple other—female, foreign, and non-Jewish, takes great risk and shows tremendous courage in challenging Jesus. At first he rebukes her, and then he is changed by her.

Depending on the context, we too have opportunities in life to confront the other as a way of forging a more open and honest friendship. Peppered throughout this book is a plea for an embrace of feelings in our everyday life. Without a doubt, feelings, especially anger, fear, rage, and sadness, are scary. They are irrational by definition and as such, admitting them, never mind embracing them, seems to go against so much we have been socialized to believe, specifically that reason trumps emotion. One of the greatest gifts we can give to others is an embrace of all the feelings in our lives so we can move forward in relationships with honesty and integrity. If we did more of this honest give-and-take and opened ourselves up to more genuine relationships—even ones of conflict—this could work to normalize emotion, creating a context for engaging those previously thought of as our enemies as friends.

BREAKING BREAD AND BREAKING BOUNDARIES

Another strategy for loving the ones that cause us fear and anger is getting to know them in a different context. A change in scenery might foster more authentic situations with the other, and potentially bridge divides. A wonderful context for building relationships with perceived enemies is eating together. Eating with one another creates a situation in which we are forced to let our guards down, so to speak, and communicate with one another on different levels.

My friend once shared a wonderful story with me about the power of food and food talk. She accompanied her husband on a dinner meeting with important clients. One of the clients was said to be painfully shy. Everyone was afraid to sit next to this person because no one wanted to be in the awkward situation of having to make small talk that never got off the ground. My friend is a skilled conversationalist, so they sat her next to the reserved client. At first, there was quite a bit of awkwardness. Then my friend mentioned baking a dessert and the client's eyes lit up. Between the meal and the food talk, the conversation began to flow. The embodied social act of eating has the potential to bring people who are uncomfortable or at odds together in profound ways.

For Christians, the sacrament of communion, of eating together in community, has the power to create connections. Jesus is portrayed in the New Testament as having his last meal on earth with his friends. Christians across the globe commemorate that event in the ritual of sharing bread and wine, just like Jesus did two thousand years ago. Everyday meals with friends, enemies, and all the identities in between can analogously celebrate hope for a renewed future together. Perhaps it's the sitting together, the tastes, the sounds, and so on, that have the potential to make the act of eating healing and a place of fresh starts.

Big Night (1996) is a heartwarming film directed by Campbell Scott and Stanley Tucci about two brothers, named Primo and Secondo, who immigrate to America from Italy and struggle to get their restaurant off the ground. The film is filled with allusions to Christian stories and themes, but it is probably the last scene of the film that has the most spiritual push. After a failed big dinner and a night of vicious arguing with one another, the brothers return to their restaurant's kitchen in silence. Their rage and disappointment toward one another is palpable. At the start of the scene, the younger brother, Secondo, methodically makes a simple plate of eggs and bread. Then his brother, Primo, enters the room. Still bitterly angry from the night before, neither brother speaks. Instead Secondo hands Primo a plate of food, and they sit side-by-side eating together. Eventually, still with no verbal words, they embrace each other's shoulders, continuing to eat. The simple meal changes their anger into love and acceptance. Not all rivalries or contentious relationships will have this happy ending through food. However, it is interesting to imagine how trying a new strategy for building relationships might change the tenor of the relationships from negative to at least neutral.

NONHUMAN ANIMAL AS FRIEND OR FOE?

Throughout this book we have investigated the potential for expanding the question of existence to include that of nonhuman animals. The reason for this is that thinking of being only in

123

terms of human being presents us with a limited understanding of the world and our human role in it. Alternatively, if we expand Christian conversations on existence to include all creatures, then we may have a better chance of understanding and perhaps even transforming the cycle of decline in which we find ourselves when it comes to environmental issues. As long as species keep dying out at the rate they are dying, we all will continue to be negatively affected. These threads of discussion provide the basis for what I have been calling a *green anthropology*, a way of understanding existence that is inclusive of all creatures.

The challenge of thinking about Christian existence in ways that are inclusive of all animals is twofold. First off, we are plagued by dualism and tend to degrade anyone who does not demonstrate "rational" properties, and hence nonhuman animals are cut out of the equation. And second, even if we desire to overcome this dualistic outlook, when we begin to imagine what our relationship with nonhuman animals might look like, we tend to fall back on anthropomorphic or human-centered categories. Recall from the previous chapter that we tend to talk about animals thinking like us, acting like us, feeling like us, or *not* thinking like us, acting like us, or feeling like us. Those are our only options.

Interestingly, when nonhuman animals look like humans in these ways, we are inclined to say they are our friends and companions. If they don't think like us, act like us, and feel like us, we are not compelled to care about them, and may even regard them as the enemy. This chapter attempts to defy dualistic ways of thinking about the relationship between human animal and nonhuman animal by framing all creatures as creatures—made good by a gracious God, each unique and other, and all dependent on one another.

BAD SHARKS AND GOOD DOGS IN POPULAR CULTURE

In popular culture, one sees the human tendency to lump some nonhuman animals into the friend category and some into the category of enemies. This is another way in which dualism disrupts our potential for human freedom. If we think a particular species is all bad, then we can treat them like objects or "its" in a rather guilt-free manner. Take for example the great white shark. It is probably safe to assume that this animal has been one of the most demonized species in popular culture. The blockbuster film *Jaws* went a long way toward raising peoples' fear of these awesome creatures. For years after the *Jaws* films were released, individuals still recounted how they were afraid to go into the water. In fact, because of these fears, hunting sharks was legitimized. Shark hunters could imagine that they were doing us a service by getting these menaces out of our waterways.

Decades later we are still feeling the terrible impact of that fear and hatred of sharks. In a previous chapter, I noted the exorbitant number of sharks killed per year, and the devastation that this slaughter brings our ecosystem. Moreover, fear of this stealth predator also became an obstacle to learning more about them; in other words, became one of our blind spots or biases. Only very recently has the public been encouraged to learn more about the wonders of these prehistoric creatures and their place in the universe.

On the other extreme is the family dog. No need to go further than Charlie Brown's pet dog Snoopy to realize how popular culture has idealized this pet. The dog, after all, is man's best friend, right? While it is wonderful to enjoy and love one's pet as one would a friend, there is not much room in our culture for that friend to act like a dog. What happens when this best friend bites our neighbor's child? Who do we hold accountable? The owner? The dog? If the dog bites enough people it could be put down. Sometimes we impute ideal human characteristics, like loyalty and affection, onto nonhuman animals to the extent that we resent them and even kill them when they do not act the way we think they should. Again these are the problems that come from a dualistic mentality, from becoming frustrated when the creatures do not act like the category we lump them into. Is it possible to conjure new ways of imagining human and nonhuman animals as coexisting together beyond the constraints of friend and enemy?

We find a special resource in the Christian tradition that fosters an ecologically engaged mindset. In the Catholic imagination, St.

Francis, the twelfth-century mendicant who went on to start the Franciscan order, was named by the church the patron saint of ecology. In fact on his feast day on October 4th, Christians throughout the world bring their animals to their local churches to be blessed. It is said that he had special relationships with birds, wolves, and other animals. In his *Canticle of the Sun*, St. Francis sings about the beauty of the cosmos, including Brother Sun, Sister Moon, and Mother Earth. It is a song celebrating the interconnectedness of life in which the threads of creation are woven together in a way that explodes any easy divide between human and animal or friend and enemy. Thinkers invested in the care of all of creation pull on these themes in Francis's spirituality. John Feehan, a prominent environmentalist, puts it most eloquently: "Francis of Assisi could talk of Brother Wolf and we approve the metaphor. But now we know it is not a metaphor. We are brother and sister, elephant and wolf and man and woman, oak and dandelion, frog and dragonfly. To think we are more is to diminish God, to imagine they are less is to diminish ourselves."[10]

SUMMARY

Above we explored how the friend/enemy dualism fails to acknowledge all the ambiguous relations in between; in other words, how it causes bias and limits our freedom. Is it the case that one person is all good or all bad, or all in the right or all in the wrong? Most of the time we find ourselves someplace other— in the middle or midst of the two. If we fail to understand this reality of the middle and that these categories of "friend" and "enemy" are in fact provisional, then we could become constrained to a life of hating the one who is deemed enemy. It is noteworthy that this friend/enemy dualism extends beyond the human world in that we find ourselves grouping various species into categories of good or bad, friend or enemy, depending on the popular views of the day. Ultimately, the friend/enemy dualism does not make sense in a tradition that teaches to love one's enemies. It eats away at the potential in all of us for freedom. How can we truly be free if we are bound to hate? In an effort to reclaim freedom, strategies were presented to break through the friend/enemy impasse. In the next chapter we will turn to the gender dualism that plagues Christianity, with a similar eye toward how fixed ideas about what makes a man and what makes a woman have the potential to limit one's freedom.

EXERCISES:
1. **Complete a journal entry on this topic.**
2. **Think-Pair-Share** (Reflect on these questions silently, find a partner and discuss them together, and then share with the class.)
   - Discuss if and how 9/11 changed the ways you and your loved ones talk about friends and enemies. It is important to be sensitive in these sorts of emotionally charged conversations.
   - Reflecting on your personal experience, consider whether Christians believe and uphold the gospel call to love their enemies.
   - Explore how memory contributes to one's understanding of who is one's friend and who is one's enemy.
3. **Creative Time**

   Plan a meal that brings people together from different religious backgrounds. Use this as a way to break bread and build community. In preparation for these meals, try to be attentive to each religious tradition's dietary restrictions. For example, see if your Jewish guest cannot eat certain foods, or perhaps if some guests are vegetarian. Be open to the possibility of a guest bringing his or her own traditional food recipe to share. While you are eating, discuss if and how eating together has changed your relationships with one another.

NOTES

1. Suzanne Collins, *The Hunger Games* (New York: Scholastic Press, 2008).
2. Luke 6:31 (NRSV).
3. Luke 6:27, 32, 35 (NRSV).
4. Matt 7:3–5 (NRSV).
5. Exod 23:9 (NRSV).

6. Deut 10:19 (NRSV).

7. Lev 19:33–34 (NRSV).

8. For more on the dangers of objectifying people, see Martin Buber, *I and Thou*, A new translation, with a prologue and notes by Walter Kaufmann (New York: Touchstone, 1996).

9. For more on the importance of self-love, see Edward Collins Vacek, SJ, *Love, Human and Divine: The Heart of Christian Ethics* (Washington, DC: Georgetown University Press, 1994).

10. John Feehan, *The Singing Heart of the World: Creation, Evolution and Faith* (Dublin: The Columba Press, 2010), 77.

Chapter 7

BLUE IS FOR BOYS AND PINK IS FOR GIRLS

Is it a boy or a girl? This question is posed to pregnant women all around the world. Aside from being a friendly question and showing interest in the upcoming birth event, it is a practical one too. With knowledge of the child's gender, one is empowered to navigate the clutter of baby clothing, toys, furniture, and accessories in baby megastores with ease. After all, blue is for boys and pink is for girls. That's all one needs to know. One may opt to buy a yellow or green blanket if he or she is unsure about the gender or does not want to be limited by the constraints of gender. It is usually more the case, though, that one capitulates to the demands of the standard color-coding.

Here we will explore how gender difference unfolds in Christian traditions and the implications of that for human freedom and justice. Thinking about male and female, boys and girls, and men and women in oppositional language has the potential to lead to gender dualism. As with the other binaries discussed, such as mind/body and friend/enemy, the male/female split, if conceptualized in too rigid a manner, eats away at personal freedom and destroys opportunities for genuine community. To begin our discussion, we will turn our attention to the perceived differences between the terms *sex* and *gender*. Then we will explore the nature-nurture debate. All this theory will then be applied to contemporary notions of gender in Catholic Christian doctrine as well as the popular imagination. Motherhood emerges as a prominent theme in the tradition. In the last section we will consider maternity in a broader context, asking whether men can mother and what mothering the earth might look like.

As mentioned above, color-coded gender thinking begins with the baby's loved ones when he or she is in utero, and in all likelihood follows the child throughout his or her life. Particularly for school-aged children, there are clear standards for what male children should wear and what females should wear—blue and pink, pants and skirts, respectively. As important as clothing is, gendered social norms go beyond dress to include gendered personality traits. Boys and girls are expected to act in distinctive ways, have distinctive interests, and relate to others in distinctive manners. For example, it is not unusual for boys to be encouraged to take part in contact sports or at the very least to be rambunctious, while girls are tracked toward playing dress up and house, and being quiet and self-contained. While these are not hard-and-fast rules, it is imaginable that many readers are familiar with some version of them.

It is important to note that as this chapter unfolds, controversial topics will be raised. For example, we will question whether in the Catholic Christian imagination there is really any role for women other than that of a mother or a celibate nun. Also, we will explore the issue of whether men can be considered compassionate, caring, and devoted if women are made for mothering. These sorts of questions, especially when engaged in a classroom setting, could result in tension. Students might need to gear up for conflict in the best sense of the word and be open to opposing viewpoints and emotional debates. That is not necessarily the point of this chapter, but is definitely a possible effect. One is hard-pressed even to think about what it means to be human from a Christian perspective without talking about these questions of what makes a man and what makes a woman. When girls feel pushed into some roles and boys into others, everyone is impacted in that everyone's freedom is on the line.

Another controversial aspect of this discussion is the "feminist" grounding of it. For some, *feminism* is a bad word. They may associate it with so called man-haters and haters in general. That is not a fair or accurate description of all feminism and feminists. For our purposes, a feminist is anyone who is committed to the idea of justice for women and men together in community. When feminism is seen this way, it wields positive connotations. There have been various stages or waves of feminism, and in the contemporary period feminists are most active in struggling for justice by working for families, the poor, and the environment. Feminist theorists are invested heavily in dismantling various forms of dualism in everyday life, because dualism tends to devalue the material world and women are so often associated with their bodies and bodily processes. Feminists as well as others concerned about these issues work diligently to argue that materiality is a good thing and an integral aspect of creaturely existence, a good that extends not only to human animals but to nonhuman animals as well.

SEX, GENDER, AND THE NATURE-NURTURE DEBATE

In order to understand gender dualism, it helps to clarify the terms of the debate. One might begin by unpacking the difference between the terms *sex* and *gender*. Simply put, sex has traditionally signified one's identity based on his or her genitalia or sex organs. What's more, it is the chromosomal matter of each of us that determines us as male or female. On the other hand, gender has been invoked most traditionally to refer to the social norms associated with those physiological markings. As a result, gender comes to mean not merely having typical male sex organs, but in addition acting like a boy—whatever that means. Perhaps that means playing on a football team instead of taking ballet class. Perhaps that means never crying in public. Perhaps that means being aggressive instead of quiet and shy.

The more one examines this binary between sex and gender, the more one sees the somewhat artificial nature of it. To be sure, it is far from easy to make such a clear distinction between sex and gender. Indeed, scholars in the fields of women's and gender studies claim that in many ways attempting to separate sex (physical appearance) from gender (social norms) is impossible. Moreover, contrasting sex with gender creates a dualism, which falsely leads one to believe that sex is natural and gender is learned, that one is biological and the other is social. We find scholars today who argue against this dualism, claiming that all we have is gender. A natural or pure sex identity that is untainted by social values and expectations does not exist, plain and simple. Put another way, as soon as we look at individuals' anatomies or genetic makeup, and classify them as boys or girls, men or women, we situate them in complex social worlds with specific norms and pressures. So a pure understanding of sex is never really feasible.

In her work *Sexing the Body*, Anne Fausto-Sterling puts it best: "Labeling someone a man or a woman is a social decision."[1] It is not about describing facts, but creating a narrative through which that person can navigate the world, and through which the community can make sense of the individual. Boys learn to be masculine and are tortured if they do not fit the male model, and girls learn to be feminine and are tortured if they do not fit the female model. The use of the word *tortured* may be a bit strong; however, its intent is to highlight the danger of trespassing gender expectations in society today. After all, some get very nervous when kids who look like boys act like girls, so much so that they may be bullied for their transgressions.

The claim that sex is never neutral and always imbued with value, and hence always already gendered, becomes much clearer when speaking about intersex situations. Intersex persons are individuals born with ambiguous genitalia or atypical genetics related to gender identity. At times, especially in the previous century, intersex babies were assigned gender through surgery pretty much before they could talk. Now there is more of a movement to let the child decide if he or she would like assignment, and if so, to which gender. There have been cases where intersex individuals did not know they were intersex. It may be the case that their appearance did not match their chromosomes, but they only realized that because of another event. Or it may be the case that their parents never told them about their being intersex and that they were reassigned a gender.

Realizing uncertain gender identity could have devastating effects. Fausto-Sterling recalls the gender trouble of one such intersex individual, Maria Patiño: "In the rush and excitement of leaving for the 1988 Olympics, Patiño, Spain's top woman hurdler, forgot the requisite doctor's certificate stating, for the benefit of Olympic officials, what seemed patently obvious to anyone who looked at her: she was female....Patiño had only to report to the 'femininity control head office,' scrape some cells off the side of her cheek, and all would be in order—or so she thought."[2] Unfortunately, it was just the beginning of a nightmare for Patiño. She failed the sex test; she had a Y chromosome. Further testing demonstrated that she had testes hidden within her labia, and she had neither a uterus nor ovaries. Her world went into a tailspin. She was barred from the games, rejected by her boyfriend, and lost her scholarship to school.

Not all intersex individuals face such challenges. Many live full, productive, and noninterrupted lives. However, the challenge is with how society views their gender identity. Does the everyday public have cognitive, affective, and moral tools for dealing with gender uncertainty? Does dualistic thinking about gender—that is, the *is it a boy or a girl* mentality—limit the way we can engage individuals who do not fit neatly into the male and female boxes? Does dualism impact the way we can deal with our own gender complexities? While we may look the boy part or the girl part, does society allow us to deviate from the accepted script about what it means to act like a boy or act like a girl? How do our social institutions, including our families, schools, laws, and religious communities, deal with gender fluidity?

NATURE OR NURTURE?

All these questions about what makes a boy and what makes a girl are rooted in what is sometimes referred to as the nature-nurture debate. Is sexual difference the sole result of biology—that is, in our nature and governed by our genetic makeup—or is it more a result of socialization—that is, the way we are nurtured? While some people believe it is a combination of both, others occupy opposing sides on the spectrum. When one believes that our biology is our destiny, he or she is typically referred to as an essentialist or holding an essentialist perspective on gender. On the other side of the spectrum, when one believes our gendered identity is all socially learned, he or she is typically referred to as a social constructionist or holding a constructionist perspective on gender identity.

This division might need some more elaboration. For essentialists, biology determines gender, so much so that from an essentialist perspective it is believed that an individual with male chromosomes or sex organs *will* develop masculine attributes, such as aggression, rationality, and so on. Likewise an individual with female chromosomes or sex organs *will* develop feminine attributes, such as shyness, emotionality, and so on. Alternatively, for social constructionists like Fausto-Sterling, gender is social and learned. It is a product of history and context. We aren't born boys, we become boys. Put another way, some individuals aren't born less emotional; on the contrary, they learn to hold back their emotions. Who we are in terms of gender identity is a product of social structures telling us what to do, and of our conforming to those social pressures. From this constructionist perspective, individuals (e.g., girls and women) aren't born with an affinity for taking care of others; rather, they are socialized to be caretakers.

ANGER, OUR SIN OR SALVATION?

When we begin to look at how girls and boys are socialized into becoming men and women, patterns arise. In general, boys are taught that it is appropriate to be rambunctious, while girls are assumed to be quiet and controllable. Boys are not expected to care about their appearances, while girls are deemed atypical if they could care less about what they wearing and how their hair is styled. Even their emotional reactions to situations are judged by social norms. For example, boys are taught not to cry, and girls are warned against being too angry. It is as if a boy cries and shows his vulnerability, he is less of a boy and more feminine. And if a girl gets too angry and is less forgiving or sweet, she is seen as less feminine. These norms related to acceptable emotions according to one's gender are worth exploring in detail, as they show how gender dualism could diminish an individual's capacity to be free.

We probably have heard the lines from the script. *No one likes an angry woman. Rageful women are unattractive and unlovable.* While I certainly think good women feel angry and experience rage, and good men feel sad and cry, part of the script of becoming girls and boys has been to suppress these tendencies, and hence to learn these lines. Here, the challenge is to ask whether these sorts of social norms impede one's capacity for human freedom. This is an especially difficult question because in some contexts, extreme anger is understood as a sin. So for girls and women, if they show anger, they are understood not only as less of a woman, but also less of a faithful Christian. What's so bad about being angry? Why does being angry make anyone less of a girl or woman? This fear of being labeled angry is at times felt in the resistance to being considered a feminist. Few haven't heard the phrase "angry feminist." What is being suggested here is that part of undoing the negative impact of gender roles is realizing a positive place for anger—not in outright rage, but rather as a way to signal that things are wrong and one's needs aren't being met.

In her work *The New Feminist Agenda: Defining the Next Revolution for Women, Work and Family*, Madeleine M. Kunin claims anger is a tool for getting individuals and groups engaged with family policy issues. For Kunin, anger can serve as a spark to incite us to reflect on what brings us joy and what causes us pain. It provides an opening for growth, in that beyond anger we might think of new ways of creating community that are more just and life-giving.[3] In suggesting the good effects of anger, I am not arguing that every emotion experienced is acceptable to be acted upon, but rather that feelings are part of our everyday life and as such they cannot be avoided. I remember speaking with a friend in graduate school who would joke about her mom vacuuming and crying. Implicit in our talks was the belief that her mom felt deep emotion, perhaps anger and rage, and only was able to express it through housework and tears. Men might have to find analogous outlets for their sadness, disappointment, and tears. After all, while it is socially acceptable for a woman to be vacuuming and crying, who of us would feel so comfortable revealing that about the men in our lives? Perhaps Christians can reimagine anger for women and sadness for men not as something to be ashamed of but as a motivating tool to lament the social norms they feel imprisoned by and to signal the prophetic hope for more genuine ways of living with one another.

GENDER DUALISM AND THE CHRISTIAN TRADITION

Christian ideas about what makes a man and what makes a woman in many ways reflect a combination of essentialist and constructionist claims. Even with this middle ground position, there are many controversial issues connected to Christian claims about gender. For instance, what is the role of women? Is their main vocation, meaning their life's path, to be mothers? How does the role of women influence the role of men and vice versa? Other touchy subjects come up as well. For example, how does Jesus' gender affect his ministry or the question of who is permitted into the priesthood? And finally, the issue of sexual desire arises here. Are we born straight or gay? If we are born gay, then how could heterosexual marriage be natural? While we will not attend fully to all of these issues, in what follows is a survey of them through the lens of scripture and doctrine.

When discussing gender in the Christian tradition, and here I focus primarily within the Catholic Christian tradition, the conversation is dominated by one theme: complementarity. This is the idea that the male and female genders complement each other and that it is natural that they are in paired romantic relationships. Sometimes when we are in serious relationships, we say that the other person complements us. What we mean by that is that the other we love possesses strengths where we have weaknesses and that our differences actually make us better; in other words, that we work well as a team.

In Catholic Christian discussions of gender difference, another type of complementarity is invoked, one in which men and women are made for each other, and it is in their very being to be together. Those who hold this position assume that men and women need each other, and the normative way of being in a romantic relationship with another is to be in a heterosexual bond. Proponents of this idea of complementary claim that the physiology of men and women prove they are a perfect fit. Their bodies are a perfect match, like pieces of a puzzle. Moreover, their personalities complement each other as well; for example, the male is competitive, while the female is nurturing. This section problematizes the implications of the theme of complementarity as it relates to the question of freedom.

While many male and female Catholics uphold doctrinal claims about complementarity of the sexes, it is important to note that some other male and female Catholics disagree with the idea of gender complementarity. Such individuals worry not about the idea that men and women might be lovers, but rather that heterosexuality is their only option. Moreover, such critics might argue that gender complementarity reduces men and women to specific, limited roles, hence reducing their freedom. In thinking through these very complex issues, we ought to pay serious attention to the concerns of an important Catholic feminist thinker of our time, Anne Carr, when she writes that while "the assertion of the natural inferiority of women is seldom found in contemporary theological discourse, one does find the notion of 'complementarity' of the sexes, which in fact resembles it in a disguised form and which offers a new rationalization for the subordination of women."[4] Women are subordinated to the role of wife and mother, while men are equally confined to the role of husband and provider. Such thinking does not allow for the fluidity between gender roles that many of us experience in our everyday lives.

What's more, when one's sexual desire and sexual orientation is limited to gender complementarity, then it becomes impossible to speak about same-sex romantic relationships as good and life-giving. With complementarity, heterosexuality is made normative. However, in many places today, same-sex relationships are regarded as positive ways to love and reflect the image of God. To convey this positive sense of same-sex relationships within theological discussions, the doctrine of complementarity would need to be reworked. It would need to be less about sexual difference and more about finding that person or creature that complements you and allows you to say yes to God and others in the fullest of ways.

SEXUAL DIFFERENCE IN SCRIPTURE

As we have already noted, the first stories of the Bible chronicle the creation of difference, with special attention to the distinctions between human animals and nonhuman animals, and of course between males and females. We read in Genesis 1 that God created humankind in God's image. According to this story, there is no mention of how sex difference occurs at all, just that God creates humankind in God's image—male and female. In many ways this is thought of as a gender-inclusive and egalitarian text, much like Paul's famous claim in his letter to the Galatians, "As many of you as were baptized into Christ have clothed yourself with Christ. There is no longer Jew or Greek, there is no longer slave or free, there is no longer male and female; for all of you are one in Christ Jesus."[5]

However in another creation story, in Genesis 2, we read a narrative about God creating the male first and the female second, to be his helper. Even if Christians and others are not reading this text literally, this story has been used to keep women in subservient roles. This is due to the fact that women are portrayed as a derivative of Adam's rib, coming into existence second. While we discussed earlier how this could be understood as a positive notion, it still has been used to enforce patriarchy, a society ruled and organized by men.

Genesis 3 also complicates gender in the Christian tradition. This is the story of the first humans dwelling in the beautiful garden, a sort of paradise on earth. God allows them to eat from every tree except one. The woman transgresses God's command, eats from the forbidden tree, and shares with her husband. They are both punished. The man is reduced to working in the field with little relief, while the woman is cursed to painful childbirth. In this scriptural text we encounter not only gender expectations regarding what men do versus what women do in life, but also gendered punishment. The woman's punishment is related to her lot in life—mothering.

One can understand Genesis 3 in a myriad of ways, including as already discussed, human beings trying to be God or dealing with what we called the "god complex." What is meant here is that we feel tremendously stressed by wanting to know more and be more, yet being ultimately limited and finite. The first humans eat from the tree because they want to be like God. It might even be understood as a story that explains why things are the way we experience them, including very concretely why men are burdened with providing for their families and why women experience pain in childbirth. The latter would be particularly edifying to people living in a non-scientific age with little to no information about human physiology.

Even with these viable interpretations, it is Genesis 3 that at the very most has led to or at the very least has reflected the prevailing negative attitudes about women in society. This connection between women's bodies and punishment has had egregious effects. The story of Eve, the first female, offers a perception of women and their bodies as sinful. Eve is portrayed as bringing sin into a good world through her greed, pride, and arrogance, and through her body. She is also constructed as tempting her husband, leading him down a bad path with her wicked ways. She becomes a symbol for sin, and a type for evil. Such misogynist readings of Eve have tainted the way all women are imagined—as temptresses and sinners. For Catholic Christians, Mary, the mother of Jesus, is presented as the antithesis of Eve, the cure all for womankind. This theological interpretation has its downsides, as we will soon see.

In addition to this story of Eve and the first sin, there are other aspects of scripture that end up creating gender divisions and power differentials between men and women. Take for example the household codes in Paul's letter to the Ephesians: "Wives, be subject to your husbands as you are to the Lord. For the husband is the head of the wife just as Christ is the head of the church."[6] In that text, there is a correlation between Christ and all men (meaning not women). This leads to gender hierarchy being rationalized and legitimized by the Bible. When read in contemporary context, what does it mean for a wife to subject herself to her husband like she is to the Lord? Does that impact her freedom? Does that impact his? Might he want a partner rather than a subject? These are all modern questions posed to ancient texts.

Nonetheless, some of these same thoughts about gender and woman's place in the church are present today.

VOCATION OF WOMEN

In addition to looking to scripture, church teachings are another important source on understanding gender in ecclesial settings. Throughout the years, the "woman question" has surfaced, and is even framed in that very awkward way. The woman question asks the following. What is a woman's role in the world? Who is she called to be for God and others? What is her vocation? While it is quite clear from ecclesial documents that the most appropriate vocations for women are being part of a religious community or being mothers, the issues permeating our conversation run even deeper. For example, what is the relationship of women religious, that is, nuns, to ordained priests when only men can be ordained? Does the reality that women are not allowed to be ordained in the Roman Catholic Church create an insurmountable power differential between the way men and women serve in the church? Are women always lesser because they cannot break through the ecclesial glass ceiling? Perhaps that is the wrong question altogether and it is more the case that both men and women are called to serve, and the difference in their vocations is not something negative or hurtful, but rather adds to the diversity of the church. Both men and women are called to serve, but in different ways. Moreover, this difference in roles does not necessarily mean a difference in the value of each role. However, not all would agree that this difference in roles does not lead to a difference in the way men and women are valued in the Christian tradition. More analysis is necessary. To begin to unpack these very important queries, we might consider the connections among Mary, mothering, and the church.

It is impossible to speak about gender or the vocation of women in the Christian tradition without referring to the ways that Mary has been read as a symbol for all believers. As noted in an earlier chapter, the Gospels reveal very little about Mary. Her power lies in the Christian imagination about her, including her yes-saying to God and her idealized motherly attributes. Both children and adults turn toward Mary in prayer and devotion for healing and compassion. In addition to being a symbol of care, she is a symbol of purity—of mind and body. Catholic Christians claim her to be the perpetual virgin, meaning that she never had sexual relations with a man for her entire lifetime.

While some Catholic Christians venerate Mary for her purity, others underscore that it is unhelpful to highlight Mary's virginity while at the same time emphasizing her mothering. The critique is that since women must have sex to become pregnant and have a child, this Marian virgin-mother ideal leads to an impossible situation in which women neither feel good enough in terms of their purity nor good enough in terms of their mothering. From this critical perspective, the virgin-mother ideal could unfold as a binary in which both women and men feel constrained to understand all women as either virgins or mothers, as pure or defiled. If women do not fit those categories, then they could be criticized and marginalized. Few of us have not heard the names uttered at women who supposedly have sex with many. Are those sorts of criticisms rooted in a dualistic view of what women could and should be?

In order to delve deeper into how Mary's identity influences gender identity, we should consider *Mulieris Dignitatem: On the Dignity and Vocation of Women*.[7] This ecclesial document was written in 1988 by Pope John Paul II and was geared toward honoring women by highlighting all they give to society, their families, their friends, and the church. In *Mulieris Dignitatem*, Mary is celebrated as the role model for women and the church, with the two highest callings being motherhood and celibacy. This document does not assume biological mothers can be virgins. On the contrary, it sets the stage for thinking that the best, most sacred choices for women are either having a male spouse with children or becoming part of a religious community, that is, becoming a nun. Both these vocations involve a type of mothering, of giving for others, sacrificing, caring, and so on.

Also in *Mulieris Dignitatem*, complementarity between men and women is embraced. Again, complementarity is the notion that the genders match up with each other. This means that men and women each bring unique gifts to the relationship, gifts that are based in biology and physical looks. From this viewpoint, one might argue that females typically have the ability to become pregnant, and hence are tracked toward mothering. Their femininity is best expressed in motherly attributes. Meanwhile, males look like Jesus physically and hence are enabled to serve the role of priests—models of Christ.[8] Their masculinity is best expressed in leadership roles. As one might imagine, these assumptions about gender roles within church documents and teaching give rise to lively conversation and debate.

It is really challenging to live in today's world where women strive to be in leadership roles in every aspect of life, including in politics, corporate life, the judicial system, the military, and higher education, to name just a few, yet women cannot be ordained as priests. If the female anatomy precludes women from being priests, why doesn't that same body preclude them from being judges, senators, police officers, and so on? The church doctrine that precludes women from being ordained seems somewhat out of place in our modern world. As one probably intuits, this conversation is extremely prickly, because one would not want to make the assumption that all Catholic women want to be priests, that all Catholic men do not want women to be priests, or that all women religious are not priests by default. Each person's perspective on this very controversial and contentious issue is distinct and nuanced. Yet, the conflation of priesthood with maleness may just be one of the most significant obstacles to the Roman Catholic Church moving forward in the twenty-first century and beyond.

RECENT CANONIZATIONS AND GENDER REVISITED

The writing on the saints, commonly referred as hagiography, is another place where believers find cues for learning what it means to be a man and what it means to be a woman. Saints in the Christian imagination are exemplary human beings who are honored after their deaths for their virtue, orthodox beliefs, and miracles. For the larger part of Christian history, what made female saints saintly was both their unconventional purity and their selfless nurturing qualities, epitomized in a spiritual type of

142

motherhood. Most female saints' histories in one way or another were penned to resemble Mary's saintly story. In modern times, particularly in the early part of this century, one detects more textured lives in the stories of female saints. However, still the ideal of perfect motherliness is highlighted.

Take for example the recent canonization of Gianna Beretta Molla in 2004 by Pope John Paul II.[9] St. Gianna was a married Italian pediatrician from the mid-twentieth century who had complications with her fourth pregnancy. Instead of having a medical procedure that would have led to the death of her unborn child, Gianna continued with her pregnancy. She is said to have stated that if it was a choice between her life and the child, she prayed that God would choose the child. As expected, the thrity-nine-year-old devout Catholic, mother, wife, and pediatrician died about a week after giving birth to her daughter Gianna Emanuela, who survived.

What is so interesting about the stories around St. Gianna's canonization is the notion that she was the first "working mom" to be canonized. Implicit in that claim about her working is the notion that the church is beginning to embrace women in a plurality of roles—not just as celibate women. So in many ways she expands the vocation of women beyond either being part of a religious community or a mother; one can be a mother and also have a professional career. After all, St. Gianna was a pediatrician. This is significant because in many places and situations, women are judged quite harshly for working outside the home. Their employment responsibilities are viewed as taking away from family life, the idea being that they cannot adequately be good mothers and spouses if they have other responsibilities. The canonization of St. Gianna challenges those commonsense assumptions about motherhood and mothering.

However, it is important to note that not everyone is eager to hail her canonization as a major achievement for Catholic women worldwide. Some might say that her canonization only solidifies gender norms for women. For one, the reason she was made a saint in the first place was for her "motherly" attributes. She sacrificed so another could live, just as in many of the saintly stories that came before her, women are valorized as long as they are sacrificing. This is not to say that sacrifice is a bad thing; in fact, it is a key component of Christian discipleship. The challenge is that women's value as women, not merely as Christians, in this worldview is tied to their sacrificing for others.

In addition to being a role model for some working mothers, as one probably intuits, the canonization of St. Gianna has become an important signifier for persons committed to the pro-life movement. She chose her unborn child's life over her own. This for many is a great gift and sacrifice for her family. Still others wonder what effect her choice had on the other children in her family. Questions such as these arise: whose life (her own or that of another) is more important; how does her story impact others in similar situations; and finally, probably most complicated, what are the connections between this modern saint and new versions of martyrdom? In this brief foray into the life and death of St. Gianna, one grasps that the connections between gender and the religious imagination are deep and varied.

REFLECTIONS ON FREEDOM

While few would deny that we all need others in our lives for companionship, feminist and other liberationist theologians challenge the notion of complementarity as the main model of companionship for a couple of reasons. First of all, there is the question of biological determinism or essentialism. Do all women act a certain way regardless of their upbringing? Do all men? Does our biology—our sex organs and genetic makeup—put us on a certain track in life? Does that track hinder our ability to be truly free for God and others? These are important threads, especially if one were to consider whether and how men could be motherly. A second challenge is the way the notion of complementarity is built on spousal and heterosexual norms. In pushing against complementarity, one wonders if there is an alternative way not only to imagine how to be male or how to be female, but also to imagine how and whom we may love. Again, the issue becomes whether one is truly free if he or she is expected to love certain people and in certain ways.

To answer these questions, we might return to the notion that human neediness is a good thing. As previously noted, we are always embedded in complex social arrangements and ultimately dependent on others. Genesis 2 is an apropos story about the importance of companionship to one's being. Being lonely is not a desirable state, and as such one story that Christians find so symbolic is the idea that God does not want Adam to be lonely. And while nonhuman animals are certainly important to the flourishing of all creatures, humans still need humans. In the current social landscape, many people, and many of them Christian, are beginning to ask more forcefully whether only a heterosexual mate can ensure one's flourishing. We all need others, but is heterosexual complementarity the only answer to that need? Could that be just one version among many of the answer to the question of human neediness? Can one imagine flourishing in all types of relationships and situations, including celibate, heterosexual, and gay and lesbian? Only in breaking out of a mentality that assumes females are made for males can we begin to entertain those sorts of queries.

This also harkens back to the question of who exactly is equipped to be a mother and engage in mothering. Is it only girls and women who are called to be nurturing, caring, and compassionate? It is not too strong to suggest that boys and men could feel stifled by the inability to freely say they have motherly gifts, particularly in a social context that does not allow for that aspect of gender crossing. If masculinity and femininity are learned, it might be the case that we all have the capacity to be motherly and ought to tap into that for our own well-being as well as for the well-being of others. Jeannine Hill Fletcher, a contemporary Catholic feminist theologian, brings this topic to the foreground when she writes about Jesus as mothering the world.[10] Hill Fletcher's work is influenced by the groundbreaking research of the American medieval scholar Caroline Walker Bynum, who has written extensively on gender, religion, and medieval Europe, and of particular importance here is her book *Jesus as Mother: Studies in the Spirituality of the High Middle Ages*.[11] Reflecting on Christian resources from the contemporary period as well as those of the past, we can begin to see that understanding Jesus as mother creates a space for women and men to both share in nurturing and leadership roles in their lives and in the community. Even more evocative, for Hill Fletcher, Jesus provides a model for a new way of Christian discipleship that does not recycle oppressive gender roles, but explodes them so that we all are invited into being like Jesus in his maternal, self-giving ways.

MOTHER EARTH OR MOTHERING THE EARTH?

Critiquing an idealized sense of motherhood and playing with an idea that mothering is a potential role and calling for all of us is one way to approach the connection between gender and ecology concerns in theology. Mothering as a metaphor is central in theology and has a special space in the conversation about ecological concerns. *Mother Earth* is a phrase used to invoke our respect for the world around us, including all the creatures in our midst and the important elements that sustain our life. We refer to the earth as our mother because it provides for us by giving us food, water, shelter, and even a sense of purpose. These days we hear more and more about Mother Earth's diminishing resources. She is worn out. She has been overworked. She cannot keep giving if we do not work to replenish her resources.

As we move toward a green anthropology—one that asks what it means to be human in a context of environmental degradation and mass extinctions—it is important to consider how human animals might pick up the slack in this fight for life. Perhaps instead of seeing the earth in terms of an idealized mother that never gets sick or tired of giving to us and that sacrifices unconditionally, we might consider that everyone has his or her limits. Every mother needs to be mothered back, even Mother Earth. This realization could help us shift our language to imagine that at one point or another someone else is called to do the work of mothering. And now, in this crisis moment, it is our turn to "mother" the earth.

What could mothering the earth look like? Returning to Seàn McDonagh's work, we need to think of concrete ways to live lightly while Mother Earth is mending or at least not deteriorating any further. One issue that must be addressed is population control. How many children ought we to have? How many is too many? Population concerns bring up all sorts of questions about the Roman Catholic Church's prohibitive view on artificial contraception. If the church began to see overpopulation as a life issue, one that is wearing away at the earth's resources, might there be fresh views on the role of contraception in the lives of married couples? While undoubtedly important, population control is not enough. Christians committed to green concerns need to reflect on their use of resources, especially in the developed nations. We need to outline concrete ways for Christians, for example in the United States, to stop overusing the world around them, and instead to mother the earth by living lightly. This involves finding alternative energy sources, reducing water use, and changing patterns of food consumption.

Moving ahead in living lightly, we are called to mother the earth in the best sense of the word, nursing the other until the other is better. Throughout this chapter it has been argued that the metaphor of mothering has been overused in the Christian tradition and is exploitative of one gender. If so, then one is right to question the value of using mother language at all here. It could be the time to move onto a different metaphor. Nonetheless, mothering is so powerful an idea that perhaps it can bring about the conversion to green thinking that so many of us desire. And while there is the perception that it is more "natural" for women to be motherly, each one of us, regardless of gender, can learn mothering ways of giving up and going without for the greater good.

SUMMARY

Is it a boy or a girl? Are they male or female? On the surface these common questions are innocuous; yet in this chapter we witnessed how these matters are in fact quite complex and wield broad implications for how we live with one another. Studying the male/female divide, or what is sometimes referred to as gender dualism, we again noticed the pitfalls of conceptualizing difference in either/or typologies. As in our discussions of the dualism between mind and body, friend and enemy, and human and animal, here we were able to see how a dualistic mentality that fosters a simplistic understanding of gender constrains the human being from being truly free and engaging in life-giving relationships. While Christians don't necessarily talk about pink and blue specifically, deep within their religious imaginations are implicit and explicit rules for what it means to be a man and what it means to be a woman. And although not all rules are problematic, some of the theological norms related to gender are harmful and even potential sites of sin. It is to the important theological ideas of sin and brokenness that we now turn.

EXERCISES:
1. **Complete a journal entry on this topic.**
2. **Think-Pair-Share** (Reflect on these questions silently, find a partner and discuss them together, and then share with the class.)
   - Reflect on your sense of gender norms. Divide a sheet of paper into two columns. On one side of the page write down all the qualities associated with being a man or masculine, and on the other side list the qualities associated with being a woman or feminine. Analyze the differences. Where did you get the messages and information from to organize this page? Do you fit your gender? Is there some crossover? Would you feel comfortable with others knowing that you have some of the other gender's qualities? Why or why not?
   - Read St. Gianna's biography on the Vatican website. Does her story follow the traditional pattern for female saints in the Christian tradition? In other words, is it about mothering and purity? If so, discuss whether that is a good or a bad thing.
   - Discuss whether the metaphor of mothering has the potential to make people think about their relation to the earth in new ways.

3. Creative Time

Search for images of Mary, the mother of Jesus, on the internet. What are some similarities among the images and what are some differences? Do these images give social cues about what it means to be a woman and/or feminine? If so, explain how. Imagine an alternative image of Mary based on the context in which you are living. What might that look like?

NOTES

1. Anne Fausto-Sterling, *Sexing the Body* (New York: Basic Books, 2000), 3.

2. Ibid., 1.

3. Madeleine M. Kunin, *The New Feminist Agenda: Defining the Next Revolution for Women, Work and Family* (White River Junction, VT: Chelsea Green Press, 2012).

4. Carr, *Transforming Grace*, 49.

5. Gal 3:27–28 (NRSV).

6. Eph 5:22–23 (NRSV).

7. Pope John Paull II, Mulieris Dignitatem, http://www.vatican.va/holy_father/john_paul_ii/apost _letters/documents/hf_jp-ii_apl_15081988_mulieris-dignitatem_en.html.

8. For more on the issues related to women and Roman Catholic teachings on the priesthood, see Elizabeth T. Groppe, "Women and the *Persona* of Christ: Ordination in the Roman Catholic Church," in *Frontiers in Catholic Feminist Theology: Shoulder to Shoulder*, eds. Susan Abraham and Elena Procario-Foley (Minneapolis: Fortress Press, 2009), 153–71.

9. Gianna Beretta Molla (1922–62), see http://www.vatican.va/news_services/liturgy/saints/ns_lit_doc_20 040516_beretta-molla _en.html.

10. Jeannine Hill Fletcher, *Motherhood as Metaphor: Engendering Interreligious Dialogue* (New York: Fordham University Press, 2013).

11. Caroline Walker Bynum, *Jesus as Mother: Studies in the Spirituality of the High Middle Ages* (Berkeley: University of California Press, 1982).

Chapter 8

PUTTING HUMPTY DUMPTY BACK TOGETHER AGAIN

No one makes it through life without experiencing some form of pain related to being physically, emotionally, and spiritually broken. While our bodies may be intact, we are torn up inside by strained relationships. We have feelings related to resentment, remorse, guilt, and anger. Our situations could be caused by our sinful actions or those of another, or both. Sin leads to brokenness. Some sins are rather inconsequential, while others can destroy all potential for life-giving relationships, that is to say, ruin our chances for genuine freedom. The depths of sin and the situation of brokenness leave us disoriented and desperate. We may even wonder if we could ever become whole again.

At these moments, we are not that different from Humpty Dumpty. Many of us are familiar with the common children's nursery rhyme: *Humpty Dumpty sat on a wall, / Humpty Dumpty had a great fall, / All the king's horses and all the king's men, / Couldn't put Humpty together again.* This chapter explores the implications of being broken like Humpty Dumpty, that is, of being cut off from others and feeling helpless and lost. In analyzing brokenness, particular questions come to the foreground. Why are we broken? How is our capacity for freedom diminished by our predicament of being broken? Whose fault is it that we are in this painful situation? How can we undo experiences of brokenness? And of course, what is the place of grace and forgiveness in all of this? For in the midst of feeling broken and unable to feel whole again, Christians are called to hope for a better, graced future.

As suggested in an earlier chapter, some of us have become so broken that we cannot even open ourselves to grace. Perhaps we have experienced trauma. Perhaps that trauma came at the hands of someone we trusted. These situations are particularly painful because they point to a cycle of brokenness in which the sins of the past prevent us from opening to life-giving relations in the present. And in these cases, brokenness presents as an inability to say yes to God.

As we begin our exploration of these issues, it is important to keep in mind that this chapter unfolds differently from the others in that it begins with a section not on sin and brokenness but on the challenge of talking about it in the first place. This is a significant challenge to deal with because if one is uncomfortable discussing sin, it becomes impossible to have a critically engaged discussion about it. After the stage is set for sin talk, Christian scriptural and traditional resources are surveyed with an eye toward the distinction between individual and social sin. Racism is then defined as a concrete example of social sin, after which nonhuman animal issues are raised, as they have been already on a number of occasions in this book.

HAVING THE "TALK"

Being frank about religion is at times as difficult as being frank about sex. Some individuals go through great pains to avoid having the sex talk with their children. They may feel embarrassed. Others may not want to give their children the wrong information. And still others may be overwhelmed by the idea of the talk altogether. They may not even know where to start because sex is connected to other very complex realities like love, power, acceptance, violence, and personal identity. Broaching religion is an equally daunting conversation. Some individuals avoid talking about it with their children because of all of the aforementioned reasons. What's more, refraining from talking about religion, never mind the notions of sin and brokenness, could be a sign of not wanting to offend others. After all, who knows where our neighbors or teachers stand on some of the more controversial subjects? Simply put, religion presents as another one of those "talks" in our lives that we wish to avoid. For example, it is difficult to have a casual conversation about pro-life/pro-choice questions because one cannot be sure what the other's position is. What's more, around December, it is hard to know whether to wish someone "happy holidays" or to be more specific. These are just two instances in everyday life in which we avoid getting into conversations about religious issues or happenings because of the emotional reverberations around some religious attitudes.

It should come as no surprise, then, that teaching about sin in theology courses is a daunting task. There are significant challenges to even beginning a discussion of sin and brokenness. For one, many students rightly hold what I like to call a *been there done that* posture when it comes to all matters related to the Christian faith. What this refers to is the reality that many students do not enter into an academic study of religion in college as a blank slate. On the contrary, they have had many interactions with the tradition either casually or in a more formal manner. They may have very pious grandparents. Or it may be the case that they were in religious education for the larger part of their childhood and adolescence. Their fatigue regarding the subject of theology in general and sin in particular, especially in the cases where students went to Catholic private schools for twelve years, is totally understandable. Educators need to be aware of this religious malaise and take it seriously.

I encounter such malaise from students every semester and try to be sensitive to it. In the undergraduate college where I teach, students are required to take courses in religious studies. Usually by the end of the term, a majority of students are engaged in the issues discussed and open to exploring them further. I cannot say the same for the first days of the class. Many of my students have taken courses in religion or theology throughout their lives, particularly if they have attended parochial schools. They are jaded and think this is more of the same. My colleagues and I have to go to great lengths to convey to them that this is not necessarily grade thirteen. We try to convince them that in college we are investigating religious and theological questions from an academic perspective and that they probably or at least hopefully will be surprised by what they learn. However, meeting students in their malaise and trying to get them to imagine what they are doing as new is difficult. In many ways it is easier to dismiss a student for not caring about ethics or the world, in other words, to accuse them of being apathetic. Such a response is neither adequate nor accurate. Instead of being judgmental or condescending toward students, instructors need to see this as an opportunity for all parties involved to build on and complicate what they already know, and to try to understand sin in relation to creaturely existence with fresh eyes.

Another challenge is trying to ascertain whether students are comfortable with the rhetoric of sin. I never am sure what students think and feel about this term. *Sin* can be such a cumbersome word. It can sound blaming and punitive. And to many secularized Christians of the first world, it can sound "churchy." What is meant by *churchy* here is that it is a word only appropriate and relevant to a specific context—practicing Christians. And because of this connotation, it may seem inappropriate to talk about sin in the public square with individuals who come from a plurality of religious backgrounds. In other words, when sin is understood only as a Christian thing, one could surmise that talking about sin in a diverse context will offend those who do not share the same Christian grammar. The word *sin* in and of itself may alienate non-Christians from feeling welcome into the conversation. Or it may be more the case that non-Christians do not think that they have the credentials to talk about sin.

On the flip side of this dynamic, an individual from a different religious tradition or philosophical perspective may become annoyed by Christians acting as if only they have a response to pain and brokenness. To be sure, being broken is a universal existential phenomenon. As such, we need to consider how others could enter into this conversation. Would a Muslim or a Jewish person feel welcome in the discussion of sin? Would an atheist feel welcome? This chapter focuses on Christian responses to sin and brokenness because it is a primer in Christian theology. However, it is important to keep in mind that other traditions have formidable approaches to this question, and we would all

153

benefit from exploring those approaches. The more support one gets in working to overcome feeling broken, the better.

A third obstacle to sin talk is the dynamic in the classroom where people do not want to offend others or be under scrutiny themselves. If an individual has left Christianity or has a complicated relationship with any part of it, he or she may think that others who are outwardly more committed to their faith could not and would not understand him or her. This gets to the heart of how emotionally charged talking about religion is, especially the topic of sin, where there seems to be a clear right and wrong.

I have my own reasons for being uncomfortable teaching the topic of sin or even discussing it less formally in my everyday life. Women are often seen in Christianity as the reasons for sin, and their bodies as vehicles of sin. Already we have dealt with some of these issues in the chapters on dualism and gender, and here they surface again. Even with my reservations, I am aware that avoidance will not be an adequate response to sinful patterns and structures in our world, nor to the perceived place of women in them.

One time a student came up to me after class. We had just finished reading about the question of vocation and motherhood in John Paul II's *Mulieris Dignitatem*. All my years of teaching college students *never* prepared me for my student's very heartfelt question. She asked, "If a mother abandons a child, is that a sin?" I stood there like a deer in headlights. It is not that I did not know what to say; it was that I had so much to say and ask before I could answer the question. Yet my student stood before me awaiting an answer. I think I said yes.

I regret saying anything. That is one of those moments where I should have said that I did not know. I should have said that while the emotions around that action—abandonment—are so strong, and that while we may want someone, here the mother, to pay for the crime, there exist other forces and structures that allow that abandonment to happen that may have nothing to do with the mother. One could imagine scenarios in which the mother has no choice, in which the best yes she could muster to God, others, and her child was to leave. Why couldn't I say that? Was I worried about hurting this student in front of me? I thought that she was perhaps abandoned, so I wanted to be my student's advocate. But I was her teacher, and I missed my opportunity to teach.

For all these reasons and personal failures, at times I want to avoid sin talk altogether, never mind examine it critically. Nonetheless, human interactions require a grammar to talk about pain, suffering, hurt, and injustice. That grammar is the language of sin. It is important to keep in mind that we can talk about pain and injustice and still be critical of our sin talk. In fact being critical is an important aspect to doing theology. Being critical does not require trashing an idea or even disagreeing with it. Critical analysis requires thoughtful study and discussion of the subject. It involves considering all relevant scholarship on the topic, opening to new questions and concerns of the day. So when studying sin, I urge students to think for themselves along with scripture and tradition in order to formulate their views. Most importantly, all individuals should be allowed to talk sin talk, not just the so-called good Christians, because part of human existence is being caught up in complicated patterns of relating, which sometimes give way to hurt and injustice. No one is immune from sin. We are sometimes the perpetrators and at other times the victims, and most of the time somewhere in the murky middle. We cannot let that gray zone deter us from conversation. We have an obligation as Christians to live like Jesus and talk back to sin and violence. We can only do this if we hone our analytical skills and get comfortable with tough conversations—the touchy subjects.

SETTING THE MOOD

If talking about sin is vital for life-giving relationships with God and others, and if talking about sin is not something many of us are comfortable with or competent at, then before talking, we need to create an atmosphere for discussion that is safe and welcoming to a plurality of perspectives. Whenever I have a gathering at my home for a birthday party or a holiday celebration, in addition to preparing food and buying drink, I try to create an ambiance in my home which sets the tone for the event. I may change seating arrangements around so as to create conversation areas. I have been told that one should never put all the food on one table; so before the guests arrive, I make a point to set plates of food in different places to keep my guests and the gathering flowing. I choose the appropriate music and lighting, and decorate in a way that enhances the party theme, if there is one. This is quite common, and what we are all trying to achieve through this detail-oriented party preparation is an opportunity for people to be comfortable and enjoy themselves. Otherwise they might as well stay home.

Getting individuals to talk—and here I mean to really be honest about their thoughts and *feelings* about sin—requires an analogous type of preparation. It begins in creating a context in which people feel like participants in the discussion of sin, not like they are going to be lectured. This is difficult as the leader or instructor may have to take a back seat in the conversation. The teacher needs to be receptive to the class as the students formulate their values and ideas. The teacher cannot dominate or overpower. Why? Precisely because he or she is in a position of power. So the more the teacher fades into the background and nurtures the concerns in the classroom, the safer everyone will feel. This does not mean that the instructor cannot offer insights from his or her expertise in the field; rather, it is about creating a space where people can feel safe making mistakes about ideas and issues, self-correcting and learning from others, and pursuing their own leads. The teacher is there to facilitate a conversation and provide resources for tackling the big issues, yet not to have the final word.

More important than the facilitator are the participants. They have to feel empowered to take ownership of the conversation. For sin talk to be meaningful it cannot be just memorizing sins or robotically citing scripture, it has to come from the ground up, reflecting the important issues and concerns of the day. Storytelling is an important piece of the conversation. Participants could talk about their backgrounds and significant events in their lives. Sharing ourselves in these ways creates intimacy, and enables us to relate to others in more genuine ways. Storytelling helps break through the defensiveness that often thwarts give-and-take conversation. It ought to go without saying that each participant needs to be respectful of the others for fellowship to emerge. Food and drink might help too. I notice that when I have shared a meal with someone I have a richer relationship with that person than with those with whom I have not eaten. Something about the vulnerability that emerges in the physical act of sitting together over some food can get people talking. Once people feel comfortable, and they have shared their stories, it might prove beneficial to discuss their reactions to basic questions about sin. For example, what are some things they consider sinful and why? From where have they received messages about sin? Only in beginning to ask and answer these fundamental questions can a deeper reflection on sin and brokenness develop.

What I hear time and again from my students is that they don't want others to judge them, so they choose not to judge others by labeling anything about who they are or how they act as sinful. From a purely sociological perspective, this may be a good thing. For what is morally wrong in one culture could be morally neutral or even positive in another culture. It all depends on one's upbringing and perspective. Whereas before modern technology, travel, and communication, we may have not been totally cognizant of this phenomenon of religious and cultural pluralism, in our current context of globalization, where mixing and moving with others occurs interpersonally and virtually, there is no way to avoid difference. This is a crucial point, since Christians are called to live like Jesus and strive to engage others with compassion, rather than judgment. At the same time, we need to be able to say that something is morally wrong and causes another pain in order to enact justice. It is this tension between not wanting to judge and being obligated to promote justice that makes talking about sin complicated business.

SCRIPTURE AND TRADITION ON SIN AND BROKENNESS

In his work *The Christian Vision of Humanity: Basic Christian Anthropology*, John R. Sachs notes three general descriptions of sin in the Hebrew Scriptures: "missing the mark" or a misdeed; the state of being twisted or turned on the inside; and rebelling against God and the law.[1] Both the notion of missing the mark and that of rebelling against God and order represent personal failures of not living up to God's commandments or purposely going against those commandments, respectively, which many experience at one point or another in their lives. Moreover, few of us leave this earth without feeling twisted or torn up, carrying guilt, and feeling overwhelmed by burdens. And unfortunately, each one of us is in danger of passing all these burdens on to those around us if they are not transformed and overcome.

While these descriptions of sin certainly convey what it means and feels like to be broken, as the early Church developed, Christians began to interpret the Hebrew Scriptures on sin in a distinctive way. It became commonplace to refer to sin in terms of "the fall," which generally describes how human beings became alienated or "fell" from God's grace. While the first two chapters of the Bible focus mainly on the idea that God created a world that was good, in Genesis 3, human beings are portrayed as experiencing the fall by succumbing to greed, narcissism, and the negative aspects of the God complex. One reads in Genesis 3 that even though God tells the first humans that they can enjoy most of the garden, they fail to curb their pride of thinking they deserve more and sin by eating from the forbidden tree. As a result of their actions, they are illustrated as feeling ashamed, and then they are punished. Tapping into the symbolic nature of this story of the fall, the experience of being alienated from God and goodness is what Christians mean when they speak about being broken. Beyond scriptural references then, Christians interpret "the fall" more broadly as a concept for understanding how all human beings at one point or another sin and feel broken, experience alienation and loneliness, and feel disconnected from the love of God and others. Put another way, in both scripture and tradition the notion of "the fall" conveys the price of not saying yes to God, and the reality of saying no.

As this section unfolds, important questions related to the symbolic nature of the fall are considered. For instance, it is necessary to reflect on the way sin is understood from a Christian perspective in the contemporary period. Which sins do Christians commit today? How does one trespass God in our time? What does saying no to God look like in everyday life? One might think that sin is an isolated event and brokenness is a passing situation, and in some ways they are. Nonetheless, sin rarely manifests in an isolated effect. It is more the case that any one sin impacts others and sin gets passed on from one generation to another.

SIN AS INHERITANCE

There are many ways to interpret the belief that sin is inherited and never is disconnected from other peoples' lives. One interpretation is that we are in patterns of sin that we pass on to others, or at least the effects of our sin get passed on to others. In other words, there is a domino effect to sin in that it may start with one person or an isolated community, but it impacts the others surrounding them. We experience this on a very basic and almost unconscious level. For example, if our parents constantly have heated arguments and disparage and hurt one another, those broken relations not only impact the two of them but everyone around them. The children often feel terrible about these conflicts; they want to fix them or make them go away. If the parents fail to change their ways, this persistent conflict in the home could taint their children's views on romantic relationships in general. This is just one example. There are many others, expanding to the global panorama. For instance, as we will see more in the pages that follow, the sinful effects of slavery in the United States and throughout the Americas did not end completely with the Emancipation Proclamation. Indeed, the United States continues to struggle with issues related to racism and racial inequality.

There is another way that Christians imagine sin being passed on, namely, through sexual intercourse. St. Augustine, a prominent thinker in the early Church, developed the idea that the sin of the first humans is passed to the next generation through sex. He traces sin back to the fall in Genesis 3, when Adam and Eve disobey God because of their pride—the pride of wanting to do whatever they want and of not heeding their creaturely limits. For Augustine, this act of disobedience is humanity's first or original sin. And as a result of this original sin, human beings are corrupt, and they experience this corruption or brokenness through bodily desire, particularly sexual desire. What's more, original sin is transmitted through sex, making sin unending and everywhere—part of the human condition. For Augustine, to overcome sin, human beings must control their bodily appetites, especially sexual ones, and even sexual desire in marriage. Ultimately, though, self-control is not enough to wipe out the inherited sin of humanity. We need baptism and God's continued grace to be cleansed and made new again. As one might imagine, Augustine's theology fosters a fear of sexual desire. Many people throughout history have felt ashamed of their sexual desires, precisely because of Augustinian theology of the body. Christians still struggle with perceived connections between sex and sin today.

A SIMPLE QUESTION, YES OR NO?

In a previous chapter, freedom was described in terms of saying yes to God, others, and life-giving relationships. Here we might want to read sin as saying no to God, others, and life-giving relationships. However, as with our discussion of freedom, it is difficult to describe sin without considering other factors and the complex web of relations in which we find ourselves. Like freedom, sin is a result of semiautonomous existence. We are always influenced by others, and sometimes these influences predispose us to sin. This does not excuse any damaging actions; on the contrary, it aids in our understanding of what went wrong and how we might avoid it in the future.

Catholic Christians have particular ways of classifying sin, as venial and as mortal. Venial sin is far less serious than mortal sin, and generally refers to acts that hinder our ability to have life-giving relationships with God and others, such as lying or getting too angry with others. Mortal or deadly sins are the transgressions that destroy one's capacity to say yes to God and others, and include the sins of wrath, greed, laziness, pride, lust, envy, and gluttony. While there is a lot of room for overlap between these two types of sin, they are helpful tools for Christians to keep in mind as they navigate their faith journeys in an attempt to say yes to God and others.

CATEGORIES OF SIN

It would not be surprising if Christians, particularly Catholic Christians, when asked what sin is, would refer to venial and mortal sin, as well as list the Ten Commandments, which are important laws given by God for communal living. The commandments to be faithful, not to kill, and to honor one's parents are just a few of the rules that most Christians are taught at an early age. While these commandments are important, to move our conversation further, instead of listing all the commandments and explaining them, it might be helpful for readers to explore sin in broad categories or frameworks. Here the work of Bradley Hanson, a Protestant theologian of our time, becomes important. Hanson was already mentioned in the first chapter, and here I want to highlight the way he divides sin into several categorical groupings, including unbelief and idolatry, pride and passivity, and concupiscence and blindness.[2] These groupings provide the scaffolding for a discussion of the power of sin and the pain of brokenness.

Idolatry refers to an individual or group putting all their faith into an entity other than God. For example, idolatry is when people are so consumed with making tons of money that they neglect all the relationships around them. Here money and status are their gods, which could end up leading to their brokenness, especially if they never seem to think they have enough or have achieved enough. Interestingly Hanson pairs idolatry with unbelief in order to demonstrate that when we are overcome with a desire for something other than God, we begin to lose faith. God and healthy relations to others become low on our list of priorities. This sense of unbelief is different than doubt, as most faithful Christians go through periods of doubt throughout their lives. With unbelief, however, it is more the case that the other god in their lives, that is, money or status, corrodes their potential for faith relationships. It is noteworthy that this sense of unbelief is not the same as deliberately choosing to be part of a different religious tradition or even an atheist. That is not unbelief; rather, it is the act of locating oneself in an alternative religious or philosophical trajectory.

Hanson also groups pride and passivity as sin. Too much pride or hubris is a problem because in the discourse of Jean Vanier, it causes the individual to become consumed by self and status, shutting him or her off from the possibility of building relationships based on vulnerability. Pride cuts us off from our humanity—that is our frailty—and builds a wall between us and all others. However, one could argue that some pride is good, especially when it helps build self-esteem. The Jewish feminist theologian Judith Plaskow, in an early work entitled *Sex, Sin and Grace*, cautions against our conceptualizing sin only in terms of pride.[3] Particularly for many women, according to Plaskow, pride is something that they have been deprived of developing. Conditioned to be subservient to others in a male-dominated culture—and, I would add, in a white-supremacist culture—some marginalized individuals and groups need to procure a bit of pride to become fully free and genuinely human.

While pride makes people boast of all that they have done and are capable of doing, passivity is the inability to imagine and do anything. This is a sin because human beings according to Christian doctrine are created with the capacity for freedom and the responsibility to further healthy relations with God and others. Passivity leads to sin because it represents a moment or lifetime of refusing to use that freedom. This is worth consideration because it is easy to assume that sin is when an individual does this or that, when one person violates another or when one group exploits another. However, Christians also talk about sin in terms of not doing anything. For example, if exploitation is happening and we know it, we need to struggle against it. We all have opportunities to take stands in life that secure another's freedom and flourishing. Today, schoolchildren are taught extensively about the perils of bullying. They are encouraged to report the one who is bullying the other as well as to not bully. Not bullying can be a form of standing up to bullies, because it shows that there is something wrong with bullying behavior. There are other examples as well. When we choose our leaders, we are faced with hard decisions. Do we choose those who seem to be on our side, or do we choose leaders who are on the side of the poor and the marginalized? Opting for the other in society on the individual or communal level is a way of avoiding the sin of passivity. This is one of the main messages in the Gospels, namely, the obligation to be on the side of and in solidarity with the poor, sick, and outcasts of society. Jesus as portrayed by the gospel writers was anything but passive.

The last grouping for Hanson is that of concupiscence and blindness. Concupiscence refers to inordinate desire for something or someone, to the point at which that desire damages the good relationships in one's life. Some assume this desire to be a sexual one. It could be; but it could also be an unhealthy, uncontrollable desire for anything worldly, including a person, place, thing, experience, and so on. We all have desires; this is part of being human in a world with others. Nonetheless, when our desires become our main focus, practically our God, then we are not free at all. We compromise our freedom and potentially that of others. For example, if the object of our desire is a certain vehicle and we take on tremendous debt to own the car, we may become less free to do other things in our lives that we find pleasurable. What's more, if money gets really tight, we may find ourselves having to borrow from others, which can potentially put a strain on them and/or on our relationship.

Finally, blindness is the inability to see or detect injustices around us that we may or may not have caused. As mentioned in a previous chapter, Bernard Lonergan, a Roman Catholic thinker, wrote about the sin of blindness as *scotoma*, which is a classical term to talk about blocked, distorted, or compromised vision. This scotoma for Lonergan manifests in being unaware or not attentive to the problems, sins, injustices, and wrongs of our time. For Lonergan, it is not the case that human beings are inherently malicious and/or stupid and that their malevolence and/or ignorance prevent them from perceiving sinful situations and acting against them. On the contrary, Lonergan argues that there exist forces, including emotional and social pressures, which prevent us from seeing the totality of the situation and acting accordingly. Perhaps fear or ignorance is in the individual's way, and this leads to situations of brokenness. Like with passivity, there is a tendency with the sin of blindness to excuse it. After all, there are outside factors that lead one to be passive or ignorant, and hence sin. However, reading Hanson's work on blindness in tandem with Lonergan's work on conversion, the Christian believer is accountable for overcoming or at least struggling against these obstacles.

SOCIAL SIN

So far we have explored sin mostly on the individual level. However, we learn from Bernard Lonergan and others that sin, largely in terms of bias, occurs on the group level as well. This is when we might begin to talk about social sin, in which brokenness is caused by entire social structures, including families, schools, laws, facilities, and so on. Sexism is a social sin. Racism is a social sin. Environmental degradation is a social sin. And perhaps speciesism, which is being more concerned for, holding a higher moral regard for, and ultimately having more value for one animal species over all others, is a social sin. In what follows, we will look at the social sin of racism, particularly in the context of the United States, and explore the questions of speciesism as well.

CHATTEL SLAVERY

Shawn Copeland, a most significant Catholic theologian of our day, has written extensively on the social sin of racism, whose roots are in the tragic history of chattel slavery in the United States. It is important to keep in mind that the social sin of racism is not about a preference for one kind of person over another—like a preference for Diet Pepsi over Diet Coke. On the contrary, it is when all social structures support the belief that humans are divided into races and that one race is superior to the other. In the Americas, race has functioned as a separation between "white" and all other persons of color. The term *white* is put in quotes because theorists claim that race is a fiction—after all, there is nothing biologically separating these groups. All belong to the same species; nonetheless, racial categories function to oppress some groups for the benefit of others to keep the fiction of race alive.

Racism manifests in individual and social sin in that it runs contrary to the Christian belief that all creatures are created good and all human beings have the capacity for freedom, that is, are created in the image of God. A person could be racist, but it is important to note that racism runs deeper. Racism occurs when virtually all aspects of society justify and legitimize the oppression of one group over another and the power of one group over another, and most importantly for Christians, deny that specific group the blessings of being created in the image of God.

Racialized categories fueled the egregious, catastrophic, and evil system of chattel slavery in the Americas, and continue to plague the United States today by dividing individuals and groups and even leading to racial violence and hate crimes. While slavery has existed all over the globe at various times and in various forms, what was distinctive about slavery in the Americas was that people were understood as objects to be bought, sold, tortured, raped, and so on. It was the complete objectification and dehumanization of human people. This particular form of slavery—which reduces humans to "its" to be used by others—is what is meant by the phrase *chattel slavery*. Moreover, according to Copeland, black women suffering under chattel slavery experienced a particular form of torture and dehumanization. Enslaved women were objects of property, objects of production, objects of reproduction (their bodies became vehicles of production for future generations of slaves), and objects of sexual violence.

Copeland's work compels all readers, and especially Christians, to come to terms with the way slavery debased all humans and God. That is the power of social sin. This is not an easy issue to digest. We are still dealing with racism and racial hatred today. All one needs as proof is to reflect on the Trayvon Martin case, the police shooting of Michael Brown, or the brutal killing of Eric Garner in order to see how these racial wounds are still fresh. Part of healing is learning the history and asking more about racial situations today in as open a posture as possible. For Christians in America, there really is no other choice but to deal with racism head on, as Copeland suggests that no one can really reflect the image of God unless all are working toward justice.[4]

SPECIESISM

Christian scholars engaged with issues related to environmental degradation make analogous claims, namely that until Christians embrace the centrality of the earth and our small place in it, they will continue to fail to reflect the image of God and to say yes to God's grace. Speciesism is one way of breaking into this conversation on social sin and the environment. It refers to when some species are regarded as having more value than others and social structures support the value differential. In all fairness, it is important to note that some would not even consider speciesism a problem, never mind sinful. Rather, those taking this perspective might argue that it is descriptive of reality. A human life is worth more than that of a gorilla or an ant. Even those who are troubled by speciesism have probably at one time or another fallen prey to its logic. Every time an individual makes a choice about which nonhuman animals to eat and which not to eat, or which nonhuman animals to bring into his or her home as a pet, he or she is making value judgments about the value of particular species relative to others. If one decides that this species has more value than another, then he or she might feel legitimized to exercise power over them and regard the other less-valuable species for his or her own use.

For most Christians the trap of speciesism is extremely difficult to avoid. In fact much of religious education is predicated on the notion of human animals being the crown of creation—so much so they are removed from nonhuman animal life altogether. This teaching became crystal clear for me when attending a meeting to prepare children for the sacrament of reconciliation. I was struck by how much talk was devoted to the human person being the crown of creation as portrayed in Genesis 1. While one appreciates the gender-inclusive language of the notion of "the human person" being created in the image of God, it comes at a cost of having to sacrifice the inclusivity of and appreciation for all of creation. I could not tell how the others around me at the meeting felt about this issue. Perhaps they were not paying attention. Maybe they were tuning it out, and were instead on their smartphones. They could not have been fully conscious because they are quite invested with their nonhuman animals. They bury their pets in their well-manicured lawns. They sacrifice time and money to get them the best healthcare. They adore them. It is true love. There seems to be a strong disconnect between what they are doing and what they were hearing, namely, that only humans are capable of full communion with God. I sat there in my struggle wondering, is this not the sin of pride, of narcissism, of anthropomorphism, that needs to be told in the confessional? In *The Dream of the Earth*, Thomas Berry argues that anthropocentrism "is largely consequent on our failure to think of ourselves as species."[5]

The term *narcissism* is thrown around quite a bit and could use some explication. Referring back to Ovid's *Metamorphoses*, Narcissus is the figure who falls in love with his own image—a reflection in water. Narcissus was not necessarily egotistical or self-absorbed; rather, he was unable to distinguish where he ended and the water began—he could not detect the borders of another. This myth has become a way for clinicians to diagnose and treat individuals with narcissistic personality disorder.[6] However, most of us employ the term *narcissistic* in a far less technical way, to describe people who are only concerned with their needs and their wants. This may be the case because they are selfish and self-involved, or worse, because they do not see the impact they are having on others. When framed in this way, it is possible to talk about the attitude of human animals toward non-human animals as narcissistic.

This is not meant to be blaming in any way. Rather, it gives language to try to understand from a theological, sociological, anthropological, and psychological point of view how we have arrived at the sixth mass extinction pattern. It is not that people are innately bad; quite the opposite, the Christian tradition affirms the goodness of all of creation. It is that in enacting freedom, some of our decisions have had a negative impact on other creatures. Humans could be acting in self-interest, or perhaps in the discourse of Berry, humans do not see their connections to other animals, and hence overstep their boundaries. With the question of boundaries, we come full circle to the Garden of Eden, back to the story of the first humans overstepping boundaries in greed, pride, and arrogance, which of course does not have a happy ending. Perhaps Christians are getting a second chance in the garden. And while it may be difficult and not feasible to view and value all the species the same way, might

Christians begin to imagine themselves as a species? Might this be one step in putting Humpty Dumpty back together again?

SUMMARY

Here we explored key issues related to the topic of sin and brokenness. First, the difficulty of having the sin talk was discussed with suggestions for how to set the stage for a productive conversation about it. Then scripture and tradition were mined for an eye toward key beliefs about sin. The differences between individual and social sin were noted. In many ways, social sin is more controversial than individual sin because one can hide personal sin, while social sin is inherently public and potentially shameful. Chattel slavery was highlighted as a major blight on U.S. history, the effects of which we are still experiencing now. Finally, the chapter concluded with some reflections on how human animals are called to rethink of themselves as one species among all other species as a way to heal some of the wounds associated with environmental degradation. Sin is a deeply personal topic and it helps to share our stories about the pain and confusion of being broken as a path toward healing. The journey for healing is longer for some than others, depending on the situation and the extent of pain and brokenness. One needs to keep going, putting one foot in front of the other, so to speak. After all, hope is crucial to the process. Ultimately the problem with the text on "Humpty Dumpty" is that it is devoid of hope. Christians believe there is always hope for healing and peace through forgiveness and reconciliation. It is to those questions that we now turn.

EXERCISES:
1. **Complete a journal entry on this topic.**
2. **Think-Pair-Share** (Reflect on these questions silently, find a partner and discuss them together, and then share with the class.)
   - Click on a news website. Locate a major problem in the community or world. How does sin unfold in that event? Is it a result of individual or social sin? How can

it be remedied? Explain what it means for the situation to be fixed in light of gospel messages about Jesus and his mission.

- Watch *Dolphin Tale* or *Blackfish*. Discuss how either of these films portrays the complexity of speciesism.

3. Creative Time

Listen to your favorite music. In which ways does a specific song illustrate the pain of being broken? Is some music more spiritual than other music? If so, what makes it more spiritual? Finally, write some lyrics that convey your experiences of brokenness; and if you are comfortable doing so, share your song with others.

NOTES

1. John R. Sachs, *The Christian Vision of Humanity: Basic Christian Anthropology* (Collegeville, MN: Liturgical Press, 1991), 61.

2. Hanson, *Introduction to Christian Theology*, 108–13.

3. Judith Plaskow, *Sex, Sin and Grace: Women's Experience and the Theologies of Reinhold Niebuhr and Paul Tillich* (Washington, DC: University Press of America, 1980).

4. See M. Shawn Copeland, *Enfleshing Freedom: Body, Race, and Being* (Minneapolis: Fortress Press, 2009).

5. Thomas Berry, *The Dream of the Earth* (San Francisco: Sierra Club Books, 1988), 21.

6. For more on narcissism, see Michele Saracino, *Being about Borders: A Christian Anthropology of Difference*.

Chapter 9

THE POWER OF
FORGIVENESS

If I polled students randomly, asking them to pinpoint an important belief in the Christian tradition, many of them would say forgiveness. There are many reasons for this. While Christians by no
means invented the idea of forgiveness, Christian scriptures, traditions, and rituals emphasize the centrality of forgiveness as a
way to live like Jesus. In the Gospels, Jesus is portrayed as forgiving individuals in the community who are thought to be sinful,
including criminals, tax collectors, and other social outcasts.
What's more, Catholic Christians participate in a particular ritual
of forgiveness referred to as the sacrament of reconciliation, and
it is believed that confessing one's sins publicly or privately is an
important part of conversion on any level. These are just two
examples of forgiveness in the Christian landscape. As the chapter unfolds, we will see many more.

Even with so much emphasis on the significance of forgiveness
in human existence, when an individual desires to forgive another
in his or her ordinary life, the ability to forgive may seem extraor-
dinarily difficult. Forgiveness is not necessarily forgetting what
happened; rather, it is being willing to let go of all the anger, rage,
and resentment one feels toward the other who violated or tres-
passed him or her. Anyone who has ever been hurt knows that
forgiveness is a painstaking, and at times a seemingly impossible,
process. In this chapter, we will explore some of the spiritual and
psychological challenges to forgiving.

We will begin by looking at iconic moments regarding forgiveness in the Christian imagination. Then we will think through our

commonsense thoughts about anger and how that blocks forgiveness, working from straightforward to more complicated scenarios. In the more thorny situations, it becomes apparent that harboring resentment and rage is an impediment to enacting one's freedom for God and others, including the freedom to forgive. In these moments, one needs to open his or her heart to something other than feeling like a victim. It is worth noting that not all forgiveness is oriented toward others; at times we may be called not only to forgive the other but to forgive ourselves.

Forgiveness takes a long time for some of us, in that it demands we transform ourselves and the way we relate to God and others. This transformation is about loving ourselves and others and letting go of unhelpful habits and old hurts. We might need to mourn these losses, since these habits and hurts have been with us for a while. In the end, letting go is the only way to become whole again. As we think about transformation in a cosmic sense, we might begin to not only let go of destructive habits and old hurts, but also any sense of creatureliness that ignores the importance of all beings. In connection with this, by the end of the chapter, we will explore how applying queer theory to our love of nonhuman animals may create avenues for reconciliation with the entire planet.

THE CALL TO FORGIVE

There are numerous references in Sacred Scripture that call believers to show mercy on those that have wounded them, and eventually to forgive them. To begin, in the Book of Daniel, forgiveness is understood as a quality associated with the Divine, meaning God: "To the Lord our God belong mercy and forgiveness, for we have rebelled against him."[1] The merciful disposition of God is displayed even more poetically and strongly in Micah: "Who is a God like you, pardoning iniquity and passing over the transgression....He does not retain his anger forever, because he delights in showing clemency. He will again have compassion upon us; he will tread our inequities under foot. You will cast all our sins into the depths of the sea."[2] This is a poignant meditation on how believers have faith in a god that angers, yet overcomes anger. This is an image of God that lets go of all hurt, rage, and resentment. The sea takes up all the negativity; water washes away brokenness.

Water is an important symbol in religious thought. For Christians, the connection between forgiveness and water is most obvious in the sacrament of baptism. Once an ancient Jewish ritual, baptism became for Christians a significant moment of being cleansed and recreated in God's image. In this universal Christian sacrament, believers are immersed into water as a sign of their commitment to faith and their being created anew in the Christian community. All sin is washed away in baptism. The Gospel of Mark begins with Jesus' baptism as an adult Jewish male. There is no reference to his infancy or his childhood. Rather, the Markan editor dives right into Jesus' adult life, when his public ministry is heating up. According to Mark, "John the baptizer appeared in the wilderness, proclaiming a baptism of repentance for the forgiveness of sins. And people from the whole Judean countryside and all the people of Jerusalem were going out to him, and were baptized by him in the river Jordan, confessing their sins."[3] Jesus was one of those baptized.

Forgiveness is connected to other places in the New Testament scriptures. Specifically in the Gospel of Matthew, Jesus is shown teaching that "if you forgive others their trespasses, your heavenly Father will also forgive you; but if you do not forgive others, neither will your Father forgive your trespasses."[4] Here forgiveness is not just one option among many, but a prerequisite for salvation. All Christians throughout the world pray the Lord's Prayer, making the plea to forgive a universal sign of Christian identity.

One of the most jarring moments in the New Testament writings is when Jesus is portrayed as praying for his murderers, immortalized in the famous phrase "Father, forgive them; for they do not know what they are doing."[5] Jesus is on the cross, near death, and enduring a most humiliating experience for a Jew under the Roman Empire. Even so, Jesus asks his father to forgive those that are doing this—to forgive his perpetrators. What Christians glean from this text is that to live like Jesus means, plain and simple, to forgive others—even in the midst of intense suffering and torture.

Some cases of hurt are more intense than others. Personal experience as well as history reveals to us that in extreme cases of pain, violation, and trauma, letting go of hurt and ultimately forgiving others becomes a lifelong journey. For example, if one's child dies at the hands of another, perhaps because of a car accident involving drunk driving, it would be an excruciating process to forgive the compromised driver. So many emotions are involved in the process, including anger, guilt, sadness, and despair, that forgiveness seems impossible. Similarly, when a community experiences trauma, as in the case of the devastating events surrounding 9/11 or of the Sandy Hook school shooting in Connecticut, forgiveness seems so far away, and almost seems to be a disservice to the victims involved in the tragedy. Even if people want to forgive the other who hurt them, they may feel like they are traitors to others if they do. They may feel guilty about forgiving what others deem unforgivable. This is what Christians are called to do nonetheless. And such forgiveness is not merely for the other, but even more than that, for the injured, so they can be restored to a state of feeling whole and able to participate in God's creation in life-giving ways.

As we move toward the possibility of forgiveness, we need to not only reflect on Sacred Scripture, but also on how the call to forgive is made sacred in sacramental life. Baptism was already discussed relative to the religious symbolism of water in the Old and New Testaments. In addition to baptism, communion is a sacrament where the salvific nature of forgiveness is revealed. In Matthew's Gospel, at Jesus' last meal with his friends, we see the spiritual connections between eating and forgiveness: "While they were eating, Jesus took a loaf of bread, and after blessing it he broke it, gave it to the disciples, and said, 'Take, eat; this is my body.' Then he took a cup, and after giving thanks he gave it to them, saying, 'Drink from it, all of you; for this is my blood of the covenant, which is poured out for many for the forgiveness of sins.'"[6] Christians all around the world on Sunday commemorate Jesus' last supper through the sacrament of communion or Eucharist. Eating and sharing in the memory of Jesus' life and mission, individuals and communities are healed by letting go of their anxieties and opening to grace. Eucharist provides a model for all our meals, in that eating together on any social occasion provides an opportunity to build relationships and become materially and spiritually nourished.

Beyond specific scriptural references and sacramental life, we see the power of forgiveness in the Christian imaginary, particularly in the symbolic nature of the cross. There is a plurality of views on the cross, and throughout the past two thousand years, various theologies of the cross have been explored. Sometimes Jesus' death on the cross is understood as a sign of victory over evil, whereby in dying on the cross Jesus stomps out evil in the world and creates a new way of living. Alternatively, one could interpret Jesus' death on the cross as a payment for human trespass. Another way the cross is interpreted is as a model for all believers, meaning that all Christians are called to sacrifice for the greater good. Like Jesus sacrificed on the cross, Christians are obligated to sacrifice in their lives in a myriad of ways to honor and imitate Jesus. Here sacrifice brings about conversion and forgiveness. There is much overlap among these interpretations of the cross. Ultimately, any and all interpretations lead to a sense that through Jesus' death, all are forgiven and opened to a new way of living. There is also the sense that forgiveness is not easy—it takes work and perhaps even sacrifice.

WHAT'S THE INCENTIVE?

It is fair to ask, then, why forgive at all, especially if the act of forgiving may be as painful as the wound that needs to be forgiven? In other words, what's the incentive to forgive? One way to answer this question is to reflect on the notion that forgiveness is not just about sacrificing for others; it is also about retrieving a healthy sense of self. It has the potential to free us up from all the negative feelings that imprison us, which prevent us from living life to the fullest and from loving others, God, and even ourselves. Thus, the payoff of forgiveness is in the individual or community being liberated to enjoy life and life-giving relationships once again.

This interpretation of why forgiveness is important helps us deal with the problem of one-sided forgiveness. This refers to situations where the one who has wronged us is not asking for forgiveness, refuses to admit any wrongdoing, or is simply unavailable (perhaps because he or she is estranged or deceased). In any of these cases, we may feel as if we cannot genuinely forgive the individual or group because they are not initiating the process; it is one-sided. In fact, their disconnectedness from the situation may frustrate us even further, making us want them to pay a higher price for their hurtful actions. While these feelings are totally understandable, if prolonged and not overcome, they could end up hurting us even more. We could become so preoccupied with our hurt that we are unable to be present in any other aspect of our lives. In such circumstances, forgiving the person who has wronged us is our best chance for survival and flourishing. Whether the other asks to be forgiven or not, it is in our best interest to forgive. Jean Vanier discusses that forgiveness in such situations is a powerful tool for opening oneself to grace. Regardless of whether the other asks for it, we have the power to let it go and symbolically—as in Micah—toss all that binds us to negativity into the sea.

Before letting it all go, one needs to deal with some of the negative effects of the hurt in the first place. Getting angry might be a first step toward making things right. I am comfortable being angry. At least that is what I tell myself. For a long time I would feel bad about myself when I got angry with someone—like I was a failure or not quite competent at the relationship or situation from which the anger originated. I was afraid that my anger would cause me to lose the other's love or acceptance. However, I have come to realize that embracing my negative feelings allows me to develop more of a tolerance for other individuals to be angry, even to be angry with me. While that feeling of wanting approval and love still lingers, I am more comfortable with being in relationships where one or another at some point is angry, because for me, that is more of a genuine relationship. It is part of the give and take of creaturely existence.

Some may share my experience and others may not. I am not speaking for everyone, and realize that each individual deals with anger differently. However, it is important to keep in mind the gender connections discussed previously, in which we considered the pressure on girls in society not to get angry or show any sort of discontent. Instead girls are rewarded for smiling; if they are not smiling, they are told to do so. As girls grow up and become women, they are held even more rigidly to a no-anger policy. It is as if a woman who gets angry is less feminine, desirable, and worthy of love. It was argued that instead of trying to suppress it at every corner, we might attempt to be more honest and open about the power of anger. It is not something to be ashamed of, but worked through. To be sure, not all anger is productive. If it feeds resentment, festers into rage, and becomes a pattern of relating that prevents life-giving relations, in other words, if it infringes on our freedom, then it is hazardous. This is when anger, rage, and wrath lead to sin.

FORGIVING ONESELF

So far the focus has been on forgiving the other. At times, one of the most challenging dimensions of being human is forgiving oneself. We hold ourselves to such impossible standards and we want to be perfect so badly, that at times we fall prey to the illusion that we can achieve perfection. We blame ourselves, hide in shame, and fear the reality of being finite and limited. That is what makes forgiving oneself so hard to do—it demands that we admit our vulnerability. Not only does our fear of exposure at times thwart our ability to make healthy connections with others, it also interrupts our capacity for freedom. Being locked up in anger and hate prevents freedom. In many ways it is easier to hold onto feelings of shame and anger about what one has done, than to ask for forgiveness and attempt to move on.

MEMORY AS IMPASSE

Part of the challenge of opening to the possibility of forgiveness is dealing with the affective dissonance, meaning emotional volatility, around memories of the event we are called to overcome and forgive. Memory is a complex cognitive and emotive phenomenon and cannot be underestimated when it comes to the topic of forgiveness. Sometimes we are not even fully conscious of how much of an impact memory has on our self-understanding or the way we relate to others.

Here is an example from my own life. Not too long ago I acquired a new piece of furniture and had to find room for it in my home. My husband suggested that we get a smaller sofa to accommodate the new piece of furniture fitting into the room. I looked at him aghast and cried, "No way, that is the sofa we had when our children were born!" Then my neighbor suggested I move a cabinet to make room, and I looked at her appalled and said, "That's from my first apartment!" Reflecting on those gut reactions, I realized that indeed I am sentimental, and more than that, my sense of who I am and who I want to be is tied up with memories of those relics.

Memories of the good and what's pleasurable stay with us throughout our lifetime. Memories of the last time someone saw his beloved uncle, of the rich taste of her grandmother's signature dish, or of the sweet sounds of birds or insects come back when least expected. Every summer, I am soothed, delighted, and catapulted into feeling nostalgic by the sounds of the cicadas. Their buzzing haunts me, reminding me of the carefree summer days of when I was a child. Its reverberations remind me that I am no longer a child and that I have children of my own. The memory of the sound of the cicada anchors me; it is part of me.

These are all pleasurable memories. What if the memories that haunt us are unpleasant? What if sounds, tastes, and sights related to a painful event begin to disrupt our lives and prevent us from having life-giving relationships in the here and now? These painful and intrusive memories, some of which are associated with trauma, make forgiving the individual that is implicated in these memories quite difficult, if not impossible. They manifest as impasse, in which we become thwarted in our efforts to progress in the forgiveness process. In these cases, we should not feel bad that we cannot forgive, but should continue to work with individuals and communities of support, including caregivers, clinicians, and so on, to get to a place where we can imagine moving forward. Here the Christian call to forgive still applies, yet is contextualized in the deep wounds of brokenness with which we find ourselves. God meets us there too.

TRUST AS FORGIVENESS

We already have begun to intuit from this discussion that forgiveness does not always come in the form of words. One does not necessarily need to say "I am sorry," or expect to hear it, to experience forgiveness. Words are certainly important, but so are heartfelt gestures, such as converting from a stance of ignorance to an understanding of the other as well as converting to a genuine openness to the other. This second aspect of showing openness is a way of beginning to trust another again and demonstrating forgiveness.

Trust in interpersonal relationship takes work and time. If someone has repeatedly hurt us emotionally or physically, a simple apology probably would not suffice. In an effort to protect ourselves from being hurt again, many of us need evidence that the person has changed. This evidence allows us to trust the other again. This sort of trust is also important in societies, even within the global landscape. In the wake of 9/11, there was a tremendous amount of backlash and prejudice against Arab Americans. It is fair to say, there continues to be anti-Arab and anti-Muslim sentiment throughout the United States. These groups are targeted, feared as terrorists, racially profiled, and harassed. The memories of that day unfortunately make it possible for good, moral individuals to pay the price for an extreme few. Most of us have nothing to do with these bias crimes or attitudes, and have nothing for which to be forgiven. However, if one lives in the United States, one is connected to these prejudices—implicated just by the fact of being here. Is it too strong to suggest that showing hospitality and trust toward our Arab and Muslim brothers and sisters would go a long way toward building community and healing wounds?

WHAT'S LOVE GOT TO DO WITH IT?

Forgiveness is connected inextricably to the capacity to love and be loved. When one is twisted with feelings of hate and resentment, loving another or oneself seems impossible. When put this way, the desire to be whole again serves as a catalyst or incentive for forgiveness. This section addresses what is meant by the term *love*. We know that teenagers daydream about it. Married couples struggle with it. The elderly and sick crave it. Advertisers make big bucks off our obsession with it. Love is a mystery. It is that feeling that draws us out of ourselves and orients us toward the other. However, not all love is the same. It is relative to each specific situation. For example, a parent's love for his or her child is not the same as a wife's love for her husband or a person's love for his or her God. The unexpected and unexplainable aspects of love are perhaps what make it such a significant aspect of our lives. And those same aspects make it difficult to talk about. Speaking about love in relation to religion becomes even more complicated, and practically taboo.

Perhaps one of the reasons we avoid talking about love is that it is by nature an affectively charged notion. There is so much emotion around loving and being loved. First of all we need to be receptive to opening to another, baring our hopes, dreams, and fears of failure. We need to trust that the other is going to do right by us and not hurt us emotionally, physically, or spiritually. We have to gear up for not only the joys of love, but the sadness and anger that emerge in relationships of intimacy. Another reason we may avoid talking about love is that we have a deep-seated fear of not being loveable. We all want love, but how many of us really feel like everything we do is loveable? This could leave us in a profound existential crisis.

These complicated aspects of love are probably what I was least prepared for in parenting—the emotional turmoil that loving another brings. It is not just juggling work, home, and kids' schedules that makes parenting tough; it is learning how to love without having all the answers and without being in control. I think this is what people really mean when they speak about *loving unconditionally*. We love others even when we cannot change them. We love others even when their actions disappoint us. We love others even when they seem to not love us anymore. Moreover, sometimes as parents our actions toward our children are less than desirable. Perhaps we are low on patience and we yell at them or ignore them. These instances leave many of us feeling unlovable. While we may be fully confident in our unconditional love for them, we may feel like they should not or do not love us unconditionally. We feel undeserving of their love.

Unconditional love is one of those complicated concepts, and hence worthy of further consideration here. Many understand the phrase *unconditional love* quite literally, meaning that one will love another without strings, expectations, or conditions. However, that has never really been my experience. I may love others even if I am disappointed by their actions; nevertheless, I still have expectations of them. I expect respect. I expect them to be present. I expect not to be hurt over and over again. So there are conditions; I just cannot guarantee that the conditions will be met because some things are out of my control. Again, this dynamic is evident in parenting, in which one is called to let go of control and relinquish the primacy of one's own ego so that of the other can flourish. This can be quite unsettling and painful, yet profoundly life-giving for the relationship in general. So when read this way, unconditional love—as love with expectations, yet no guarantees—is a powerful concept.

Having to let go of the notion that one can control the other is probably at the core of why loving is so affectively charged, and becomes one of those touchy subjects. We like to think we have the right answers in life, including about God, religion, and love. And when we encounter others who challenge us or our ideas, we could become anxious. This is an opportunity to expose our feelings to another as a way to build relationship. As said in previous chapters, letting go pretenses of having the only right perspective could create situations where we develop genuine friendships and are able to pursue romantic partners. Indeed, in letting go, we make space for God in our lives. It is not surprising that some theologians have correlated our feelings for other creatures with our feelings for God. For Bernard Lonergan, religious conversion is typified by falling in love with God. What he means by that is that an authentic faith relationship is not merely knowing or acting—even though those aspects are certainly significant—but rather, the fullness of relationship comes with feelings of love.

LOVE AS JOURNEY

When love is presented in film and television it tends to be distorted into a simplistic story with a beginning, middle, and end—and hopefully a happy ending. We always expect the princess to find her prince, the wounded to be healed, and everyone (at least the good guys) to live happily ever after. While framing love in terms of this neat narrative definitely has an appeal, we cannot forget that every love story does not have a happy ending. In fact, each love relationship changes throughout life. The importance of the story is not in its end, but in all the moments along the way. Love is a journey. The use of the word *journey* allows for talking about the ups and downs of relationships. For in any love relationship, we might hurt the other, be hurt by the other, ask for forgiveness, be asked for forgiveness, or any combination of these possibilities. Not all we do in love is perfect and pleasant, but we need to be able to forgive to keep on loving. Put another way, love—a basic feeling that all of us crave—is not possible without an openness to forgive and be forgiven.

TYPES OF LOVE AND LOVING

So far we have discussed theoretical issues about love, and have conflated romantic love with familial love and with charitable love. It might help to explain more fully these three important ways of loving for Christians, including Eros, philia, and agape. Eros describes romantic, passionate, and erotic love for the other. It is what we mean when we speak about sexual desire and love. It is what drives us to do great things in our lives and aspire to success. The capacity for Eros is an important dimension of human existence. After all, falling in love with another in the physical sense has the potential to ameliorate feelings of loneliness and isolation. Moreover, erotic love could lead to the creation of new human beings. It is precisely this connection between erotic love and procreation that is worth exploring further, as reflecting on Eros has implications for what was discussed in the chapter on gender.

The challenge of speaking about Eros here is *not* to conflate it with heterosexuality. To be sure, heterosexual desire is an expression of Eros, but Eros also can manifest in other relationships, including same-sex ones. Having said this, it is important to note that much of the Christian tradition rests on an idea of heterosexuality being the norm, whereby gender complementarity leads to a "natural" romantic state for human beings. It is really only in the more contemporary theological and ethical writings that these assumptions are challenged. Theological reflections that expand Eros to other romantic configurations implicitly and explicitly question the assumption that heterosexual relationships are more just than other types of romantic relationships. Indeed, some ask whether it is possible to have a more life-giving sexual relationship with a member of the same sex than with one of the opposite sex. These contemporary theologies underscore the idea that how we love is just as important as who we love. They lead to the conclusion that both heterosexual and same-sex relationships have the potential to be life-giving and ways to honor God and all of creation.[7]

Much of the theology and ethics that rejects the idea that there is only one way to desire is indebted to the field of study called queer theory. This field of study examines and critiques the norms associated with love and desire in a particular culture. Integrating queer theory in this chapter, we not only imagine good love in same-sex relationships, but also in relationships between human animals and nonhuman animals. Queer love experiences may give us insight into how to imagine human existence differently in an age of mass extinctions.

Continuing to map how love is understood in the Christian tradition, we see that in addition to Eros, there is philia, which refers to the love between friends, family members, and other communal connections. It refers to non-romantic love, or love that is free from sexual desire. This is the love that comes with companionship, and it often feeds the bonds with others we have in our schools, workplaces, and homes. We tend to think of human animals as friends. It is worth reflecting on how we might think of all relationships between human animals and nonhuman animals in terms of philia—love friendships.

Beyond Eros and philia, Christians are called to agape, which is a selfless love of the other that does not expect anything in return. Agape refers to the life of charity and hospitality for which we are chosen, and which may or may not accompany our romances or friendships. When we share our resources—our time, money, and space—with others, we demonstrate agape. When we love the other even if he or she does not love us or cannot love us in the same way, we demonstrate agape. This sort of love demands an openness to self and other that is compassionate, forgiving, and asymmetrical. It is the deepest of all loves and what opens us to say yes to God.

Again, in reflecting on love, it is easy to assume we are talking about relationships between human beings: friends, lovers, and family members. We have already seen with agape that human beings are drawn out of the earthly realm to a relationship with the Divine. Now, let us consider the love that emerges between species, the love of human animal and nonhuman animals' bonds. Perhaps through such reflection we can continue to develop an understanding of being human with a greater awareness and embrace of all creatures, taking the power of forgiveness to a higher plane.

QUEER LOVE STORIES

Love stories with nonhuman animals are quite common. We hear of neighbors, friends, relatives, and colleagues who have pets as companions in the fullest sense of the word. They eat with them, sleep in the same space as them, play with them, cry with them, hold them, and care for them. Kathy Rudy puts it best in her work *Loving Animals: Toward a New Animal Advocacy*, when she argues that this is another way of talking about queer love. Taking the lead from queer theorists and applying their thought to animal studies, Rudy writes, "Queer theory teaches us to recognize various forms of intimacy that are often erased or invisible in our culture. It challenges us to resist the dominant forms of heteronormativity and celebrate differences of all sorts. Most important, it schools us to recognize that sexuality and intimacy have deep and varied connections." In pressing on with queer love as animal love, Rudy shares her "border-crossing" love for her dogs: "These canines teach me more about life and love than one human ever has or could. And so I ask again, isn't this queer?"[8] Rudy's reaction reminds me of when Louis Herman, an expert in dolphin cognition, described his dolphins that died from infection as "colleagues" and "children."[9] He had no other words for his queer love of his dolphin companions. His love for them did not fit into traditional categories.

I have been struck by the queer love stories on a reality television show on the National Geographic Channel called *The Incredible Dr. Pol*. Each show tracks the cases of a Dutch-born Michigan farm veterinarian. I am shocked by the emotional reactions some farmers have to their animals. One farmer, when two of his calves were stillborn, spoke about how sometimes dealing with the pain of loss is unbearable. Another farmer had to put her pig, Penelope, out to slaughter, because she could no longer breed. The grief on the farmer's face was powerful and unsettling. I tried to understand and thus overcome my disorienting emotion for the farmers' stories. After all, this is their business, shouldn't they know what to expect and be prepared for these difficult situations? Shouldn't they know better? After reading Rudy's work, I began to think that their queer love interrupted any easy conceptualization and knowing of these relationships. These are the queer love stories that fill our lives and have the potential to change the way we view the world and our place in it.

WHEN QUEER LOVE HITS HOME

I don't have pet mammals, such as dogs, cats, or rats. My son has fish and I constantly worry if they are okay, dreading another dead tetra. I eat meat. I am conscious of how the animals are raised and treated, and where the animal flesh comes from; however, I still consume animal products. I wear makeup, more out of habit than anything else, and I try to be conscious of how the cosmetics have been tested and whether animals have been exploited. This is not meant to be a confession of any sort, rather, a reality check for me and possibly others before I get enamored with any green anthropology that I cannot make real in my life. This self-story makes me feel somewhat awkward advocating for the flourishing of nonhuman animals at all. It seems like one would need to experience queer love for other creatures to write about them and fight for their survival. However, personal love for this or that creature is not what inspires me, rather, it is another's perspective.

My son was a late talker. He had a wonderful speech therapist who came over twice a week to kick-start his verbal skills. Even without spoken words, his love for marine animals was clear and present. Etched in my memory is the day they were reading a book on sharks—his queer love. He saw an image of shark finning, where sharks are hunted for their fins. The fins are sliced off when the sharks are alive, only for the sharks to suffocate and die when they are thrown overboard, because without fins sharks cannot swim and hence cannot acquire oxygen. My son had no verbal language to say anything; yet the grief on his face has stayed with me. *I* was converted by that experience. Sometimes story, feelings, silence, or other unpredictable moments create opportunities for new ways of thinking and acting—for conversion. My son's subjectivity seemed to be awakened by the slaughter—by the demand of the naked, finned, face of the shark other. At the same time, I as bystander was called to attention. My son's presence served as an as interruption to any private consumption of the reading material. He called me by his silent grief to recognize the violence we have done to the nonhuman animal other. His queer love has challenged me to think about my trespass and to ask for forgiveness. Being open to love in unexpected places can catapult us into new ways of relating with one another. It allows us to confess how we live in the world with sin, how our lives might be patterned in brokenness, and how we can enact forgiveness in light of these realities.

TRESPASS AND THE COSMOS

What does forgiveness look like in consideration of environmental concerns and extinction issues? Does it mean forgiving the shark for attacking human animals or forgiving other human animals for eating nonhuman animals? These may sound like ridiculous questions, but our feelings about nonhuman animals have an impact on how we value them and how we treat them. As already mentioned, the great white is one of the most demonized species of animals on the planet. When people are demonized this way, it usually follows that they are dehumanized and commodified, such that they are not seen as human anymore, allowing them to be bought and sold, used and abused as one would an object. What do we say when that happens to other animals? We cannot say they are dehumanized, but a certain commodification occurs.

With the case of the great white, historical episodes of children being attacked by sharks and of course movies, most specifically the *Jaws* films, have led many in the public to hate sharks, so much so that the slaughter that shark populations currently endure has gone unchecked until recently. This change of mind has come with the realization that the drop in shark populations poses negative consequences for the entire aquatic ecosystem.

These are political and scientific shifts. What is the obligation of the Christian believer in light of these ecological challenges? What are we to do theologically? Do we start to claim that all creatures have some sort of soul, and thus their dignity and lives ought to be protected? Do we rethink what we mean by creaturely existence and freedom, and situate human animals and other species as partners in being? These streams of questioning are certainly important, so much so that we weighed their merits in previous chapters. Here we need to push the conversation further and ask how forgiveness and love come into play.

Learning about nonhuman animals and understanding their roles in existence is a type of forgiveness. Understanding asks questions instead of assuming answers. Understanding involves not only relying on one's immediate experience, but questioning that experience and overcoming any bias that might skew one's understanding of the experience. It is important for individuals to get beyond the guilt factor. Sometimes the problem of ecological degradation seems so overwhelming. We need to let go of that guilt, mourn our place of being the most important at the border, and begin a new life with all creatures. We need to forgive ourselves for past acts in order to be freed up to make changes in the present.

LETTING GO AND LETTING DOG

This section heading is a play on the popular phrase, "Let Go and Let God." When I hear this phrase, I usually think that I need to stop trying to control every aspect of my life and my surroundings. I need to listen more to what's going on, instead of talking over people. I need to enjoy life and creation and not try to master everything. This letting go of the illusion of control, perfection, and mastery is disorienting. By replacing *God* with *dog*, the reader is nudged into thinking that it is time to decenter the human animal, by paying attention to the needs and plight of the nonhuman animal. Letting go and letting dog happens in a couple of ways. To begin, individuals and communities need to stop seeing themselves as the center of the universe. Then, they have to grieve— mourn their loss of privilege of being the most important creatures in the world, as well as mourn the very real loss of life that is happening all around us. Species are dying out at exponential rates because of human ignorance, overuse, and abuse. Perhaps this is the trespass for which Christians must ask to be forgiven.

Mourning may seem like a strange word here, so it is worth explaining its significance a bit further. On the surface, mourning usually signifies grieving some sort of death, perhaps the loss of a friend or family member, and anyone who has ever grieved knows it takes an emotional, physical, and spiritual toll. Some feel lost. Some feel angry. Some feel guilty. Some cannot pray. Some cannot sleep. This is all part of the healing process, to feel one's way through loss. This is what opens one to the possibility of a future. Otherwise, we say one is stuck in denial or melancholy. In our lament, in our letting go of a sense of self that is embedded in a human-centered mentality, we need to learn more about how overfishing troubles the aquatic ecosystem, leading to sharks and other marine animals dying out. We need to learn that trees are more than just pretty and protection from the sun. They are our life source, as we cannot exist without oxygen and the best source of oxygen is trees. We need to appreciate a broader connection with all of the animals and plants of the cosmos. We need to emphasize relationality over individualism. For a possibility of a future, we need to relinquish and mourn a person-centered mentality and embrace an antianthropocentric anthropology, one that resists making humans the center of the study. Finally, as Christians we are challenged to work toward creating solidarity with and among all animals and plants in the world. Only then can we imagine a green anthropology that admits its trespasses and hopes for mercy.

SUMMARY

Forgiveness was explored here as a way of broaching the problem of sin from the previous chapter. We often think of forgiveness as something that is good for the other, a gift to the one that has hurt us. Here forgiveness is presented as a way to become healthy and whole again, for the one who is hurt. It is another key to our freedom. Without forgiveness we cannot love, and without love, forgiveness is not possible. In the last section we imagined what forgiveness might look like in terms of environmental degradation. Queer love experiences were presented as openings into thinking about how to rebuild relationships among all the creatures of the world. And ultimately, while one cannot forgive a shark and a shark cannot forgive a human in the same way humans forgive one another, forgiveness could take shape through trust and understanding. Forgiveness is an integral part of the journey of being human. It is to the idea of that journey that we now turn.

EXERCISES:
1. **Complete a journal entry on this topic.**
2. **Think-Pair-Share** (Reflect on these questions silently, find a partner and discuss them together, and then share with the class.)
   - Reflect on some of your experiences of queer love with nonhuman animals. Do those stories have the ability to make you want to change your ways of relating to all creatures? Why or why not?
   - Close your eyes. Try to relax. In a classroom with other people around you, this might seem awkward, but try to focus by breathing and clearing your mind. Once relaxed, silently recall an event in your life where an individual or group hurt you. As you bring the events to mind, imagine them offering you an apology. What are your feelings? How are you going to proceed? Do you forgive them? Either way, try to name some of the feelings and thoughts you experienced during the exercise.

Then, pair in groups of two and share those feelings. (It is not necessary to share the events, in order to maintain your privacy.) Did any of your thoughts or feelings about the situation resonate with your group partner? If so, what does that tell you?

3. Creative Time

Create a skit in which a mother and a daughter or two lovers resolve a conflict and forgive each other in a way that allows them to move on. Perform the skit. Discuss how watching the skit makes the audience members feel. Is everyone comfortable? Why or why not?

NOTES

1. Dan 9:9 (NRSV).
2. Mic 7:18–19 (NRSV).
3. Mark 1:4–5 (NRSV).
4. Matt 6:9–15 (NRSV).
5. Luke 23:34 (NRSV).
6. Matt 26:26–28 (NRSV).
7. For more on these issues, see Margaret A. Farley, *Just Love: A Framework for Christian Sexual Ethics* (New York: Continuum, 2006); Todd A. Salzman and Michael G. Lawler, *The Sexual Person: Toward a Renewed Catholic Anthropology* (Washington, DC: Georgetown University Press, 2008); and Christine E. Gudorf, *Body, Sex, and Pleasure: Reconstructing Christian Sexual Ethics* (Cleveland: The Pilgrim Press, 1994).
8. Kathy Rudy, *Loving Animals: Toward a New Animal Advocacy* (Minneapolis: University of Minnesota Press, 2011), 41.
9. Morell, *Animal Wise,* 177.

Chapter 10

ARE WE THERE YET? REVIVING A SENSE OF VOCATION IN EVERYDAY LIFE

Who hasn't been on a road trip when someone has uttered the familiar phrase, *Are we there yet?* Parents cringe when their children scream it. School bus drivers probably mutter it to themselves after dealing with a long day of moving squirrely children. We all want to know when we are going to get home, to the vacation spot, or wherever our final destination is. Christians also have ways of talking about arriving at their destination. That end could be an earthly end, like finding peace and happiness in our everyday lives, or it can be an otherworldly end, like heaven, hell, and all the spaces in between. In this chapter, we will focus on what it takes to find peace and happiness in the here and now, as well as discuss how the process of being in relationship with God is as important as the final destination. Ultimately, life is a journey of potential yes-saying.

For Christians, the journey is complicated by two different senses of time, *kairos* time and *chronos* time. *Kairos* time is God's time; it is metaphysical time. It is beyond our complete knowing, yet prophesized in scripture as the moments in which God changes the world. Christians learn about this sense of time from biblical stories and tradition. In the Gospel of Mark, Jesus calls attention to God's time when he proclaims, "The time is fulfilled, and the kingdom of God has come near, repent, and believe the good news."[1] There Jesus signals an important cosmic event, specifically peace and justice on earth. In addition to scripture, *kairos* time is present in Christian sacraments. Every Sunday, Christians celebrate God breaking into the world in the incarnation and in giving up his only son for humanity.

While *kairos* time is important to the life of the believer, in our everyday lives, many of us find ourselves in a constant struggle with *chronos* time. This is the sixty minutes in an hour, the twenty-four hours in a day, seven days in a week kind of time. It is evidenced in our scramble to get to work or school, and to make it to the store before it closes. Perhaps it is present in the anxious journey to find Mr. or Mrs. Right before it's too late.[2] Christians are called in their journey to say yes to God and others and hope for those transcendent, *kairotic* moments, in the midst of *chronos* time. In what follows, readers are invited to explore the connections between *chronos* time and *kairotic* time through a specific lens, namely that of vocation. All human beings have the potential to discover who they are and what they are meant to be in the journeys of their lives. It is not at all easy, but Christians are called in their freedom to live with an openness to God's grace. A significant aspect of openness is determining how one should live, including what one should do for a living and whom one should love.

Sometimes when I bring the notion of vocation up to my students, they seem puzzled, wondering if I misspoke and really meant vacation. After some kidding around, we return to the question of what they want to do with their lives, and if they see that as a "calling" in any way. This sometimes brings more confusion as many students presume that vocation is only for people who are becoming ordained or are religious—for priests, brothers, and nuns. What's more, they tend to think from a religious perspective that one vocation should be regarded as better than another; for example, that a priest is more valuable than a mom. It is important to break down this commonsense hierarchy of vocations, reflecting on how each one of our callings is important. The challenge is for us to even imagine that we are so significant as to have a calling, and then ultimately to be open to it. Simply put, the question for us is this: How do all Christians, not just the ordained and religious, begin to think about their commitments in life as their vocations? Embarking on such a thought process undoubtedly involves reflection on what we decide to do for our careers and who we choose to be our friends and partners. These are crucial dimensions of our vocations.

It is worth making one point clear: in the pages that follow we will not conceptualize vocation as merely one's job, but rather as one's intentional decision to plan one's entire life in response to who he or she is called to be. This is not a decision one makes overnight. It is a lifelong journey that makes us question the essence of our humanity. In fact, for Jean Vanier, our very humanity is a product of this journey. We may be born human beings, but becoming human is something else; it is about self-discovery: "[It] is a journey from loneliness to a love that transforms, a love that grows in and through belonging...It is the process of truly becoming human."[3]

STACCATO EXISTENCE

Even as we move to embrace the idea of creaturely existence in terms of a journey, we need to be clear about the challenges to that way of life, namely, the interrupted existence many of us experience with the use of electronic technology and social media. To be sure, few could have imagined the impact that email would have on daily life. When it first was emerging, reading one's email was an event. One had to have access to a computer that supported the technology, and it was basically used as an extra form of communication with friends, loved ones, and colleagues who lived far away. Today, email has changed the way we live. In conjunction with smartphones, email allows us to receive and check messages anytime and anywhere. I hear my whistle notification alert when I am in the grocery store, falling asleep at night, or even in class if I forget to turn my phone on mute. When I hear any notification, I wonder if it is for me. I am not alone. When someone's phone rings, everyone starts to check their bags and pockets. We are so used to checking at a moment's notice, that we may even get distracted when driving or cooking and look to see who is calling us. This could lead to trouble.

There is an interruptive quality to these notifications in that they pepper our everyday existence and lead to a sort of staccato existence. When a musical note is played staccato, it is played short and separated from the others. At times the notifications on our devices mimic that shortness and abruptness, leading to a fragmented experience of everyday life, in which the journey seems more like a montage of quick, disconnected moments than a developing story. In this way, it is fair to say that staccato time complicates the journey of the Christian believer.

When speaking about the dynamic between *kairos* time and *chronos* time, it is important to be attentive to the staccato time brought on by electronic technology. Not a waking moment goes by, or even a sleeping moment, when people are not interrupted by the rather disconnected notifications—buzzes, beeps, chimes, and so on—from their electronic devices that indicate that another is communicating with them. While connecting with others is a good thing and sociality is an important aspect of being human, in the pages that follow we are called to reflect on whether the staccato rhythms of digital life are beneficial to us and help us to create life-giving experiences.

A staccato way of life challenges much of what has been argued for throughout this book, which is that Christians are called by God and through others to a thoughtful, intentional embrace of life's journey. We are obligated to deal with the ups and downs of *chronos* time. We have to struggle with memory and feelings related to joy and brokenness in order to move forward. Sometimes we need to improvise, but that improvisation is not willy-nilly; rather, it is hopefully deliberate and other-oriented. A staccato way of life is not necessarily willy-nilly either; but nor is it necessarily planned-out. There is a random quality to it that has the potential to undermine the Christian sense of journey as well as obscure our responsibility and connectedness to others.

It is not that we do not feel responsible for the other in an age of electronic technology; it is that we feel responsibility differently. With smartphones, at every moment we are on, someone can call, and we are expected to respond immediately, because the message is immediate. We constantly feel responsible for being on. It takes a tremendous amount of self-discipline to say, "I am going to turn my phone off now." Some feel that they need to be available for work calls or calls from their child's teacher and so on. So wherever we are, regardless of what we are doing, many of us have our phones on. Why do we feel like we have no choice? Why is this where we feel most responsible? We feel like we need to respond, but the quality of our responses—how caring they are—does not seem to matter, or at least is ambiguous.

Having said this, many of us go along with developments in electronic technology without protest. Even those who have held off on getting a smartphone or the latest device are eventually pressured into it not only by fads but also because there are few other options. When and if we do try to remain with the same technology, say for instance if we just want to replace our batteries on our old devices, we often find that it is more cost-effective to buy a new device than replace the old batteries. We are prodded along by industry. Some people thrive on new developments, and feel like they make life easier and offer more opportunities to connect with others. They can catch up with old friends in an instant and deal with work crises from distant locales. Others are far less enamored with social technology, yet feel as if they have no choice but to respond to all email and always be available. Staccato existence becomes the norm by default. We need to be cognizant of the pitfalls of staccato existence as we struggle to hear and be open to our callings.

CONTEMPORARY FRAMES FOR IMAGINING VOCATION

Important thinkers of our time have reflected on the development of human beings, implicitly acknowledging vocation as a process. For example, Bradford Hinze, a Roman Catholic thinker who focuses on the doctrine of the church, carefully weaves theoretical, theological, and clinical threads together in the question of human development, focusing on the process of individuation. For Hinze, individuals do not develop who they are and who they are called to be in isolation; rather, such development is always in conversation and communion with groups and associations. At times, in our drive for success and perfection—that is, our drive to be unique individuals—we tend to downplay the influence that others have on our lives. Extrapolating from Hinze's work, we might argue that for a holistic commitment to vocation to unfold, we need to support the idea that individuals will only develop in life-giving ways when strengthened and challenged by others. What's more, for Hinze, attention to the complex process of individuation "provides a conceptual structure to explore the struggle, endemic to the human journey, against a false and distorted sense of the self, bounded and contorted, diminished and potentially destroyed by personal and social sin. At the same time, it provides a way of charting a graced journey of discovering one's created uniqueness and charismatic giftedness."[4] Clearly, from this perspective, the mentality of *are we there yet* obscures the struggle and transformation in each individual's journey.

Another important voice in our conversation about vocation is not from a Christian perspective, but from that of a Buddhist monk. In his work *Being Peace*, Thich Nhat Hanh develops a practice of engaged Buddhism, which ordinary people can integrate into their lives.[5] As the overall title of his book suggests, being peaceful and becoming awakened, which are also aspects of Christian notions of anthropology, take work, meaning physical, emotional, and spiritual discipline. In other words, we cannot take peace for granted, just like we cannot take our humanity for granted. It is not an object that one totes around to use in isolated situations, like an umbrella to take out on a rainy day. Rather, becoming peace involves taking on a certain posture of openness and calmness, and converting negative emotions into neutral ones. Being peace also demands acknowledging our connectedness or interconnectedness with all around us. This too takes great discipline, as we have seen how societal pressures force us to separate ourselves from others, consequently feeding a dualistic mentality. From this perspective, reflecting on one's life choices—how we live—is not just a Christian precept; on the contrary, it is a human one that transcends creed and culture and involves the whole person—mind and body.

In addition to the others, Mary Catherine Bateson provides an aesthetic model for thinking about how we live our lives; she speaks about how each one of us "composes" a life.[6] This metaphor of composition has an intentionality to it; one that is concerned with beauty and joy. So many of us feel overwhelmed by everything that is going on in our lives, at school, work, and home. We tend to try to juggle it all—and that becomes the default way of speaking about our vocation. Bateson is not in favor of the term *juggling* as a way to describe what we are doing and why we are doing it. Juggling as a way of describing our life can leave us feeling overwhelmed, out of control, and trapped. It is like we are caught up in an unending game, and there is no way out. While this may be how many of us feel at moments, there are other ways to frame our experience to help us feel more empowered and confident. Instead of thinking that we have to frenetically juggle all of our responsibilities and obligations, Bateson uses the notion of composing as one would a literary, musical, or visual piece of work. Our lives are works of art. Each stroke, lyric, and alliteration adds to their richness.

Christians could apply Bateson's idea of composing a life to their own questions of vocation, specifically in relation to how life is a journey with ups and downs, twists and turns. Sometimes a change we make, perhaps related to a relationship or a job, doesn't work out like we planned. Instead of falling to pieces or feeling like failures, Bateson says that we need to improvise. Continuity for Bateson, meaning that things stay the same, is not a reality for most. We need to be able to handle change, which is ever-occurring. We can do this by improvising—not juggling. This way of thinking about life and vocation may be appealing to some because it connotes a sense that we have some choice and freedom in what we do, who we love, and how we respond to unexpected situations. The notion of improvising, moreover, allows us to be flexible in the midst of staccato existence.

In relation to our discussion of a green anthropology, one last perspective on the question of being human as a process is worth noting. As mentioned in preceding chapters, Kyle Kramer develops a notion of vocation for our everyday lives. In his twenties, while doing graduate work in the field of Christian theology, Kramer made a life change that he calls a "vocation of location."[7] He bought a plot of land in Indiana and created a sustainable home life. Committed to his vocation of location, he and his family constructed a farm on their land to grow food for their household as well as to sell to others to supplement their living. For Kramer, vocation is not just about what one does for a living, but even more than that, is about creating a home both literally and symbolically that embraces the goodness of all of creation. Interestingly, in his working the land, building his barn and house, courting his wife, and parenting, Kramer notes that he has many vocations—all in the same space. Moreover, he claims that committing to a life of sustainability allows him to overcome the pathological need to control everything and everyone in his life. Reading his work, one sees how he gives himself over to everyday acts of exposure, opening himself to becoming vulnerable to the land and those he loves. Kramer's spirituality on vocation echoes the inspirational work of Vanier, challenging his readers to reflect on their life stories and choices. Moreover, one finds connections between Kramer's and Bateson's works when he claims life is a "messy process of improvising" through which we gain the potential to experience God's unimaginable grace.[8]

Thinkers like these, despite coming from different scholarly and religious trajectories, arrive at a common point: that healthy being, subjectivity, and peace are not givens. They emerge from an active process; a journey of working out and transforming patterns of brokenness into neutral or life-giving ones. This process is creative, imaginative, and improvisational. It demands a multitude of individuals and groups along the way. As a process, the *are we there yet* mentality falls short. It obscures the importance of the journey for the end, and misses the point that how we live our lives is inseparable from our end.

OBSTACLES TO BUYING INTO THE IDEA OF VOCATION

As one would imagine, pondering the above frames for vocation is somewhat accessible in educational settings since students are in school to do something with their lives, so to speak—to get the credentials to work in this or that arena and to develop in ways that allow them to participate most fully in their communities. In addition to classes, some students devote their time and resources to service projects and volunteer experiences. These opportunities have the potential to expose students to complicated situations of poverty and social sin, whether in faraway locales or in their own neighborhoods.

To be sure, individuals are transformed by academic courses and service experiences; yet it is not always easy to integrate what they have learned back into their daily lives. While one's college years are for experimentation and exposing oneself to all different philosophies, cultures, and so on, it is sometimes difficult to connect these moments in one's self-story into one's larger vocation. One reason it is difficult to cultivate a rich sense of vocation in ordinary life is that in the developed nations, and here the United States comes to mind, we have an overinflated sense of living comfortably. We think we need this or that creature comfort to survive. We conflate our desires with our needs. In light of this way of living large—the pressure to have big cars, big houses, and so on—making a commitment to a sense of a vocation that encourages lifelong learning and service to others demands that each one us ask difficult questions. Do I really need x or just want it? Will x really make me happier? Will my having x negatively impact the well-being of another?

This line of questioning relates to popular conceptions of success. What is success? Is it attending college with the goal of ultimately getting a job? To be sure these are important steps, and we all need to think about how to be fiscally responsible and pay the bills. Nonetheless, where along the way do we have the opportunity to begin to see our jobs as part of our vocations? A job is not enough to keep us human in the fullest sense; we need to satisfy our longings for connections with others. If vocation is larger than what we do for a living, we also need to consider how our friends and partners fit into our journeys. Do they support us in our processes of yes-saying? Do they challenge us to grow?

CHRISTIAN RESOURCES FOR THE JOURNEY

Believers have resources and practices from the tradition they can draw upon as they take on the question of vocation and begin their journeys. Prayer and sacramental life are important markers along the way, providing sustenance for the weary traveler. They create opportunities to invite a deeper relationship with God and others. Additionally, stories about saints in the Christian tradition become models or guides for the journey. These holy role models inspire Christians to say yes to God in extraordinary ways. Finally, believers ought to look to the actions and commitments of Jesus as a resource for the journey. As was the case for Jesus, heeding one's call may not be easy, but can be profoundly life-giving.

PRAYER AND SACRAMENTAL LIFE

Prayer is any form of communication with God. It incorporates moments of silence and moments of speech. A believer may ask things of God, express gratitude, or petition God as to why he or she is in this or that situation. Moreover, prayer entails listening for and responding to God's word. Much of prayer life is developing an affinity for the sensual aspect of religious experience, of being drawn into God's mystery and being attentive to God's calling. Not all prayer is easy. In fact much of prayer is complicated because it is communication with another whom we cannot know fully, but whom we love intensely. We may have other feelings for God as well, including anger, and this potentially brings conflict and struggle into our lives. We may not feel comfortable with the direction that our meditations are leading us. Perhaps we feel called to a relationship or job that is not going to make others happy. We may want to turn off the prayer; yet such discontinuities require further prayer as well as an examination of our conscience. Prayer is an important part in the journey because it keeps us going, gives us strength, and strengthens our relationships with God and others.

There is no right way to pray. Prayer unfolds in different forms. We might pray differently at various stages in our lives. There is informal prayer—we can praise, thank, and request of God anywhere and anytime. There are more formal prayers that we learn as part of our religious tradition. Liturgy is the public prayer in which we celebrate with others during communal worship. In working toward a green anthropology, one begins to imagine new venues for prayer, perhaps favoring locations connected to nature and outside the box or church, so to speak.

Even when responding to the question of vocation—of how we are living our lives and why we are living them in those ways—not all prayer is directed toward inquiry about what types of jobs are best and what kind of relationships are life-giving. Even more than that, when reflecting on the question of how to live, we must deal with the concrete reality that we all have been living in patterns and situations already. Some of them are sinful, especially in relation to the social problems related to environmental degradation. In light of these experiences of social sin, prayer might involve less praising God and asking for direction, and more expression of our remorse for what perverse enactments of freedom have done to the whole of creation. Prayer here becomes lamentation, an expression of sorrow and sadness. Whatever the form and content of one's prayer, these meditative moments invoke the transcendent in one's everyday life, giving way to *kairotic* moments in *chronos* time.

In addition to prayer, sacred rituals or sacraments mark *kairotic* time in that they announce God's mystery breaking into ordinary life. Sacraments help us organize our lives in ways that provide us with deep meaning. Participating in sacraments is a way for Christians to say yes to God's offer of grace. One could think of them as stops on the journey. It is noteworthy that while baptism and communion are two rituals that *all* Christians celebrate, Catholic Christians celebrate five others, including confirmation, reconciliation, anointing of the sick, holy orders, and holy matrimony—the last two of which are related to a narrow sense of vocation, concerned specifically with what one should do with his or her life.

As mentioned in the last chapter, baptism is the ancient Jewish rite, which Christians learn about from the gospel accounts of Jesus being baptized in the Jordan River by John the Baptist. Jesus' baptism, like the baptisms of Christian believers today, is portrayed as a turning point in his life and mission. It marks the beginning of his public ministry. For Christians today baptism signifies their initiation into the faith tradition. The importance of water as cleansing cannot be overstated here, especially as so much of our conversation has been geared toward thinking about a green anthropology. Water is a natural resource that so many in the world need and so many of us squander. Every baptism ought to remind believers of the centrality of water to creaturely flourishing, and serve as a path for their journeys to respect the global need and scarcity.

Communion is the other ritual that is common to all Christians. Most Christians participate in a meal together once per week, on Sunday. This is called communion and commemorates Jesus' last meal with his disciples before his death. As an embodied activity, communion binds us together as a Christian family in a material way. We already discussed how eating together is a social activity, bringing people together who might be at odds with one another or are just plain lonely. When Christians come together for sacraments they say yes not only to God, but also to the particular Christian community they are a part of, and in doing so implicitly whisper, "we are almost there!" None of us can make it through our ordinary days without eating. This everyday practice of *chronos* time is made *kairotic* through the sacrament of communion.

This sacrament also weighs heavily on our conversation about moving toward a green anthropology in that Christians committed to ecological justice might want to reflect on how their meals honor the plants and animals of all of creation. As some scholars have shown, it is not always feasible for everyone to commit to organic eating or growing. Christians, like all people really, are called in their daily lives to consider what constrains some from a greener eating lifestyle and how they might participate in change and transformation.[9] This would undoubtedly involve vigilance to impoverished communities and a critical eye toward the

201

structural sin that leads to poverty, as well as a commitment to the survival of all life.

GUIDES FOR THE JOURNEY

The most inspiring stories about saints for me are the ones that chronicle the holy person's lifetime of struggling to say yes to God and others. Struggle is important for me, not because I like to see people fail—rather, I relate to people when they think they are in danger of failing because at times I feel like a failure. Feelings of failure can be devastating, especially in a culture that seems to privilege "success," whatever that means, and perfectionism, as unrealistic of a goal as it is. When we fail, we don't just miss the mark, but at times feel unlovable and just plain not good enough. Vanier names the fear of failure as one of the most debilitating emotions we may experience, because it could lead to shame and often leads to giving up before we even start to say yes.

Knowing this reality and seeing it in the lives of saints eases the pressure of yes-saying in our world, and perhaps makes it even more relevant. An important part of the Christian imagination, saints are regarded as holy people who led lives of service during their earthly lifetimes and now work in heaven on behalf of the living. Saints are friends and companions in an uncertain and complicated world. Saintly stories, referred to as hagiography, have the power to inspire believers to say yes to God and give them the courage to make difficult decisions along the way, serving as guides for one's life journey.

In Roman Catholicism, there are official requirements for a person to become canonized as a saint that became institutionalized by Pope Urban VIII in the seventeenth century, including doctrinal purity, heroic virtue, and miraculous intersession. The first requirement refers to the expectation that the candidate for sainthood must teach and be an icon of orthodox teachings, meaning that they cannot have demonstrated heretical beliefs in any aspect of their lives. Heroic virtue means that during their lifetime they exhibited extraordinary forms of the Christian virtues, such as faith, hope, charity, prudence, and fortitude. The last requirement, referred to as miraculous intersession, is the belief that the holy dead persons are working in heaven with Christ on behalf of the living, answering prayers and enacting miracles.

While these requirements are worth noting, it is also important to consider other less formal saintly individuals and stories in one's lives. These inspiring persons also serve as guides. Martin Luther King Jr., Gandhi, and even Princess Diana are role models for many individuals—icons of service, commitment, and sacrifice. Perhaps we have special relationships with teachers, professional mentors, and even grandparents, which aid in our deciding how we live our lives. What is so powerful about official and unofficial saints are the stories we tell about them. In *The Practice of Everyday Life*, French theorist Michel de Certeau explains how stories arrange one's sense of reality: "In modern Athens, the vehicles of mass transportation are called *metaphorai*. To go to work or come home, one takes a 'metaphor'—a bus or a train. Stories could also take this noble name: every day, they traverse and organize places; they select and link them together; they make sentences and itineraries out of them. They are spatial trajectories."[10] In the discourse of de Certeau, an integral aspect of our journey is taking stock of the many stories that inform our lives, those that shape who we are, what we want out of life, and how we are connected to others.

Already we have spoken about St. Francis of Assisi's story. This twelfth-century Italian mendicant devoted his life to living the gospel out on the streets, supporting an ethic of poverty and humility, and embracing all of creation. He is known as the patron saint of animals and the environment, and was canonized in 1228. A more recent canonization and resource for this green anthropology is St. Kateri Tekakwitha. Canonized in 2012 by Pope Benedict XVI, this daughter of a Mohawk warrior is the first Native American to be canonized. Known as Lily of the Mohawks, this seventeenth-century woman demonstrated many important Christian virtues as well as radiated an appreciation of nature and all of creation, making her, like St. Francis, a patron of the environment and ecology. Native American spirituality is deeply tied to the sacredness of the land and all of creation. In canonizing Kateri, the Church shows an appreciation for that sensibility and offers a model for others to follow. These green saintly stories have the potential to open Christians to new discussions about what charity might look like, what love might look like, and what self-discovery might look like. Instead of being human-centered, these saintly stories call believers to love a God that cares for all of creation. In being like God, we are called in all our finitude and frailty to embrace the nonhuman animal others in our midst, perhaps incorporating that vision to our vocations.

WHAT WOULD JESUS DO?

It is not uncommon when discussing vocation for some individuals to express feelings of surprise and confusion over the demands that Jesus makes in the Gospels. When reading key texts on hospitality, like the story in which Jesus tells his followers to invite not only their friends and families into their homes and lives, but strangers in need as well—the sick, poor, lame, and blind—some could become puzzled and concerned. They might equate these others that Jesus refers to with the others in their lives, with the homeless person they pass on their way down to the subway, with the woman struggling with mental illness at the local pub who sits alone talking to herself, and even with those individuals who are incarcerated. How could Jesus have meant this, that to be a follower one must give up his or her status and safety, and risk being in relationship with social outcasts? However, this is precisely how Jesus is portrayed in the Gospels, as advocating a lifestyle unfettered by worldly desires and attachments, engendering a call to live lightly.

For example, in the Gospel of Luke, Jesus clearly claims that following him involves a life of relinquishment: "Now large crowds were traveling with him [Jesus]; and he turned and said to them 'Whoever comes to me and does not hate father and mother, wife and children, brothers and sisters, yes, and even life itself, cannot be my disciple. Whoever does not carry the cross and follow me cannot be my disciple….So therefore, none of you can become my disciple if you do not give up all your possessions'"[11] Luke portrays a messiah who advocates for a notion of vocation that is not consumed with money or status, but rather with ministry.

Even though it is advocated for in the Bible, and seems to be what Jesus would do, some of us recoil from such a seemingly extreme, austere lifestyle and sense of vocation. When these gospel passages are juxtaposed with what we are actually doing with our lives or planning to do, it is uncomfortable, if not downright painful, to entertain the idea that the plans we have made for our lives are not good ones. People wonder if they have made the right choice. They begin to ask the tough questions. Should I have become an accountant? Should I have gotten married? These are normal thoughts, and it is not as if there is no support to help sort through these questions, as religious leaders and clinicians are available to facilitate thinking about one's life. Rather, it is a culture that insists that we are certain, rather than open to improvisation, that makes entertaining these questions all the more difficult. This is where some of the threads on vocation and personal journey become important. If we look at life with an eye toward exploration, improvisation, creativity, and finding home in a variety of places, perhaps we can deal with these thoughts with more openness and honesty.

Ultimately, our living like Jesus might demand we choose a vocation that goes against the grain of society. In the words of Vanier, we may need to occupy the position of the dissident; namely, someone who challenges the norms in society, including laws, social customs, and mainstream lifestyles. The dissident has the potential to play the part of the prophet, pointing out damaging aspects of society and communicating healthier ways of living. All the while the dissident needs to be prepared for enemies because upsetting the status quo unnerves people, especially those who fear change.[12] The Gospels portray Jesus as a dissident in that he threatened the Roman authorities with his questions and activities, especially since many of his actions, including being in solidarity with the marginalized, were countercultural and would have caused quite a stir. In response to thinking about vocation in relation to the question of *What would Jesus do?*, perhaps the answer is being a dissident by choosing a vocation that does not go along with societal norms about money, love, and happiness.

RETURNING TO THE GARDEN

So how do we decide how to live? We have seen Kramer's turn to the land as a "vocation of location." However, when figuring out how we are going to live, in reality buying a farm might not be a choice for everyone, nor should it be. We need bankers, lawyers, teachers, medical professionals, plumbers, engineers, and so on. In what follows, we begin to imagine ways that we can commit to a healthier relationship with the cosmos in less extreme ways. This need not be overly daunting. According to Elizabeth Johnson, thinking about vocation in terms of a commitment to ecological flourishing is already happening: "Whether framed in these terms or not, numerous people around the globe are beginning to live the ecological vocation, caring for the living world as their neighbor."[13] In the spirit of Johnson's work and in deference to Seàn McDonagh's plea for living lightly, we need to be cognizant of massive waste and overuse of the world's resources in our everyday lives. We need to find ways to think about these issues in *chronos* time.

Perhaps in our rather mundane decision making about what to eat, what to wear, and how live, we could begin by recognizing that at times we are driven by greed and narcissism before charity. Recall how narcissism is not about being conceited; on the contrary, it reflects a mentality in which one does not recognize personal boundaries and hence does not recognize the other or the other's needs. Are there places in our lives where we might give more weight to the needs of the other—or as a start, recognize the other at all? This other can be a human animal or nonhuman animal other, or even a plant.

While we may not farm, there exist other ways we can get more in touch with nature. We need to return to the Garden of Eden we read about in Genesis 3 in order to understand the cost of ignoring boundaries between self and other. When human beings try to be too much like God, they end up losing. When they trespass boundaries, they end up broken. Short-term gain does not have long-term payoffs. Although they do not reside in Eden, Christians today have the opportunity and obligation to admit limits, to admit that they have been overusing resources—plants and nonhuman animals—and that there is a cost. As always, a first step in change is education. Learning can be part of one's everyday life—one of his or her many vocations. Learning involves engaging these sort of queries. Does my sense of what it means to be fully human depend on being a consuming subject, regardless of the cost to others—and the world? How much meat is too much, especially in light of the fact that forests are being cleared to raise cattle for my consumption? Whose bodies matter more—my body, that of the tree, or those of local people who depend on those trees? These are just examples of the work of vocation as education, or what we might call gathering the data for intellectual conversion.

A second step might be getting on board with nature. This would include leaving our smartphones behind for a while in order to go outside, get planting, and observe the world around us. We need to embrace our connections to the earth, from which we have emerged and are intimately connected. We need to be ready to get our hands dirty. There was a popular saying when I was growing up, *cleanliness is next to godliness*. What I took it to mean is that God wanted us to be clean, and perhaps that being dirty is sinful. In this world, creaturely existence as we have known it is being threatened. Hence, it might be time for a new mantra—that *dirt is close to godliness*. This new ecological moment calls those invested in a life of saying yes to God to become comfortable getting dirty and messy. The dualistic mentality that separates human beings from the rest of the cosmos does little to work on healing the earth and sustaining life.

As already mentioned in a previous chapter, in *The Singing Heart of the World: Creation, Evolution and Faith*, John Feehan develops the notion of a deeper consciousness of connectedness with other creatures and the cosmos. For Feehan, Christians have failed in making more of an informed and educated commitment to evolutionary theory. He urges readers to consider that with the appropriate changes in scientific and theological attitudes, we might be able to reimagine our embodied beings as attuned to nature and geography in a way that makes us feel part of the natural world, rather than over and against it. We might begin to believe that "creation is the absolute revelation, the very embodiment of divinity," and in becoming conscious of this reality, take on responsibility for our connectedness.[14] This is a tremendous claim in that it implies that God is part of everything, including squirrels, slugs, cockroaches, ferns, dirt, rain, snow, tornadoes, and so on. Feehan links this broader consciousness with questions of evolution. He asserts that evolution is not merely a biological process, but a spiritual one as well. We might be evolving into this type of creature-inclusive community as one would in a "family."[15] Embracing the idea that we are one family in the cosmos is going to take a lot of *chronos* time and more *kairotic* moments. We are not there yet.

SUMMARY

The focus of this chapter is an exploration of how we live our lives and why we live them the way we do. This idea is referred to as vocation and is conceptualized as a lifelong process of improvisation, development, and homemaking that is neither easy nor quick. It is an extended process that takes place in everyday time and sacred time. Indeed, spiritual moments, such as prayer and the sacraments, have the potential to enrich one's journey. Thinking through everyday life as well as contemporary theories on vocation and self-discovery, it becomes clear that an *are we there yet?* mentality when it comes to human development is inadequate, as it doesn't account for change and conversion. Thinking about vocation in terms of a green anthropology raises the question of how Christians ought to live their lives in the face of environmental degradation. Do they need to commit every aspect of their lives to green causes, or is there another way? These questions about what Christians are called to do in the here and now connect to our discussion of the hereafter, and it is to that topic that we now turn.

EXERCISES:
1. **Complete a journal entry on this topic.**
2. **Think-Pair-Share** (Reflect on these questions silently, find a partner and discuss them together, and then share with the class.)
   - What do you plan to do with your life? Consider where you got the messages from about what you should and shouldn't do. Are there unexplored areas of your vocation?

- Do you see a connection between what you do for a living and the friends and loved ones in your life? How is it possible to have many vocations?
- Are you comfortable with life being improvisational? Why or why not?

3. Creative Time

Go for a nature walk or mediate or pray in an outside location. Is there a way one could integrate these activities into his or her sense of vocation?

NOTES

1. Mark 1:15 (NRSV).

2. For a witty foray into parenthood and *kairos* time, see Glennon Melton, "Don't Carpe Diem," http://www.huffington post.com/glennon-melton/dont-carpe-diem_b_1206346.html (accessed November 4, 2013).

3. Vanier, *Becoming Human*, 5.

4. Bradford Hinze, "Individuation and Communion: Implications for the Church's Identity and Mission," in *Believing in Community: Ecumenical Reflections on the Church*, ed. Peter De Mey, Pieter De Witte, and Gerard Mannion (Leuven, Belgium: Peeters Press, 2013), 26.

5. Thich Nhat Hanh, *Being Peace* (Berkeley: Parallax Press, 2005).

6. Mary Catherine Bateson, *Composing a Life* (New York: Grove Press, 1989).

7. Kramer, *A Time to Plant*, 65.

8. Ibid., 82.

9. See Michael Pollan, *The Omnivore's Dilemma: A Natural History of Four Meals* (New York: Penguin, 2006).

10. Michel de Certeau, *The Practice of Everyday Life*, trans. Steven Rendall (Berkeley: University of California Press, 1984), 115.

11. Luke 14:25–27, 33 (NRSV).

12. Vanier, *Becoming Human*, 74–75.

13. Johnson, *Ask the Beasts*, 281.

14. Feehan, *Singing Heart of the World*, 10.

15. Ibid.

Chapter 11

HAPPILY EVER AFTER

Every Disney movie seems to end up happy, at least in the short run. What is meant by *happily every after* is that the main characters, perhaps the princess and the renegade, are able to be together in peace and contentment with no threats to their love. When there is not a happy end, some viewers end up feeling disappointed and unfulfilled. Even though these narratives run deep in our psyche, the lives most of us lead are not the stuff of fairytales. We have to deal with everyday life. We have to navigate *chronos* and staccato time with the hope of *kairos* time. This chapter explores the challenge of keeping up hope for a Christian happy end in a world complicated by stressors and pressures. We will see that the happy end that Christians hope for is not merely an earthly one of romance and riches. Indeed, it transcends the here and now and extends into the hereafter. The Christian notion of a happy end includes being in the presence of God for eternity and being reunited with loved ones in heaven. That is the stuff of salvation.

Christians learn from an early age that this world is not the end for creation. They are encouraged to hope and pray for the beatific vision, which means to be in the company of God and enraptured by God's grace. The idea of the beatific vision is one way of speaking about heaven and salvation for Christians; nonetheless, it is just the beginning of the conversation. Other dimensions of the topic are important as well, such as whether everyone will eventually be with God or if only some will be saved. Moreover, as we move toward a green anthropology, we might want to imagine a broader sense of salvation beyond the human/divine encounter. In thinking through some of the questions engaged in this book, we might imagine a renewed sense of the beatific vision, which includes nonhuman animal partners. This does not mean to sound silly or trite. It is not a flip response to a very real question for some: *Will I see my pet in heaven?* Rather it is a meditation on how to imagine grace everywhere—not just in our human relations but in all creaturely entanglements. As we work through the many meanings of a happy end, including ideas related to the beatific vision, heaven, and salvation, this chapter mediates on the idea that such an ending is only possible with God's grace and by working to heal broken relations among all of God's creatures.

In the previous chapter, creaturely existence was framed as a process and a journey. We tend to know things about that process because we are conscious. When speaking about the hereafter, all certainty goes out the window. As we tackle questions about the connection between the here and now and the hereafter, we have no empirical evidence. We cannot know what is going to happen with scientific accuracy. Hence in this chapter I do not argue for a specific reality once an individual dies; rather, I underscore the issues at play in the conversation about salvation. Ultimately we are all amateurs in this world, and perhaps that frame of being an amateur can alleviate some of our anxieties about knowing for sure our ultimate end.

DO YOU HAVE A PLAN?

I love having a plan. It makes me feel organized, in control, and ready to tackle the day. Having a vision enables people to focus their energies on specific issues and tasks that matter deeply to them. Christians are taught that they are created for a specific purpose or end—in other words, that God has a plan for them. This is a broad claim and is interpreted in many different ways. It is quite common to hear that something "happened for a reason" and "it was meant to be," all under the umbrella idea that God has a plan. These phrases in one way or another usually suggest that there is a higher force driving reality and our yes-saying. This sentiment that God has a plan continues from this world to the next and is evident in the indisputable claim for Christians that there is a *telos*, "end" or "plan," for the world, specifically that humans are created in God's image and for God into eternity.

What is debatable is what we mean when we say that God has a plan for creation. The challenge arises when one tries to pin down this claim to specific beliefs. Saying God has a plan does not mean that God plans every event in our lives and controls us as if we are puppets on a string. When read this way, the *God has a plan* and the *it's meant to be* sentiments obscure the importance of freedom in relation to heaven, hell, purgatory, and the spiritual spaces in between. This is an important point because an individual can feel disempowered by the *meant to be* mindset. While it is good to embrace that we cannot control every aspect of our lives, Christians are called to accept the responsibility of saying yes to God throughout their lifetimes. Freedom is a gift that comes with tremendous obligation. Hence when the *meant to be* mentality takes on too great a weight, it potentially could be an excuse to do nothing or an obstacle to enacting one's freedom. This *meant to be* mentality is sometimes framed in terms of fate. We may say it was our fate to end up with this person or with that job. The problem with taking the idea of fate to an extreme is that it seems to give up on the idea that we have agency in our lives. Christian believers would not want to give up on the idea of possessing and enacting the gift of freedom.

Moreover, when thinking about one's spiritual destiny, the *happened for a reason* sentiment can be challenging in another way. It is related to the quest for freedom, but even more to the problem of evil. If and when tragic events occur, what kind of response is it to say that the tragedy is all part of God's plan? What kind of portrait of God allows for terrible world events, like genocide, to happen and even to be part of God's plan? Is this what Christians mean when they say it happened for a reason? Probably not; in fact, they are probably referring to something on a much smaller scale. Yet this is a potential result of that line of thinking. So here when speaking about a Christian sense of God's vision and end, we refer less to the plan for the here and now and more about what will happen when we die. This theological topic is known as a study of the eschaton or eschatology.

THE DREADED QUESTION:
What Happens When We Die?

Most of us probably wish we had a concrete answer to this basic question. Whether we lose a friend, partner, or grandparent, this question haunts us. When children ask this, a respectable answer seems even more urgent. One could say that the deceased loved one is in heaven; nevertheless, one never knows if that retort is helpful, edifying, or satisfying, especially when one is then compelled to explain what heaven is and is not. When I am confronted with this question, I usually fumble around, reporting what this religious group believes and what that religious group claims. I explain how the end for Christians involves a longing for being with God, and that this otherworldly communion with God is what is meant by the term *heaven*. Then I ask the child what he or she thinks. Children get a bit frustrated with this question, because they, like most of us, desire certainty. Older children usually end up engaging some of the science around death and expressing hope that there is a heaven, because they want to see their loved ones again. This response is quite typical.

Kids are some of the first to ask about nonhuman animals and the afterlife. What happens to their beloved dog, cat, or iguana when they stop breathing? Will they see them in heaven? These questions might seem sweet and silly at the same time; nevertheless, they have real theological teeth to them. Adults need to take care in how they respond to these queries from children. Our answers could impact a lifetime of attitudes toward other creatures—both human and nonhuman. As with the death of human animals, when speaking about nonhuman animals one could talk about being embraced by God's love and infinite grace, and returning to the creator-savior-spirit of all.

PLANNING FOR A
SPIRITUAL RETIREMENT

From a young age those of us living in a consumer culture have been getting mixed messages, and lots of them are about how to make money and what to do with it once we get it. This relates to

213

the previous chapter on vocation. On the one hand, we are taught to save money for a rainy day and for our golden years. We are encouraged to plan, meaning to work in school to get good grades, to get into the best schools we can, and to get good paying jobs so we can afford a comfortable life. All the while, many of us are gearing up for finding our one true love. Whether we are looking ahead to our first job, home, marriage, or retirement, we are taught to keep our end goals in mind as we work in the present. We are always looking ahead and planning, so much so that many of us wish we could live more in the present and enjoy the moment instead of calculating our next move.

Here comes the mixed part of the message. In the midst of all this planning, somewhere along the way, we are told to spend, spend, spend, and with reckless abandon spend more—after all, we deserve it. We get ourselves into debt buying things we probably do not really need and certainly cannot afford, and then we have to pay the price. In doing this, we risk losing the goodwill of our loved ones, our sense of self-respect, and sometimes even our livelihood. We learn after the fact that freedom is not necessarily the ability to have everything we want when we want it; rather, freedom is an opportunity to lead productive life-giving lives.

An analogous type of journey happens when we plan spiritually. We are told from a young age all the important ingredients for a good life and death, including living with open hearts and being welcoming to all. Somewhere along the way, we close ourselves off and our plan for the future disappears. Heaven and hell seem remote, so many of our efforts for a good and genuine life disappear along with the relevance of those theological ideas. Perhaps revitalizing these categories—heaven, hell, and all the spaces in between—can reinvigorate our obligation to live in the image of God as a way of being ultimately with God.

HEAVEN, HELL, AND ALL THE SPACES IN BETWEEN

There are different ways of imagining the afterlife for Christians. Imagining and imagination do not mean that the afterlife is made up or untrue; rather, these words refer to the finite language and imagery employed to describe what is ultimately infinite and a mystery. In all probability, when people think about heaven and hell, they have in mind some version of Milton's *Paradise Lost* and of Dante's *Inferno*. These are not wrong per se, just literary frames for imagining what being with God or alienated from God after one's death looks like. Nonetheless, Christians have a rich tradition of teachings on what happens next. It might help to look at how some of the theological ideas about the end or eschaton developed in order to get a fuller sense of how all of the topics discussed so far, including vulnerability, freedom, sin, and forgiveness, impact not only the earthly existence of the creature, but the otherworldly one as well.

A HISTORICAL LOOK

What we find in the early years of the Jesus movement is an apocalyptic eschatology. The term *eschatology* refers to Christian teachings on the end of life and issues related to salvation. Salvation is one way of speaking about the happily-ever-after for Christians—for being in heaven. From the vantage point of the early followers of Jesus, an apocalyptic eschatology signified a sense of the end that would be ushered in by the messiah and in which good would win over evil. There was to be a cosmic and spiritual battle, typical of apocalyptic films like *Star Wars*. What's more, demonology and angelology are common aspects of this type of apocalypse.

Threads of apocalyptic eschatology are present in gospel renditions of Jesus' ministry. We note in the Gospel of Mark that during his life Jesus was said to preach the coming of the kingdom and urged people to heed the new time: "Now after Jesus was arrested, Jesus came to Galilee, proclaiming the good news of God, and saying, 'The time is fulfilled, and the kingdom of God has come near; repent, and believe in the good news.'"[1] Today Christians conflate "kingdom of God" with heaven. However, when Jesus is said to have uttered those words in a messianic context, he was most likely referring to an earthly kingdom, one of peace and justice and freedom from the exploitation promulgated by the Roman Empire.

This kingdom or new way of life ushers in an ethical eschaton, in which a person's actions are influenced by the hope of the kingdom. For Christians, a common way of thinking about this is that the kingdom of God is already here and not yet fulfilled. Until the second coming of Jesus and the final judgment, we need to act on behalf of the world in the here and now. This demands great vigilance on the part of the Christian believer. We cannot be sleepy or fail to pay attention. We have to say yes in the face of complacency. This creates opportunities for all of us to rethink the end in a more holistic, inclusive manner. This is where apocalyptic and ethical eschatology converge in that the struggle is over how we act in response to God's offer of peace and justice. The New Testament portrays both this apocalyptic sense as well as an ethical one, in which Jesus is presented not only as the one who defeats evil and corruption, but also as the one whose death and resurrection usher in a new life and way of being.

As already intimated, the early followers of Jesus were hoping for the second coming—Jesus' return—in their lifetime. As time passed and generations followed, doctrine developed on the afterlife to match the prolonged waiting for Jesus. Christians became less confident of the imminence of the end of time. This in-between time gave rise to more nuanced interpretations of what happens to one's soul when an individual dies, and what happens at the end of time.

The long-standing teaching of the mainline Christian churches is that death is the end of natural life, but not the loss of personal existence. Catholic Christians believe that the soul continues to live on after the death of the body, and exists in the afterlife as the individual's real, personal identity. At the moment of death, each soul is judged by God on the basis of his or her words and deeds in life. In this event, called the particular judgment, some are judged to eternal damnation, or hell, and some are judged worthy of the beatific vision, or heaven. In this Catholic imaginary it is assumed that most of those who are judged favorably are not yet worthy of the beatific vision, and must spend time in the third supernatural "place," purgatory, to be purified of their sins. At the *kairotic* end of time, called the Last Judgment, Christians believe that the bodies of all the dead will be miraculously raised to life and reunited with their souls, and all human beings throughout history, whether saved or damned, will stand before Christ to be judged together as this world passes away and heaven and hell endure forever. In the past, because Christians were concerned about the souls of unbaptized children and the souls of patriarchs who died before the coming of Christ, and who thus were not considered capable of responsible judgment, teachings emerged about limbo—a place for them until the second coming. Interestingly, limbo is no longer an orthodox teaching in the Roman Catholic Church.[2]

Belief in the resurrection has its roots in Judaism; it is an idea that was appropriated by Christians and became central to their worldview and part of the Christian creed. Christians believe Jesus was raised from the dead, that he will come again, and that at that time all believers will be resurrected for a final judgment. New Testament scholars debate exactly what is meant by resurrection in early Christian writings. Does it mean that individuals will be raised in their actual bodies or a more spiritualized type of body? An early leader in the Jesus movement, Paul, refers to a spiritual resurrection in his Letter to the Corinthians: "So it is with the resurrection of the dead: What is sown is perishable, what is raised is imperishable. It is sown in dishonor, it is raised in glory. It is sown in weakness, it is raised in power. It is sown a physical body, it is raised a spiritual body....What I am saying brothers and sisters, is this: flesh and blood cannot inherit the kingdom of God, nor does the perishable inherit the imperishable. Listen, I will tell you a mystery! We will not all die, but we will all be changed, in a moment, in the twinkling of an eye, at the last trumpet. For this perishable body must put on imperishability, and this mortal body must put on immortality."[3] This notion of the spiritual body raises many issues, especially those related to the ambivalent feelings about flesh in the Christian tradition. Ultimately for Christians the idea of a final resurrection and judgment is not contested; rather, how that all unfolds is what is debated.[4]

A CONCEPTUAL LOOK

What are heaven and hell exactly? Most assume heaven is a good thing and hell is a bad thing, but aside from that, interpretations vary widely. Christian teaching does not suggest they are physical places per se; rather, they are states of existence post-mortality. Hell could be the instance of our souls being twisted and contorted due to sin and brokenness; alternatively, heaven could be complete peace. Where people stand depending on their social context has a lot to do with the way they conceptualize these final realities. For example, if someone is doing well in his or her life economically, socially, and otherwise, his or her conception of heaven might look very similar to where he or she stands now. However, even those who are doing well experience pain and brokenness. In such cases, heaven might represent an eternal reprieve from that emotional and spiritual burden. Alternatively, those who experience material exploitation and dehumanization in their daily lives would certainly not want to push their present into eternity. Heaven is anything but the suffering they experience in the here and now.

This type of thinking gives rise to Marxist and neo-Marxist critiques of Christianity. The modern period brought a questioning of everything from the feasibility of an afterlife to the existence of God. Karl Marx's questioning of religion in general and Christianity in particular raises questions for those who are not so well off in the here and now. For example, does a heaven promised in the far future prevent individuals and groups from fighting against injustice in the here and now? If so, does Christianity become a tool of the oppressor to keep some individuals and groups in positions of power and others marginalized, exploited, and disenfranchised? All these philosophical and sociological matters come into play when discussing the theology of the end time.

ARE YOU SAVED?

It is not out of the ordinary for an individual to be approached by a stranger and asked this question. The backstory to this situation is whether the person in question lives by the gospel and has accepted Jesus Christ into his or her heart. Christians talk a lot about salvation—it is in the creed, it is in prayer, and it is in Christian art. Salvation is often connected to the idea of judgment. The problem with talking about judgment is that while it keeps us from being sleepy, it has the potential to make us judgmental. What happens when mere humans start to make claims about who will be saved? Recall how Jesus commands his followers not to judge others. So how can one be sure about who is saved and who isn't? This is a real dilemma as it calls into question the heart of Christian existence and identity. For some may wonder, what is the point of being Christian, of trying to live like Jesus, if anyone can be saved? While others may assert that if to live like Jesus means to live with an open heart and mind to others, then salvation is available for all, regardless of culture or creed.

So far much of the conversation about salvation has been oriented toward the question of salvation of human animals. It is worth noting that this green anthropology is committed to the premise that all of life is important to the story of salvation. So a logical next step is trying to imagine what an eco-friendly and queer-storied salvation, which includes human and nonhuman animals, might look like. However, such a vision is impossible when some claim that salvation is only for humans, and even more than that, only for humans that are committed to Jesus. For example, if some say that our Muslim brothers and sisters *cannot* be saved because they do not believe Christian claims about Jesus, then how can one even begin to speak about the orca or the ant being saved, when humans do not share similar language systems with them or have the same sorts of souls or spirits as them?

PARTICULAR VERSUS UNIVERSAL SALVATION

For human animals, there are two general categories for speaking about salvation: particular and universal. Particular salvation refers to the idea that not everyone is saved. Some Christians believe that only a limited number of people are saved, and that the individuals who are saved are most probably Christian. This definition is quite vague, and inevitably leads to a multitude of questions and concerns. For instance, some might wonder which Christians in particular are saved. Is salvation only possible for a specific denomination or does salvation span across Christian churches? Others may wonder if individuals' actions are more important than their being Christian or being a member of a certain Christian sect. In other words, regardless of his or her religious affiliation, has the individual in question lived a moral life, a life of charity, or a life of which Jesus would have approved? When talking about salvation in any rigorous way, it quickly becomes apparent that we need some clarification on what it takes to be saved, aside from God's grace. What are the deal breakers, especially in a religion where forgiveness is such a powerful and transformative act? Is there really any one thing that can keep someone out of heaven? Ultimately, all these questions lead to an even more complicated one: If anyone can get into heaven, then why be Christian at all?

Universal salvation is the idea that all human beings have the potential to be in communion with God into eternity. In some interpretations of this idea, the grace of Jesus Christ will be so irresistible at the second coming that everyone—even non-Christians—will be called into his forever embrace. One issue that arises here is, once again, related to the question of freedom. If Christians are created with the freedom to say yes to God, then are they really free if the grace of God is so irresistible to them? What if some Christians want to say no? Are they free to do so?

Criticism of this idea of universal salvation has not been directed toward freedom alone. In fact, many of the reasons why some Christians argue for the position of universal salvation are the same reasons they resist it. In a global world, where many of us encounter individuals from other religious traditions on a daily basis, it is becoming increasingly difficult to claim that only Christians will be saved, and more than that, that only some Christians will be saved. When our neighbors are atheists, Muslims, Jews, and so on, and moreover when we consider them to be good people, how is it possible that we cannot imagine that a good God would show mercy on them at the end? At the same time, why do Christians need to have their "other" friends and loved ones be saved by a Christian savior? Is that not a bit imperialistic in today's world? These issues get at the core beliefs of Christian identity and mission in a world of religious pluralism.

NOSTRA AETATE

During the Second Vatican Council (1962–65), the Roman Catholic Church shifted gears on many issues, including understanding the importance of the other world religions. The Council was intended to modernize the Church in many ways, meaning to open Catholic Christians to important issues of the day. Sixteen documents were published as a result of the Council. Here we will reflect on one document for a deeper look into the questions of religious pluralism and the possibility of universal salvation—the Declaration on the Relation of the Church to Non-Christian Religions, *Nostra Aetate* (1965).[5]

Most broadly, *Nostra Aetate* emphasizes the connections and commonalities among the world's religions—how even the Eastern traditions of Hinduism and Buddhism share values with monotheistic religions, including a desire to understand "the unsolved riddles of human existence."[6] The declaration also concentrates on the common stories and prophets within Judaism, Christianity, and Islam, as all three world religions trace their roots back to the beloved patriarch Abraham—a connection that is vital to moving forward and healing any past hurts. *Nostra Aetate* states that Islam honors Jesus and Mary as important religious figures in world history and in the story of Islam, as well as that Muslims embody an upright morality rooted in their prayer, charity, and fasting.

Furthermore, the document extensively accounts for the "common spiritual heritage" between Jews and Christians, a spiritual patrimony, which lends itself to "mutual understanding and appreciation."[7] The declaration is so committed to healing Jewish-Catholic relations that it calls for Catholics to renounce "displays of anti-semitism."[8] In sum, *Nostra Aetate* implicitly calls Catholics to celebrate their interreligious beginnings, highlighting their shared ancestry with those of the Jewish faith: "This sacred council remembers the spiritual ties which link the people of the new covenant to stock of Abraham."[9]

These claims to a common brotherhood and sisterhood among the Abrahamic religions and respect for all of the world's religions represent a giant step forward for the Church in terms of being other-oriented and charitable to people of different faiths. However, there are some controversial points of the document. At the same time as *Nostra Aetate* illuminates the interconnections among the world's religions, it designates a clear difference between Christianity and all the "others" when it states the following: "The Catholic Church rejects nothing of what is true and holy in these religions. It has a high regard for the manner of life and conduct, the precepts and doctrines which, although differing in many ways from its own teaching, nevertheless often reflect a ray of that truth which enlightens all men and women. Yet it proclaims and is in duty bound to proclaim without fail, Christ who is the way, the truth and the life (Jn 14:6). In him, in whom God reconciled all things to himself."[10] In these few phrases, *Nostra Aetate* erects a border between Christianity and all other religions, implicitly affirming that while there may be respect and solidarity among the religions of the world, there is one pure and true story that leads to salvation, Jesus' story.

There are diverging responses to this claim about the ultimacy of Jesus in *Nostra Aetate*. Some Catholic Christians believe that this claim of the primacy of Jesus undermines the Council's good efforts at reaching out to other religious traditions. Others, however, assert that such a claim about Jesus is necessary in order to maintain Christianity's essence and integrity, as well as respect the difference of other traditions. To be sure, these issues continue to be discussed privately and publicly as questions about group identity and mission unfold in our communities, in places of worship, and in the global panorama.

STRATEGIES FOR SALVATION

Christians need to navigate the murky waters of this salvation question. They have to strike some sort of balance between choosing to be part of Christianity because of its ultimacy, and at the same time being open to others in practice and in theory about salvation. This is a difficult situation to manage. As such, we need to be cognizant of how we approach these situations. We need strategies. We have to be intentional about how to live ourselves into the future. In what follows are various frames for conceptualizing one's journey toward salvation. This discussion is an extension of the conversation on vocation, building on the idea that Christian discipleship in the here and now has an impact on the future and one's experience of the hereafter. It will not be surprising, then, that all four frames, namely those of the pilgrim, exile, creative creature, and amateur, highlight important dynamics in one's journey from the here and now toward the hereafter.

PILGRIMS AND PILGRIMAGES

The act of participating in a pilgrimage is familiar in religious circles. For example, Muslims are obligated to journey to Mecca as part of their participation in the Hajj. Christians too go on pilgrimages to holy sites. They visit the relics of saints and even journey to the Holy Land. Here we might imagine a pilgrimage as even more than an earthly journey. Indeed, everything a Christian believer does in his or her life is in preparation for the end. Living in the here and now purposefully and with intentionality with an eye toward salvation is a spiritualized pilgrimage. After all, what is more holy than being in the presence of God—the beatific vision —a religious destination all Christians hope for? Every pilgrim must prepare for the journey by acquiring the proper material and spiritual supplies. Every pilgrim must gear up for encountering others, that is, for dealing with all types of difference. Christian pilgrims have a responsibility to engage the other (human and nonhuman) with a grace and charity exemplified by Jesus. And finally, in reflecting on pilgrimage as a frame for understanding how we live out issues related to salvation, perhaps like pilgrims we must develop faith and courage in the face of the unknown, ultimately giving up on the sense of control and power over everything and everyone on the road we travel.

HOMELESS AND EXILED

Being an exile is another important theological trope that could prove helpful when imagined as a strategy for navigating this life into the next. The history of God's chosen people, the Israelites, is one of their being exiled from the land promised to them in sacred story. As exiles, they experienced resistance and even rejection from the current occupants of the land. The Israelites were otherized and marginalized. Recall how God commanded the Israelites to remember when they were in Egypt, alienated from their home, and how those feelings of loss could serve as catalysts for treating others in their midst with more compassion and hospitality. In being homeless, they had an experience that could transform their lives in radical ways and profoundly impact the lives of others.

Some may argue that homelessness and being an exile are not good things, so how in the world could they be strategies for navigating life into death? The challenge of using exile as a frame for understanding one's faith journey is that it tends to obscure one's sense of freedom. As with homelessness, virtually no one wants to be an exile—to be forced out of one's home and deprived of all sense of belonging. Being an exile means being a victim, with limited control and agency to influence one's destiny. Yet, even the exile has freedom. He or she can remember what it is like to be without and can work on behalf of others to heal situations of injustice.

To push this line of thinking further, remembering exile and living as if one does not have total control over one's surroundings and home could honor what Jesus meant in the Gospels when he urged his followers to leave all their possessions behind. Moreover, a metaphorical homelessness may be what Seàn McDonagh has in mind when he calls Christians to live lightly in the midst of ecological degradation. Ultimately, the homelessness being referred to here is not homelessness in the sense of not having the resources to be able to have a roof over one's head and provide for one's family; rather, it is embracing the call to let go of one's attachments to the excesses of life, to status, and to a false sense of self.

CREATIVE CREATURE

Keeping with the green theme of this anthropology, thinking of the journey from this life into the next as the journey of a creative creature could push us into thinking beyond the salvation of the human animal. In addition to highlighting two central themes of this book, vulnerability and freedom, imagining oneself as a creative creature levels the playing field among all animals. It is not only my salvation that is at stake: it is that of the entire cosmos. I have agency in saving or at least changing the trajectory of mass extinctions that we are on now. That commitment alone honors the kingdom of God that is already and not yet.

We are all creative, meaning that we are resourceful, imaginative, and capable of making changes in our environment as a way of saying yes to God and others. The use of the word *creature* highlights that we are animals, all part of the cosmos. We cannot hide behind our humanity and avoid our connections to nonhuman animals. In fact, perhaps we will become more of who we were meant to be if we acknowledge that we are creatures like the great white, the orca, the lion, the lemur, the fire ant, and so on. Creative creatures might envision a heaven that is not only populated by human and nonhuman animals, but that is also green and peaceful, ultimately recovering from degradation. Hell might be a continuation and acceleration of our current ecological trend.

AN AMATEUR EFFORT AT SALVATION

An overarching theme of this book has been that nobody is perfect. Freedom does not need to be perfect: it just needs to be enacted responsibly. We all make mistakes. We all are broken. These existential realities need to be part of the frame when living and loving ourselves into the hereafter. This is not an excuse not to try; rather, a reality check that even with our best efforts and best intentions, living and loving is a bumpy ride at best. Perhaps that is the beautiful idea about purgatory, namely, the notion that we are meant to be with God but we are not really ready yet. We are amateurs both here and now and in the hereafter. Amateurs are working at living and loving. They are pilgrims who struggle with others and with their lack of control; they are homeless giving up on the idea of perfection; and they are creative creatures always striving for peace and justice. When Kyle Kramer used this idea of amateur to speak about vocation, some may have bristled. After all, why would anyone want to settle for being an amateur? However, there is a freedom that comes with embracing being an

amateur as a strategy for life and death, in that amateurs never stop working, but forgive themselves when they hit their creaturely limits.

SUMMARY

In this chapter, issues of the afterlife were explored. Special attention was given to the question of what salvation might look like and who is included in God's plan. Indeed, the whole idea of God having a plan is problematized; since at times that type of language can lead Christian believers to think they are powerless in making the spiritual journey from this life into the next. As with choosing a vocation, in preparing for one's spiritual future, great care must be taken. Christians are called to balance their own desires for peace and salvation with the needs of others in their midst—human and nonhuman. This is difficult work because it calls them to question why they are Christians in the first place. Ultimately, it is argued that in being intentional about how we live from this life to the next, we are all amateurs. Perhaps we can take some comfort in that reality.

EXERCISES:
1. **Complete a journal entry on this topic.**
2. **Think-Pair-Share** (Reflect on these questions silently, find a partner and discuss them together, and then share with the class.)
   - Read *Nostra Aetate* (http://www.vatican.va/archive /hist_councils/ii_vatican_council/documents/vat-ii _decl_19651028_nostra-aetate_en.html). How open is the Catholic Church to other traditions? Does this document go far enough or too far? What impact does this have on your understanding of the world to come?
   - What might change if Christians in large numbers began to buy into the idea that all creatures—human and nonhuman—are capable of salvation? What are the issues and problems with such a theological claim?

3. Creative Time

Draw pictures of your visions of heaven and hell. Analyze them. What do they say about you and your social context?

NOTES

1. Mark 1:14–15 (NRSV).

2. For a contemporary constructive theological approach to eschatology, see John E. Thiel, *Icons of Hope: The "Last Things" in Catholic Imagination* (Notre Dame, IN: University of Notre Dame Press, 2013).

3. 1 Cor 15:42–44, 50–53 (NRSV).

4. For an elaborate discussion of resurrection, see Claudia Setzer, *Resurrection of the Body in Early Judaism and Early Christianity: Doctrine, Community, and Self-Definition* (Brill Academic Publisher, 2004).

5. Declaration on the Relation of the Church to Non-Christian Religions, *Nostra Aetate* (*NA*), October 25, 1965, in *Vatican Council II: Constitutions, Decrees, Declarations*, ed. Austin Flannery, OP, A Completely Revised Translation in Inclusive Language (Northport, New York: Costello Publishing Co., 1996), 569–74.

6. Ibid., 569.

7. Ibid., 573.

8. Ibid.

9. Ibid., 572.

10. Ibid., 570–71.

Epilogue
WHAT'S TRENDING?

Throughout this book we have explored Christian teaching about how to be human in the midst of others—different people as well as different species. A prominent thread running through this work is that being human involves paying attention to the plight of all species, and specifically to how human animals are connected explicitly and implicitly with the entire cosmos. Topics related to what it means to be created in the image of God, to be vulnerable, to enact freedom, to overcome dualism, to open to conversion, to forgive and love, and to embrace life as a journey both in the here and now and in the hereafter served as lenses for understanding the complicated connections between human beings and all others.

Admittedly, in some chapters it was easier to connect the plight of human animals with that of nonhuman animals than in others. At times, it may have even seemed like the connection between human animal and nonhuman animal was a forced one. One reason for this is that in light of specific theological teachings, such as those related to the afterlife, the human animal and nonhuman animal divide is so overwhelming that it is awkward to argue for connections between the two. To overcome this disconnect, examples from everyday life were employed to explicate and underscore the interplay among all creatures and the importance of the survival and flourishing of all.

In attempting to connect theological teachings with ordinary life, complex social trends and realities that profoundly befuddle the conversation about how to be human were revealed. Some of these trends are related to changes in science, medicine, and technology. In this work, the conversation has only begun; these

228

trends in our everyday life need to be analyzed more closely in an effort to understand what it takes to be human in the twenty-first century.

Take for instance the trends in science. As researchers make more advances in genetic engineering, the public at large is faced with tough decisions about how much control one should exert over human existence and performance. When we have the ability to choose what genes we wish to alter, we must consider factors that influence our decision-making process. Difficult questions emerge. Do we feel forced into societal norms about what is normal when we make these choices? In other words, do we wish to choose and change genetic makeup in order to conform to what society deems beautiful? Other existential questions come to the fore as well, such as whether our tolerance for human imperfection will decrease as we obtain the capability to become even more seemingly perfect. Reaching back to the chapter on human neediness, one might ask, in the face of such scientific developments, how can vulnerability unfold as a virtue when we are able to genetically choose not to be vulnerable?

There are other trends that complicate being human in a world with God and others. Developments in the pharmaceutical and cosmetic industries bring challenges analogous to those of genetic engineering. In the face of chronic and terminal illness, we are grateful for the latest drug therapies that keep our family and friends alive and thriving. Nonetheless, some may wonder if there is no end to what we treat and how we treat it. Put simply, how much medical intervention is too much? Moreover, in concern for global economic justice, one might ask whether the extensive treatment of those in the developed nations take away resources from those suffering poverty and illness in underdeveloped countries, especially since resources are far from infinite. Finally, as with some forms of genetic engineering, with pharmaceuticals and cosmetics are we trying to be perfect and immortal through the newest therapies? One only needs to reflect on the rhetoric around cutting edge age-lock skin technology to see how afraid many of us are of appearing older and showing visible signs of our true age. While there is nothing wrong with taking pride in how one looks and keeping oneself in good shape, what is being considered here is whether we have taken that pride to an extreme. Are we petrified of aging because we are reluctant to be thought of as weak or, even worse, irrelevant?

The trend most consistently engaged in this book relates to the developments in social networking and communication technology. Several chapters encompassed discussion of how electronic technology, including social media, texting, Skype, Facebook, Twitter, Instagram, and the like, impacts creaturely existence in both positive and negative ways. Traditional ways of understanding vocation and time were understood to be challenged by the staccato rhythms of our devices. To be sure, students today have grown up with social networking as a norm of human existence. This is one fundamental difference between how their experience has been shaped in comparison to that of previous generations. Even those not part of that demographic have experienced the power of electronic technology. Few can work in an office environment and not use email. Few parents today can avoid using portals to access important information about their childrens' education. What's more, you may be reading this book on an electronic device or blogging about a certain aspect of it for a homework assignment. These are the realities of our time; and as such, their existence is not in question in this book. Rather, our question is how these technologies have altered human existence and how they impact our relating with others. Put another way, from a Christian perspective, do blogging, emailing, texting, FaceTime, online dating, social networking sites like Facebook and Myspace, and video sharing sites like YouTube prove to be life-giving, death-dealing, or someplace in between?

All of the trends will continue to play a prominent role in the conversations about theological anthropology in the future. The jury is still out on how any of these trends and advances will change creaturely existence. What believers need to do is not avoid social trends; rather, they need to get ahead of the curve and use new realities to further their journey for God and others. Many are doing just that, and hopefully still more will follow.

EXERCISES:

1. Revisit Journal Entries.

Students should revisit their journal entries from the first week and discuss where they have and have not changed intellectually, emotionally, and spiritually with their classmates in small groups.

2. Think-Pair-Share (Reflect on this question silently, find a partner and discuss them together, and then share with the class.)

- In addition to trends in science, medicine, and technology, list some other hot topics that complicate being human in a world with others. Explain how those trends impact human existence today.

3. Creative Time

Imagine you are the author of a book on theological anthropology. What might your table of contents look like? Try to sketch some key questions and topics for discussion.

BIBLIOGRAPHY

Bateson, Mary Catherine. *Composing a Life*. New York: Grove Press, 1989.

Bellitto, Christopher M. *The General Councils: A History of the Twenty-One Church Councils from Nicaea to Vatican II*. Mahwah, NJ: Paulist Press, 2002.

Berry, Thomas. *The Dream of the Earth*. San Francisco: Sierra Club Books, 1988.

Beste, Jennifer Erin. *God and the Victim: Traumatic Intrusions on Grace and Freedom*. American Academy of Religion Series. Oxford: Oxford University Press, 2007.

Buber, Martin. *I and Thou*. A new translation, with a prologue and notes by Walter Kaufmann. New York: Touchstone, 1996.

Bynum, Caroline Walker. *Jesus as Mother: Studies in the Spirituality of the High Middle Ages*. Berkeley: University of California Press, 1982.

Carr, Anne E. *Transforming Grace: Christian Tradition and Women's Experience*. Harrisburg, PA: Continuum, 1996.

Center for Biological Diversity. "The Extinction Crisis." http://www.biologicaldiversity.org/programs/biodiversity/elements_of_biodiversity/extinction_crisis/.

Collins, Suzanne. *The Hunger Games*. New York: Scholastic Press, 2008.

Copeland, M. Shawn. *Enfleshing Freedom: Body, Race, and Being*. Minneapolis: Fortress Press, 2009.

Crisp, Oliver. *Divinity and Humanity: The Incarnation Reconsidered*. Cambridge, UK: Cambridge University Press, 2007.

de Certeau, Michel. *The Practice of Everyday Life*. Translated by Steven Rendall. Berkeley: University of California Press, 1984.

Farley, Margaret A. *Just Love: A Framework for Christian Sexual Ethics*. New York: Continuum, 2006.

Fausto-Sterling, Anne. *Sexing the Body*. New York: Basic Books, 2000.

Feehan, John. *The Singing Heart of the World: Creation, Evolution and Faith*. Dublin: Columba Press, 2010.

Fletcher, Jeannine Hill. *Motherhood as Metaphor: Engendering Interreligious Dialogue*. New York: Fordham University Press, 2013.

"Gianna Beretta Molla 1922–1962." http://www.vatican.va/news_services/liturgy/saints/ns_lit_doc_20040516_beretta-molla_en.html.

Groppe, Elizabeth T. "Women and the *Persona* of Christ: Ordination in the Roman Catholic Church." In *Frontiers in Catholic Feminist Theology: Shoulder to Shoulder*, edited by Susan Abraham and Elena Procario-Foley. Minneapolis: Fortress Press, 2009.

Gudorf, Christine E. *Body, Sex, and Pleasure: Reconstructing Christian Sexual Ethics*. Cleveland: The Pilgrim Press, 1994.

Haight, Roger. "Sin and Grace." In *Systematic Theology: Roman Catholic Perspectives*. 2nd ed. Edited by Francis Schüssler Fiorenza and John P. Galvin. Minneapolis: Fortress Press, 2011.

Hanson, Bradley C. *Introduction to Christian Theology*. Minneapolis, MN: Augsburg Fortress Press, 1997.

Haraway, Donna. *The Companion Species Manifesto: Dogs, People and Significant Otherness*. Chicago: Prickly Paradigm Press, 2003.

———. *Simians, Cyborgs, and Women: The Reinvention of Nature*. New York: Routledge, 1991.

Hinze, Bradford. "Individuation and Communion: Implications for the Church's Identity and Mission." In *Believing in Community: Ecumenical Reflections on the Church*, edited by Peter De Mey, Pieter De Witte, and Gerard Mannion. Leuven, Belgium: Peeters Press, 2013.

Johnson, Elizabeth A. *Ask the Beasts: Darwin and the God of Love*. London: Bloomsbury, 2014.

Jones, Serene. *Trauma and Grace: Theology in a Ruptured World*. Louisville: Westminster John Knox Press, 2009.

Jones, Serene, and Paul Lakeland, eds. *Constructive Theology: A Contemporary Approach to Classical Themes*. Minneapolis: Augsburg Fortress Press, 2005.

Kramer, Kyle T. *A Time to Plant: Life Lessons in Work, Prayer, and Dirt*. Notre Dame, IN: Sorin Books, 2010.

Kunin, Madeleine M. *The New Feminist Agenda: Defining the Next Revolution for Women, Work and Family*. White River Junction, VT: Chelsea Green Press, 2012.

Lamott, Anne. *Bird by Bird: Some Instructions on Writing and Life*. New York: Anchor Books, 1995.

L'Arche USA. http://www.larcheusa.org/.

Leakey, Richard, and Roger Lewin. *The Sixth Extinction: Patterns of Life and the Future of Humankind*. New York: Doubleday, 1995.

Levinas, Emmanuel. *Otherwise than Being or Beyond Essence*. Translated by Alphonso Lingis. Pittsburgh: Duquesne University Press, 1998.

Lonergan, Bernard. *Collected Works of Bernard Lonergan*. Edited by Frederick E. Crowe and Robert Doran. Vol. 3, *Insight: A Study of Human Understanding*. Toronto: University of Toronto Press, 1992.

——. *Method in Theology*. Toronto: University of Toronto Press, 1971.

——. *The Subject*. Milwaukee, WI: University Press, 1968.

McDonagh, Seàn, SCC. *The Death of Life: The Horror of Extinction*. Dublin, Ireland: Columba Press, 2005.

McFague, Sallie. *The Body of God: An Ecological Theology*. Minneapolis, MN: Fortress Press, 1993.

——. *Models of God: Theology for an Ecological, Nuclear Age*. Minneapolis: Fortress Press, 1987.

Melton, Glennon. "Don't Carpe Diem." *The Huffington Post*. http://www.huffingtonpost.com/glennon-melton/dont-carpe-diem_b_1206346.html.

Morell, Virginia. *Animal Wise: The Thoughts and Emotions of Our Fellow Creatures*. New York: Crown, 2013.

Nhat Hanh, Thich. *Being Peace*. Berkeley: Parallax Press, 2005.

Oceana: Protecting the World's Oceans. "Shark Finning." http://oceana.org/en/our-work/protect-marine-wildlife/sharks/learn-act/shark-finning.

Paulsell, Stephanie. *Honoring the Body: Meditations on a Christian Practice*. San Francisco, CA: Jossey-Bass, 2002.

Plaskow, Judith. *Sex, Sin and Grace: Women's Experience and the Theologies of Reinhold Niebuhr and Paul Tillich*. Washington, DC: University Press of America, 1980.

Pollan, Michael. *The Omnivore's Dilemma: A Natural History of Four Meals*. New York: Penguin, 2006.

Pope, Harrison G., Katharine Phillips, and Roberto Olivardia. *The Adonis Complex: How to Identify, Treat, and Prevent Body Obsession in Men and Boys*. New York: Simon & Schuster, 2000.

Pope John Paul II. *Mulieris Dignitatem: On the Dignity and Vocation of Women on the Occasion of the Marian Year*. http://www.vatican.va/holy_father/john_paul_ii/apost_letters/documents/hf_jp-ii_apl_15081988_mulieris-dignitatem_en.html.

Rahner, Karl. *Foundations of Christian Faith: An Introduction to the Idea of Christianity*. Translated by William V. Dych. New York: Crossroad, 1994.

Ratzinger, Joseph Cardinal (Pope Benedict XVI). *Behold The Pierced One: An Approach to a Spiritual Christology*. Translated by Graham Harrison. San Francisco: Ignatius Press, 1986.

Robbins, Jim. *The Man Who Planted Trees: Lost Groves, Champion Trees, and an Urgent Plan to Save the Planet*. New York: Spiegel & Grau, 2012.

Rudy, Kathy. *Loving Animals: Toward a New Animal Advocacy*. Minneapolis: University of Minnesota Press, 2011.

Sachs, John R. *The Christian Vision of Humanity: Basic Christian Anthropology*. Collegeville, MN: Liturgical Press, 1991.

Salzman, Todd A., and Michael G. Lawler. *The Sexual Person: Toward a Renewed Catholic Anthropology*. Washington, DC: Georgetown University Press, 2008.

Saracino, Michele. *Being about Borders: A Christian Anthropology of Difference*. Collegeville, MN: Liturgical Press, 2011.

———. *Clothing: Christian Explorations of Daily Living*. Minneapolis: Fortress Press, 2012.

Scruton, Roger. "Hiding Behind the Screen." *The New Atlantis: A Journal of Technology and Society*. http://www.thenewatlantis.com/publications/hiding-behind-the-screen.

Setzer, Claudia. *Resurrection of the Body in Early Judaism and Early Christianity: Doctrine, Community, and Self-Definition.* Boston: Brill Academic Publisher, 2004.

————. "Three Odd Couples: Women and Men in Mark and John." In *Mariam, the Magdalen, and the Mother,* edited by Deirdre Good. Bloomington: Indiana University Press, 2005.

Thiel, John E. *Icons of Hope: The "Last Things" in Catholic Imagination.* Notre Dame, IN: University of Notre Dame Press, 2013.

Thompson, Deanna A. *Hoping for More: Having Cancer, Talking Faith, and Accepting Grace.* Eugene, OR: Cascade Books, 2012.

Turkle, Sherry. "The Flight from Conversation." *New York Times.* http://www.nytimes.com/2012/04/22/opinion/sunday/the-flight-from-conversation.html?_r=0.

United States Conference of Catholic Bishops. "Catholic Social Teaching." http://www.usccb.org/beliefs-and-teachings/what-we-believe/catholic-social-teaching/.

Vacek, Edward Collins, SJ. *Love, Human and Divine: The Heart of Christian Ethics.* Washington, DC: Georgetown University Press, 1994.

Vanier, Jean. *Becoming Human.* Mahwah, NJ: Paulist Press, 2008.

Vatican Council II: Constitutions, Decrees, Declarations. Edited by Austin Flannery, OP. A Completely Revised Translation in Inclusive Language. Northport, New York: Costello Publishing Co., 1996.

Wendell, Susan. *The Rejected Body: Feminist Philosophical Reflections on Disability.* New York: Routledge, 1996.

MERCY
The Essence of the Gospel and the Key to Christian Life

WALTER KASPER

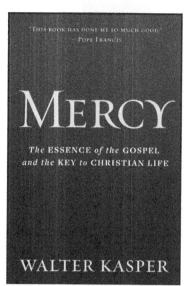

"This book has done me so much good."—Pope Francis

From one of the leading intellects in the Church today—one whom Pope Francis has described as a "superb theologian" —comes perhaps his most important book yet. Available for the first time in English, Cardinal Kasper looks to capture the essence of the gospel message. Compassionate, bold, and brilliant, Cardinal Kasper has written a book which will be studied for generations.

978-0-8091-0609-7   Hardcover

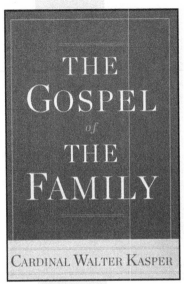

THE GOSPEL OF
THE FAMILY

CARDINAL WALTER KASPER

Cardinal Kasper, in an address to the consistory, published in English exclusively by Paulist Press, advocates a stronger appreciation of marriage and the family—even on sensitive issues such as divorce and remarriage.

978-0-8091-4908-7   Paperback

POPE FRANCIS' REVOLUTION OF TENDERNESS AND LOVE
Theological and Pastoral Perspectives

CARDINAL WALTER KASPER

Outlines the significant influences that have led Cardinal Kasper to call Francis a pope leading a radical revolution of tenderness and love—radical because it is rooted in the gospel.

978-0-8091-0623-3   Hardcover

THE TRINITY
How Not to Be a Heretic

STEPHEN BULLIVANT

The Trinity is an invitation to Christians who are sure that they believe in something called "the Trinity," but are unsure as to what exactly that means, and uneasy about having to talk about it to others.

978-0-8091-4933-9 Paperback

INVITATION TO
PRACTICAL THEOLOGY
Catholic Voices and Visions

EDITED BY CLAIRE E. WOLFTEICH

A leading Catholic scholar in the field
of practical theology gathers significant
voices to write on the many aspects to
be considered in the study of this
emerging field.

978-0-8091-4890-5   Paperback

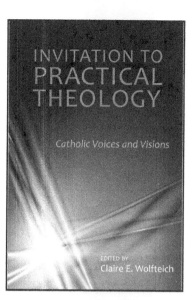

FAITH AND UNBELIEF

STEPHEN BULLIVANT

Explores the reasons for, and the realities of, modern atheism, especially through the interface of the Christian faith and modern-day culture.

978-0-8091-4865-3   Paperback

GOD AND THE MYSTERY OF HUMAN SUFFERING
A Theological Conversation across the Ages

ROBIN RYAN, CP

A survey of the Judeo-Christian tradition and the contemporary theological conversation concerning ways of speaking of God's relation to suffering people and to a world in which suffering is such a stark reality.

978-0-8091-4713-7   Paperback

Hope
Promise, Possibility, and Fulfillment

Edited by RICHARD LENNAN and
NANCY PINEDA-MADRID

HOPE
Promise, Possibility, and Fulfillment

EDITED BY RICHARD LENNAN AND
NANCY PINEDA-MADRID

Crafting a theology of hope, this book
addresses both the possibility that hope
offers and the capacity of hope to
respond to the challenges that life presents to us all.

978-0-8091-4777-9   Paperback

A PRIESTLY PEOPLE
Baptismal Priesthood and Priestly Ministry

Jean-Pierre Torrell

FOREWORD BY

Msgr. Kevin W. Irwin

Emphasizes that as believers in Christ, from baptism onward, we are all members of a royal and prophetic priestly community.

978-0-8091-4815-8   Paperback

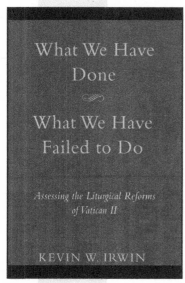

WHAT WE HAVE DONE, WHAT WE HAVE FAILED TO DO

Assessing the Liturgical Reforms of Vatican II

KEVIN W. IRWIN

Sheds light on and invites discussion about the experience in which Catholics have been engaged since the Second Vatican Council in implementing and praying the liturgy as reformed after the Council.

978-0-8091-4848-6   Paperback